Mormonism 101

Books by Bill McKeever

Answering Mormons' Questions
Questions to Ask Your Mormon Friend (with Eric Johnson)

Mormonism 101

Examining the Religion of the Latter-day Saints

Bill McKeever and Eric Johnson

BakerBooks

A Division of Baker Book House Co
Grand Rapids, Michigan 49516

Published by Baker Books
a division of Baker Book House Company
P.O. Box 6287, Grand Rapids, MI 49516-6287

Printed in the United States of America

Library of Congress Cataloging-in-Publication Data

McKeever, Bill.
    Mormonism 101: examining the religion of the Latter-day Saints / Bill McKeever and Eric Johnson.
        p.   cm.
    Includes bibliographical references.
    ISBN 0-8010-6335-3
    1. Church of Jesus Christ of Latter-day Saints—Doctrines. I. Title: Mormonism one hundred one. II. Title: Mormonism one hundred and one. III. Johnson, Eric, 1962– IV. Title.
BX8635.2.M39   2000
289.3—dc21   99-089663

All Scripture is taken from the King James Version of the Bible.

For current information about all releases from Baker Book House, visit our web site:
http://www.bakerbooks.com

To our children: Kristen, Kendra, and Jamin McKeever, and Carissa, Janelle, and Hannah Johnson. Psalm 127:3 says, "Lo, children are an heritage of the LORD: and the fruit of the womb is his reward." May you always realize the love your dads have for you, but especially the abundant love and mercy of your Father in heaven who gave His Son so that we might experience everlasting life.

Special thanks to Lane Thuet, Dick Baer, and Suzanne Schimmeyer, as well as a number of other friends, for the many hours they devoted to proofing our first draft and for offering a number of valuable suggestions, many of which were implemented in the final manuscript. May God bless all of you.

Contents

IV. Examining the LDS Concept of Salvation

V. Examining the LDS Concept of Ordinances

VI. Examining the LDS Concept of Revelation

Appendices

Preface

Mormonism is Christianity; Christianity is Mormonism; they are one and the same, and they are not to be distinguished from each other in the minutest detail. . . . Mormons are true Christians; their worship is the pure, unadulterated Christianity authored by Christ and accepted by Peter, James, and John and all the ancient saints.

Apostle Bruce McConkie, *Mormon Doctrine,* 513

The leaders of the Church of Jesus Christ of Latter-day Saints, also known as the Mormon Church or the LDS Church, have made a concerted effort in recent years to make their organization appear more like that of mainstream Christianity. Because it is not uncommon for Latter-day Saints (Mormons) to tell their Christian friends or coworkers, "We're Christians just like you," many outside of this unique religious faith may wonder just what is the actual doctrinal position of the LDS Church. Many have sought a resource that compares the teachings of the Mormon leaders, both past and present, with those of the Bible. We believe the book you hold in your hands will meet this need.

Of course, the big question is just what constitutes Mormonism? Are we to judge the LDS Church by the opinion of the average lay member? While on the surface this may sound like a good way to evaluate a religious system, our experience has shown that far too many Latter-day Saints have not taken the time to do an in-depth investigation into the history and doctrines of their faith. Should we base our study on the latest trends coming out of Brigham Young University? We admit that BYU has employed some great minds, but do professors at a church-owned school have the authority to interpret doctrine for the rest of the LDS Church?

Like many religious traditions, the LDS Church has its own unique set of scriptures. While it officially includes the Holy Bible as one of its texts (specifically the King James Version), Latter-day Saints also use the *Book of Mormon,* the *Doctrine and Covenants* (abbreviated throughout as *D&C*), and the *Pearl of Great Price.* These are known as the standard works.

However, page 55 of the LDS Church manual *Gospel Principles* states that, in addition to these four books of scripture, the inspired words of the living prophets and LDS Church publications can also be used to guide its members in the ways of truth. If this is the case, then we would be remiss if we ignored the many statements that have come forth from these leaders who many Mormons feel are called by God to not only lead the church but clarify its scriptures as well.

The Mormon Church government is a hierarchy that at the very top comprises:

- The First Presidency, composed of the Prophet/President and his two counselors
- The Council of the Twelve, otherwise known as the Twelve Apostles
- The Quorums of the Seventy

Our experience shows that many Latter-day Saints have a great respect for their leaders, both past and present. However, when members are confronted with an embarrassing statement from one of their general authorities, it is not uncommon for them to quickly distance themselves from the quote, claiming it is the mere opinion of that individual. While this may certainly be true, the student of Mormonism still needs to carefully weigh what LDS leaders have said and are saying, since it gives us an idea of what kind of men they really are. For example, if certain LDS leaders continually make irresponsible comments, we must take that into consideration. Also if it can be demonstrated that such an "opinion" was believed by church members to be true, then it places into serious question the LDS claim that its prophets cannot lead the church astray.

To be sure, the current presentation given by LDS Church leaders is much different than earlier years. When Joseph Smith began his new religious movement in 1830, there was no great effort to meld or compromise the teachings of the Mormon Church with those of nineteenth-century Christianity. Instead, early leaders prided themselves on their uniqueness and they boldly and publicly proclaimed their differences. They made little or no effort to associate with what they considered "apostate Christendom."[1]

More recently, however, some members of the LDS Church have felt it was time to declare to the world that the differences are only superficial or, at best, a problem of semantics. Some Mormon apologists have even declared that the divide between Christianity and Mormonism is not all that wide. Having studied this movement for a great portion of our lives, we find such concessions incredible, for if this is really true, it brings into question the Mormon concept of a so-called "complete apostasy."

We can see this shift to an ecumenical spirit in the Mormon Church's offering of free Bibles in TV and magazine advertisements, making this religion seem just like a Christian denomination. It appears that the LDS public relations department is purposely trying to minimize any doctrinal differences in order to appeal to a larger base of potential converts. We are convinced that if the Mormon Church leaders were to be more forthright with their unique teachings, the conversion rate would be much lower.

While many have been led to believe that there is nothing intrinsically wrong with LDS theology, we find that a number who hold this position base it on emotion rather than on a careful doctrinal comparison. We are not denying that Mormons, for the most part, are honest, sincere, and hardworking people. However, such virtues have never been a qualifying factor for deciding whether one is a Christian. Many religions throughout the world have such people within their ranks. The logical question should be, Can an individual or organization willfully deny or distort the basics of the Christian faith and till be considered Christian?

Due to space limitations, we will often use ellipses in a quote (indicating that some material was skipped) to concentrate on the pertinent information. While there is always a danger of taking quotes out of context, especially when ellipses appear, we have purposely made an effort to not alter the meaning of any quote. We invite readers who would like to study further the issues in this book to look up the quotes in their complete context.

Finally, it is unfortunate that some Latter-day Saints may assume that we were motivated to write this book out of hatred or bigotry. Be assured that we are moved with the same compassion felt by the LDS missionaries and lay members who attempt to defend what they believe to be true. While the facts as presented in this book may be ignored by certain readers who would question our motives, we echo the apostle Paul when he addressed the church of Galatia: "Am I therefore become your enemy, because I tell you the truth?" (Gal. 4:16). This book is the result of our concern for those who belong to the LDS faith as well as for those Christians who want to better understand the beliefs of their Mormon friends, relatives, and neighbors.

To God be the glory!

For more information about the differences between Mormonism and Christianity or to receive our free quarterly newsletter, *Mormonism Researched,* please write us!

> Mormonism Research Ministry
> Dept. 101
> P.O. Box 20705
> El Cajon, CA 92021

Also visit our web site at *www.mrm.org.*

Introduction

It was tenth LDS President Joseph Fielding Smith who said that Mormonism must "stand or fall on the story of Joseph Smith." This story begins on December 23, 1805, when Joseph was born to a farming couple in Sharon, Vermont. Like many other families searching for a better life, the Smiths would move west, settling down in 1816 thirty miles east of Rochester, New York, in a town called Palmyra. The story of Mormonism really takes shape in Palmyra. Today Smith's faithful followers view him as a prophet of God, chosen by the Almighty God to "restore" true Christianity after a seventeen-century absence from the earth. To many non-Mormons, he is a manipulator who deceived his followers and introduced teachings that hardly reflect the Christian faith.

Though there have been several versions of what Joseph Smith experienced in those early years, most Mormons are familiar with an account written by Smith in 1838. It tells of a fourteen-year-old Smith who wanted to know which of all the churches was true. He said that a passage from the New Testament Book of James led him to a grove of trees near his family's farm where he was visited by two personages, God the Father and Jesus Christ. The young Smith claimed these personages told him that all of the Christian churches were wrong, their creeds were an abomination, and their leaders were all corrupt.

As expected, his message of a complete apostasy of the Christian faith did not sit well with the local clergy. Many Christians immediately cast a suspicious eye on the young man who claimed to have had an audience with God and lived to tell about it. Bear in mind that the United States was at that time experiencing the effects of the Second Great Awakening. Revivals were commonplace. For Smith to claim that God did not approve of what many Christians thought was a great work of the Holy Spirit was unthinkable and even blasphemous. Undaunted, Smith continued to insist that his vision was true.

In 1823, while Smith prayed in his bedroom, he claimed he received another heavenly visit, this time by an angel who introduced himself as Moroni. During his earthly life, Moroni was a great warrior who lived among an ancient people called Nephites. He was a descendant of a Jewish family who escaped the capture of Jerusalem by sailing across the ocean to the Western Hemisphere about six hundred years before the birth of Christ. It was allegedly this same Moroni who, prior to his death, buried a set of gold plates on which was inscribed a record of the ancient American people. Smith was chosen to retrieve that record, but it was several years before he was given permission by the angel to do so. Before leaving, Moroni also warned Smith that he should show the plates to only a select few. Eventually a total of eleven men were chosen to "see" the gold plates, although some later confessed that they saw them only with the eye of faith.

The angel is said to have appeared to Smith on several other occasions until the time finally came to retrieve the Nephite record. On 22 September 1827 Joseph Smith, now almost twenty-two years old, was entrusted with the gold plates and commenced the translation of the "Reformed Egyptian" characters into English.

In April of 1829 Smith was joined by Oliver Cowdery, a third cousin of Joseph's mother, Lucy Mack Smith. Cowdery, a schoolteacher by profession, became Smith's principal scribe. Both Cowdery and Smith claimed to have been visited by John the Baptist while praying in the woods near the Susquehanna River in May of 1829. It was here that both men were ordained and received the Aaronic Priesthood, known in Mormonism as the lesser priesthood. At a later point in time the two men were ordained to the Melchizedek Priesthood, or greater priesthood, by Peter, James, and John. Even LDS historians do not know when exactly this event took place.

On 6 April 1830 Joseph Smith founded the "Church of Christ" (not affiliated with the Church of Christ denomination) with five of his close followers. By the end of the year, this number grew to almost three hundred members. Smith's prophetical inclinations compelled him to move his church to several locations. In August of 1831 a small group of Latter-day Saints moved into an area twelve miles west of Independence, Missouri. Smith prophesied that it was in this area where the New Jerusalem would be built. On August 3 Smith laid a cornerstone for a temple and even though he predicted that this location would become a gathering place where the Saints would wait for the millennial reign of Jesus Christ, his prophecy would never be fulfilled. The great influx of Mormon settlers into the area, coupled with Smith's predictions that "Zion" would be established and the time of the "Gentiles" would soon come to an end, led to many hard feelings between the Mormons and the non-LDS Missourians. The all-important gathering of the Saints was short-lived. Within three years the Saints were forced to leave Independence, and the temple never became a reality.

The Saints moved north where they settled for a while in an area called Far West, Missouri. Smith again predicted that a temple would be built, but eventually the Saints were forced to leave this place as well. Hostilities between the Mormons and their Missouri counterparts erupted in such violence that both sides came to an impasse. In October of 1838 Mormons attacked a group of Missouri militiamen who were holding three LDS men prisoner. This led to the slaughter of seventeen Latter-day Saints at Haun's Mill one week later. Joseph Smith was arrested and charged with treason. He spent several months in the dungeon of the Liberty Jail until he was allowed to escape in April of 1839.

In the meantime, the Saints had moved to a swampy area on the banks of the Mississippi River known as Commerce, Illinois. Enduring sickness and disease, they were successful in turning the once uninhabitable land into a city that attracted followers from all areas. Commerce later became the city of Nauvoo and within a short period of time, it rivaled Chicago in size. But even here, trouble did not elude Smith and his followers.

The rapid influx of Latter-day Saints to Nauvoo once again made the church both an economic and political threat in the eyes of the local residents. Joseph Smith was elected mayor, and several of his close associates eventually came to hold a number of political offices as well. Compounding the problem was the increasing number of dissidents who had grown to distrust the Mormon prophet. Many of these men were once close advisors to Smith, and some were successful businessmen in Nauvoo. Accusations between Smith and his detractors fueled the tension. Eventually some of the dissidents printed a newspaper called the *Nauvoo Expositor.* As its name implied, the purpose of the paper was to expose Joseph Smith as a false prophet who had exceeded his authority as mayor and was involved with secretly practicing "spiritual wifery," or polygamy.

The Nauvoo city council quickly reacted by declaring the *Expositor* a nuisance. Under the orders of Joseph Smith, the city marshal destroyed the offending publication and the printing press as well. Of course, this only infuriated Smith's enemies all the more. Immediately negative sentiment increased in Nauvoo and its neighboring communities. Amid threats of violence against himself and his followers, Smith placed Nauvoo under martial law on 18 June 1844. In doing so, he mobilized the Nauvoo Legion, an army of several thousand men who had sworn to protect Smith to the death.

When news reached Illinois Governor Thomas Ford, he intervened and suggested that Smith order his army to back down. He then ordered Smith to turn himself in to the authorities in nearby Carthage in the hope of settling the many differences that had escalated over the past several days. On June 25 Smith traveled to Carthage, taking up residence at a local hotel. However, he was once again arrested and incarcerated in the "debtor's cell" at Carthage Jail. With him were his brother Hyrum, John Taylor, and Willard Richards.

On June 26 the Illinois governor went to Smith's cell for a personal interview. After the meeting, Governor Ford traveled to Nauvoo but left a small contingency of guards known as Carthage Greys (many of whom were hardly sympathetic to the Mormon prophet). In the late afternoon of the next day, a mob attacked the jail, rushing up the stairs to the cell that housed Smith and his colleagues. Leaning against the door, the incarcerated men attempted to defend themselves. Smith, who was armed with a pistol smuggled to him by one of his visitors, Cyrus Wheelock, opened fire on the attackers. His six-shot pistol discharged only three times, but according to eyewitness John Taylor, all three bullets hit their mark. Still, there was no way the small group of men could overpower the mob. A musket ball penetrated the cell's wooden door and hit Hyrum in the face. He fell back, his last words being "I am a dead man." John Taylor was shot several times but was able to find cover under the bed. According to the official account, Smith then leapt toward the window of the cell and cried out, "Oh Lord, my God." Some believe he was attempting to give the Masonic signal of distress, but his unfinished cry went unheeded. As he reached the window, he was shot three times and fell two stories to the ground below. The mob then finished the deed by shooting Smith one more time. Only Willard Richards escaped without injury. Today the Latter-day Saints hail Smith as a martyr, "a lamb led to the slaughter."

None of those involved in the murders were found guilty. For a time, there was an uneasy peace between the Mormons and their non-Mormon neighbors. The big problem now facing the Saints was finding a successor to Smith. It came down to two men: Sidney Rigdon and Brigham Young. Rigdon had been a part of the Mormon movement almost from the beginning. He was a former minister who once espoused the teachings of Alexander Campbell. In addition, he was a gifted orator who, after joining the fledgling church in the early 1830s, quickly became the right-hand man of Joseph Smith. Rigdon was not someone to avoid controversy, as he was known for speaking his mind; on more than one occasion this trait had caused conflict with both Smith and his colleagues.

Standing in the way of Rigdon was Brigham Young, a convert to the church in 1832. Young did not see Rigdon's close association with Smith a reason for his becoming Smith's successor. Young claimed that the authority to choose a new prophet lay with the Council of the Twelve. It was decided that both men would have their opportunity to address the Mormon membership. When all was said and done, Young became Mormonism's second prophet, seer, and revelator. Rigdon later fell into obscurity.

The church remained in Nauvoo, and the temple that Smith had begun years earlier was finished and dedicated in April 1846. However, when it seemed apparent that those who were bent on seeing the Saints leave the area would never cease in their efforts, plans were made to move west to avoid further clashes. On 24 February 1846 hundreds of Latter-day Saints left Nauvoo and crossed the frozen Mississippi River into

Iowa. By the middle of May, it was estimated that nearly twelve thousand Mormons had fled.[1]

Many Mormons chose to live on Indian land in Iowa in an encampment that would be called Winter Quarters; others traveled to nearby Council Bluffs. Thousands of Latter-day Saints were scattered in Iowa until the spring of 1847, when the first party of emigrants headed toward the Salt Lake Valley. On 21 July 1847 a detachment of Saints led by Apostles Orson Pratt and Erastus Snow was the first to cast eyes on Mormonism's new home. Brigham Young, suffering from an attack of "mountain fever," arrived three days later on July 24. By the time Young arrived, Pratt's company was already busy building irrigation ditches.

Salt Lake City became the new headquarters of the LDS Church and though many of the Mormons set up their abode in the Salt Lake Valley, many more began settlements throughout what is today the state of Utah. Young would become the territorial governor in September 1850. Any privacy the Saints once had would soon be lost, thanks in large part to the gold rush of 1849 as well as the completion of the transcontinental railroad, both of which brought many non-Mormon "Gentiles" west.

In 1852 Apostle Orson Pratt, under the direction of Brigham Young, proclaimed as a belief of the LDS Church the doctrine of plural marriage. This teaching became so prominent in the Latter-day Saint faith that some leaders even claimed it was necessary for salvation. However, the controversy surrounding this teaching threatened to prevent Utah from achieving statehood. To alleviate this and other problems, the doctrine was officially abolished with what has become known as the Manifesto in 1890. But the stigma of polygamy still haunts the Mormon Church today.[2]

Misunderstandings and mistrust plagued the Saints for years following the Mormon emigration to Utah. The most serious conflict would arise in 1857 when, unknown to Brigham Young, President James Buchanan had him replaced as territorial governor. Having been led to believe that the Mormons were in a state of rebellion against the United States, Buchanan sent a contingent of soldiers to ensure that Young would relinquish his position. Apparently the president failed to explain this to Young, who assumed the Mormons were once again going to be forced from their homes. When Captain Stewart Van

Vliet entered Salt Lake City to make arrangements for provisions, he was surprised to find that the Mormons were expecting a hostile invasion. Despite denials from Van Vliet that the army had no intention of driving out the Saints, the Mormons continued to prepare their defense. Young devised a strategy that bought the Saints some time. Rather than fight the encroaching army, small units of Mormons delayed their arrival by blocking roads, creating cattle stampedes, and setting fires. These delays prevented the army from arriving in Salt Lake City before winter set in. The tactic worked, and the "Utah War" of 1857 failed to become the potential bloodbath many Mormons feared.

Although tragedy on a military level was diverted, the Utah War did have its casualties. A wagon train of emigrants from Arkansas on their way to California traveled through Utah during this tumultuous time. The Mormons were instructed not to sell supplies to outsiders because of the perceived threat. This circumstance compelled the wagon train to travel south into an area north of St. George, Utah, called the Mountain Meadows. This treatment served to infuriate the emigrants who began to make their feelings known. Rumors circulated that some of the emigrants had participated in the Missouri persecutions, and it was also rumored that they had the gun that killed Joseph Smith. Soon tensions escalated. While the Arkansas emigrants camped at the Meadows before crossing the desert, local Indians attacked them. This led to a conspiracy between local Mormon leaders and the Indians, and as a result a total of 120 men, women, and children were viciously killed in what has become known as the "Mountain Meadows Massacre." All of the Mormon participants took an oath of silence, and the Indians were blamed for the atrocity. Although Brigham Young knew the details within days of the incident, no one was held accountable for another twenty years. In 1877 John D. Lee became the lone scapegoat for this tragedy. He was executed by a firing squad as he sat on his coffin.

For many years a small monument marked the grave of several victims of the massacre, but few details were given to explain what exactly happened on that day in 1857. In 1990 a new set of markers was placed on the site, yet it added no information of the Mormon involvement in the massacre. Finally, in what many hail as an effort of reconciliation, the Mormon Church dedicated a new memorial in

September 1999 that admitted to Mormon participation in the event. Perhaps closure will finally come.

It is doubtful that the struggles of the nineteenth century will ever become a vague memory among Latter-day Saints. The suffering and hardships faced by the early Mormon pioneers will continually be pushed to the forefront by LDS leaders who understand that loyalty to heritage is a very powerful force. It is this legacy that compels many Mormons to remain in the faith, regardless of the myriad doctrinal problems. Still, the doctrinal inconsistencies cannot be overlooked, for if one is to be a true worshiper of God, he must worship Him in truth (John 4:24).

It was Brigham Young who declared, "I say to the whole world, receive the truth, no matter who presents it to you."[3] He also stated that Latter-day Saints should

> Take up the Bible, compare the religion of the Latter-day Saints with it, and see if it will stand the test. The doctrine that we preach is the doctrine of the Bible, it is the doctrine the Lord has revealed for the salvation of the children of God, and when men, who have once obeyed it, deny it, they deny it with their eyes wide open, and knowing that they deny the truth and set at naught the counsels of the Almighty.[4]

Although Young's challenge is a reasonable one, we disagree with his conclusion that Mormon doctrine is compatible with the Bible. In the following pages we will present our case in the hope that our readers will see that Mormonism has, unfortunately, "set at naught the counsels of the Almighty."

Examining the LDS Concept of God

God the Father

Men with keen intelligence got together . . . [at] Nicea and created a God. They did not pray for wisdom or revelation. They claimed no revelation from the Lord. They made it just about like a political party would do, and out of their own mortal minds created a God which is still worshiped by the great majority of Christians.

President Spencer W. Kimball,
Teachings of Spencer W. Kimball, 426

If the above quote from Mormonism's twelfth president is correct, then the God proclaimed by the Mormon Church is not the same God who is worshiped by millions of Christians today. Few would debate that the concept of God is paramount in any belief system. If two people hope to consider themselves of the same faith, they need to agree on their definition of the Almighty God. If they cannot agree on this vital point, they would be deceiving themselves and others to say that their faiths are the same.

Despite Kimball's claim, many laypeople in the Mormon Church insist that the God they worship is the same God worshiped by millions of Christians throughout the world. The problem with this assumption is that it does not concur with many statements made by the LDS leadership. Probably the most vocal leader on this subject was Apostle Bruce McConkie. He not only conceded that there is a difference in Gods, but he made it clear that worship of the God of Christianity's creeds will not result in salvation. For instance:

> From the beginning of history the great masses of men have worshiped false gods. Those who believe the creeds of Christendom profess to worship an incomprehensible, unknowable, immaterial essence that fills the immensity of space and is everywhere and nowhere in particular present. . . . There is no salvation in the worship of false gods. For such false worship the Lord imposed the death penalty in ancient Israel.[1]

> The false gods of Christendom bear the same names as the true Gods of the Bible. Beyond this they have little resemblance. They are described in the creeds that the Lord told Joseph Smith were "an abomination in his sight."[2]

> And be it remembered that the gods of the creeds, which are the gods of Christendom, are just as false as are the gods of the Assyrians, Babylonians, Muslims, Amorites, Hittites, or any other peoples, excepting only the members of the true church.[3]

> It follows that the devil would rather spread false doctrine about God and the Godhead, and induce false feelings with reference to any one of them, than almost any other thing he could do. The creeds of Christendom illustrate perfectly what Lucifer wants so-called Christian people to believe about Deity in order to be damned.[4]

Apostle Dallin H. Oaks said the following in a 1995 general conference speech:

> In contrast [to ideas believed in Mormonism], many Christians reject the idea of a tangible, personal God and a Godhead of three separate beings. They believe that God is a spirit and that the Godhead is only one God. In our view, these concepts are the evidence of the falling away we call the Great Apostasy. . . . The consequences persist in the various creeds of Christianity, which declare a Godhead of only one being and which describe that single being or God as "incomprehensible" and "without body, parts, and passion." One of the distinguishing features of the doc-

trine of The Church of Jesus Christ of Latter-day Saints is its rejection of *all* of these postbiblical creeds.[5]

To be sure, historical Christianity has never advocated the belief in a tangible deity. Like many other LDS leaders, Oaks mistakenly assumes that a nonhuman God cannot be a personal God. Numerous biblical passages definitively prove how God desires to have an intimate relationship with humankind. In fact He gave His only Son to make it possible! Consider, for instance, 1 Peter 5:7, where Christian believers are told to cast all their cares on God. Why? Because He is a personal God who cares for His creation. To those who have sinned, God lovingly calls them to "reason together" with Him (Isa. 1:18).

When Christians say that God is "incomprehensible," they do not mean that God is an irrational or confusing being. It is difficult, if not impossible, for finite humans to fully understand the infinite God. While describing the greatness of God in 1 Timothy 6:16, Paul explained that God dwells in unapproachable light. Because of our limitations, we can never expect to fully apprehend every aspect of the Creator. As Isaiah 55:8 says, "For my thoughts are not your thoughts, neither are your ways my ways, saith the LORD." When we compare the attributes of the God of the Bible to the attributes that LDS leaders have applied to their God, it is apparent that major differences do exist.

NOT ETERNALLY GOD

In 1844 a Mormon elder by the name of King Follett was "crushed in a well by the falling of a tub of rock." At Follett's funeral Joseph Smith delivered a sermon that has come to be known as the King Follett discourse. In this message Smith declared, "We have imagined and supposed that God was God from all eternity. I will refute that idea, and take away the veil, so that you may see."[6] According to Mormonism, Elohim, known as God the Father, or Heavenly Father,[7] lived on a planet similar to earth. LDS Apostle Orson Pratt explained:

We were begotten by our Father in heaven; the person of Father in Heaven was begotten on a previous heavenly world by His Father; and again, He

was begotten by a still more ancient Father; and so on, from generation to
generation. . . .[8]

Apostle Orson Hyde said:

Remember that God, our heavenly Father, was perhaps once a child, and
mortal like we ourselves, and rose step by step in the scale of progress, in
the school of advancement; has moved forward and overcome, until He
has arrived at the point where He now is.[9]

Still another apostle, James Talmage, wrote:

We believe in a God who is Himself progressive, whose majesty is intelligence; whose perfection consists in eternal advancement—a Being who
has attained His exalted state by a path which now His children are permitted to follow, whose glory it is their heritage to share.[10]

Page 132 of the LDS manual *Achieving a Celestial Marriage* reads,
"By obedience to eternal gospel principles, he progressed from one
stage of life to another until he attained the state we call exaltation or
godhood." The idea that God *progresses* and *advances* is foreign to
biblical Christianity. Logic would demand that if the Mormon God
had to *attain* the position he now holds, then he could not be the eternal God of the Bible. Meanwhile, Mormonism teaches that men and
women were created to become gods and goddesses in the next life.
President Brigham Young insisted:

The Lord created you and me for the purpose of becoming Gods like Himself; when we have been proved in our present capacity, and been faithful
with all things He puts into our possession. We are created, we are born
for the express purpose of growing up from the low estate of manhood, to
become Gods like unto our Father in heaven. That is the truth about it, just
as it is. The Lord has organized mankind for the express purpose of increasing in that intelligence and truth, which is with God, until he is capable of
creating worlds on worlds, and becoming Gods, even the sons of God.[11]

President Spencer Kimball concurred:

Man can become like God. In each of us is the potentiality to become a
god—pure, holy, influential, true and independent of all these earth forces.

We learn from the scriptures that each of us has an eternal existence, that we were in the beginning with God. And understanding this gives to us a unique sense of man's dignity.[12]

Regarding this subject, Kimball also wrote:

To this end God created man to live in mortality and endowed him with the potential to perpetuate the race, to subdue the earth, to perfect himself and to become as God, omniscient and omnipotent.[13]

According to the LDS-produced *Ensign* magazine:

The stunning truth, lost to humankind before the Restoration, is that each of us is a god in embryo. We may become as our heavenly parents. We, too, in exalted families, may one day preside in our own realms, under him who is our God and our Father forever.[14]

Despite the limitations that Mormon leaders place on God, the Bible is very clear that God has neither beginning nor end. Words such as *eternal* and *everlasting* emphasize the fact that God's perfection transcends time. He always was God and always will be God. Consider the following:

Before the mountains were brought forth, or ever thou hadst formed the earth and the world, even from everlasting to everlasting, thou art God (Ps. 90:2).

Thy throne is established of old: thou art from everlasting (Ps. 93:2).

Hast thou not known? hast thou not heard, that the everlasting God, the LORD, the Creator of the ends of the earth, fainteth not, neither is weary? (Isa. 40:28).

For thus saith the high and lofty One that inhabiteth eternity, whose name is Holy (Isa. 57:15).

NOT IMMUTABLE

According to LDS teaching, God gradually progressed to the position and power he now holds. It is with this idea in mind that Seventy Milton R. Hunter wrote:

Yet, if we accept the great law of eternal progression, we must accept the fact that there was a time when Deity was much less powerful than He is today. Then how did He become glorified and exalted and attain His present status of Godhood? In the first place, aeons ago God undoubtedly took advantage of every opportunity to learn the laws of truth and as He became acquainted with each new verity He righteously obeyed it.[15]

This sentiment was also expressed by Apostle John Widtsoe when he wrote:

Therefore, if the law of progression be accepted, God must have been engaged from the beginning, and must now be engaged in progressive development, and infinite as God is, he must have been less powerful in the past than he is today.[16]

Biblically speaking, God's perfection means that He never needs to change in a metaphysical or moral sense. As His nature remains constant, so, too, His desires and purposes never change. As the psalmist correctly pointed out in Psalm 102:27, "But thou art the same, and thy years shall have no end." In an expression that could not be made any clearer, Malachi 3:6 says, "For I am the LORD, I change not." And James 1:17 declares that there is no variation or "shadow of turning" when it comes to the Father of lights.

There is no fluctuation in God's divine character. The perfect God of the Bible has no need to change. If He were to better Himself, it would show that He *was* not perfect. Should He make Himself worse, it would show that He *is* not perfect. In the words of Christian theologian Herman Bavinck, "Whatever changes ceases to be what it was."[17] The idea that God is immutable should bring comfort to His people, since they can be assured God would never change anything affecting their salvation. While humanity struggles with sin and thus alters its relationship with God, it is not God who wavers, because He is always constant.

Some have asked why the Bible speaks of God as "repenting." It would seem that if God was the one who declared all things to happen in precise order, nothing could possibly catch Him unawares. Was God really unaware that Adam and Eve would sin and produce some of the most evil offspring imaginable? Was God surprised when the wicked citizens of Nineveh repented in the Old Testament Book of Jonah, thus "sidetracking" God's impending judgment? Not at all. The Bible often uses anthropomorphic language—words describing God in human terms.

Since it is God who declares the end from the beginning, it would be inconceivable to think that God could change His mind as humans do. We change our minds as a result of previously unavailable information. God, however, knows all things. There is nothing new for Him to evaluate. When God chose not to bring judgment on Nineveh, it was not because He literally "changed his mind." Quite the contrary, His decision to spare the city was actually an example of His immutability, or His constant nature. Jonah recognized this, for in his anger he confirmed that God was gracious and merciful, slow to anger and abundant in lovingkindness (Jonah 4:1–2). Jonah understood why God would not destroy the city. It was based on the fact that God consistently forgives those who are repentant. Jeremiah 18:7–10 sheds light on this issue:

> At what instant I shall speak concerning a nation, and concerning a kingdom, to pluck up, and to pull down, and to destroy it; if that nation, against whom I have pronounced, turn from their evil, I will repent of the evil that I thought to do unto them. And at what instant I shall speak concerning a nation, and concerning a kingdom, to build and to plant it; if it do evil in my sight, that it obey not my voice, then I will repent of the good, wherewith I said I would benefit them.

What appears to be a case of God changing His mind is really nothing more than God's unchangeable response to people changing their minds. Should Mormons fail to see this attribute as defined in the Bible, they would do well to read Moroni 8:18 in the *Book of Mormon*. It says, "For I know that God is not a partial God, neither a changeable being; but he is unchangeable from all eternity to all eternity." Mormon 9:19 strongly adds these words:

> And if there were miracles wrought then, why has God ceased to be a God of miracles and yet be an unchangeable Being? And behold, I say unto you he changeth not; if so he would cease to be God; and he ceaseth not to be God, and is a God of miracles.

According to Mosiah 3:5 and Moroni 7:22, God is God "from all eternity to all eternity" and from "everlasting to everlasting." Third Nephi 24:6 and Mormon 9:9–10 add that He does not vary or change. If this is so, at what time did He exist as a man? While we would certainly not claim that the *Book of Mormon* is a valid scripture, it is interesting how Mormonism hinges on the idea that God is a glorified man who lived, died, was resurrected, and eventually progressed to godhood, when it contradicts Mormon scripture.

NOT SELF-EXISTENT

Unique to Mormonism is the idea that all humans (and gods) once existed as undeveloped "intelligences." By following laws and principles that Mormons believe are eternal, each intelligence progresses until godhood becomes possible. Joseph Smith taught that his God, by his obedience to these eternal laws, now has "power to institute laws to instruct the weaker intelligences, that they may be exalted with himself, so that they might have one glory upon another."[18]

However, Mormonism does not trace this long procession of deities to one specific first cause. Instead, it is assumed that a myriad of gods preceded the LDS God and that he himself is the offspring of one of these gods. President Joseph Fielding Smith not only testified to the fact that there was a long procession of gods, but he also insisted that these gods could number in the millions:

We are informed that there are many earths or worlds which have been created, and were created by the Son for the Father. This was, of course, before he was born a Babe in Bethlehem. Evidently his Father passed through a period of mortality even as he passed through mortality, and as we all are doing. Our Father in heaven, according to the Prophet, had a Father, and since there has been a condition of this kind through all eternity, each Father had a Father, until we come to a stop where we cannot go further, because of our limited capacity to understand.[19]

The knowledge is now revealed that there are throughout the universe millions, in fact, innumerable galaxies—island universes—of stars. . . . Evidently each of these great systems is governed by divine law; with divine presiding Gods, for it would be unreasonable to assume that each was not so governed.[20]

On this subject Brigham Young taught the following:

How many Gods there are, I do not know. But there never was a time when there were not Gods and worlds, and when men were not passing through the same ordeals that we are now passing through. That course has been from all eternity, and it is and will be to all eternity.[21]

Young admitted that trying to understand how the first God came to be God was difficult.

Many have tried to penetrate to the First Cause of all things; but it would be as easy for an ant to number the grains of sand on the earth. It is not for man, with his limited intelligence, to grasp eternity in his comprehension. . . . It would be as easy for a gnat to trace the history of man back to his origin as for man to fathom the First Cause of all things, lift the veil of eternity, and reveal the mysteries that have been sought after by philosophers from the beginning.[22]

While it is admittedly difficult to comprehend the existence of a God who has always existed, it is neither implausible nor unbiblical. On the other hand, Mormonism's view of God is both implausible and unbiblical. It is also illogical since it raises several questions as to how the first intelligence was able to elevate himself to the position of deity. What allowed for this first intelligence to be first out of the "starting gate" toward godhood? How was he able to comply with the many requirements necessary to reach such a position? Following this logic, other questions are raised:

- As mentioned earlier, the Mormon God is subject to laws that are alleged to be eternal. How can this be if there is no such thing as an eternal lawgiver in Mormonism?
- If becoming a human and living in a sin-tainted world is necessary for godhood, how did the first God get his human body? Who made the world that he supposedly lived on?

- If the purpose of going through mortality is to overcome sin, who was it that defined sin? How could this first God overcome something that could not have been defined?

Mormonism's lack of a first cause is what makes understanding this LDS doctrine problematic. Joseph Fielding McConkie and Robert L. Millet claim that "God is the giver of the law, the author and maker of it."[23] This statement could only make sense if the God of Mormonism was eternally God. Since he was not, he cannot be credited with making laws that are eternal.

The Bible very clearly teaches that God is *the* First Cause. He is self-existent, or *uncaused,* and therefore not dependent on anything for His existence. God is life, and it is because of Him that we have life. All creation exists due to the purpose and will of God Himself. To assume that there were other gods before the God of the Bible refutes Isaiah 43:10, which declares, "I am he: before me there was no God formed, neither shall there be after me." When God said in Isaiah 48:12, "Hearken unto me, O Jacob and Israel, my called; I am he; I am the first, I also am the last," He allowed no room for any assumption that He came along later in the creation process.

NOT TRANSCENDENT

God is distinct from His creation and the universe. When discussing the transcendence of God, we need to consider a number of aspects. Not only is the "person" of God unlike human beings, but His moral character is also unique. He is infinitely exalted above all that He has ever created.

Mormon leaders have not hidden the fact that they believe God is an exalted human being. Apostle John Widtsoe said, "God and man are of the same race, differing only in their degrees of advancement."[24] Apostle Parley P. Pratt agreed, adding, "Gods, angels and men are all of one species, one race, one great family."[25] According to Apostle Orson Whitney, the difference between the human and the divine was just the mere matter of "education and development." He went on to say, "Gods and men are of the same species, and it is just as reasonable that God's children should attain to the fullness of his spiritual stature, as that man's children should grow to the fullness of his physical stature."[26]

Bruce McConkie gave the following description of his God:

> That there is a God in heaven who is infinite and eternal; who has a body of flesh and bones as tangible as man's, and who is in fact a resurrected, glorified, perfected, and exalted Man; who has all power, all might, and all dominion, and who knows all things; and who in the ultimate and full sense is the Creator, Upholder, and Preserver of all things, both this earth and all worlds, the sidereal heavens, and all things that in them are.[27]

Despite the many quotes supporting the idea that God was once a human, President Gordon B. Hinckley made it appear that he was not clear on whether such a concept was part of Mormon belief. In 1997 Don Lattin, a journalist for the *San Francisco Chronicle,* had the following conversation with Hinckley:

> *Lattin:* There are some significant differences in your beliefs. For instance, don't Mormons believe that God was once a man?
>
> *Hinckley:* I wouldn't say that. There was a little couplet coined, "As man is, God once was. As God is, man may become." Now that's more of a couplet than anything else. That gets into some pretty deep theology that we don't know very much about.
>
> *Lattin:* So you're saying the church is still struggling to understand this?
>
> *Hinckley:* Well, as God is, man may become. We believe in eternal progression. Very strongly. We believe that the glory of God is intelligence and whatever principle of intelligence we attain unto in this life, it will rise with us in the Resurrection. Knowledge, learning, is an eternal thing. And for that reason, we stress education. We're trying to do all we can to make of our people the ablest, best, brightest people that we can.[28]

Several months later President Hinckley still sounded confused. On 18 July 1997 a public television program titled *Road to Salvation* featured the LDS Church. In the broadcast, interviewer Richard Ostling noted, "President Gordon Hinckley says the concept of God having been a man is not stressed any longer, but he does believe that human beings can become gods in the afterlife." Then, in the 4 August

1997 edition of *Time* magazine, reporter David Van Biema wrote on page 56:

> On whether his church still holds that God the Father was once a man, he sounded uncertain. "I don't know that we teach it. I don't know that we emphasize it. . . . I understand the philosophical background behind it, but I don't know a lot about it, and I don't think others know a lot about it."

It would certainly be erroneous to assume this teaching has not been stressed in modern times. Writing for the LDS magazine *Ensign,* BYU Professor Robert L. Millet in 1996 wrote, "Knowing what we know concerning God our Father . . . he is an exalted and glorified being; that he was once a man and dwelt on an earth."[29] When referring to some of the criticisms that were raised following these interviews, President Hinckley made it clear that he was very familiar with what he believed. However, Hinckley has not only been evasive with the secular media, but he has also not been forthright with his own people. For instance, at the October 1998 LDS general conference, he gave the message "What Are People Asking about Us?" He prefaced his talk by saying that he wanted to respond to some of the questions "asked by those of the media and other churches."

First on his list was the question, "What is the Mormon doctrine of Deity, of God?" Hinckley began his answer by quoting Joseph Smith, who had stated in 1844, "It is the first principle of the Gospel to know for certainty the Character of God, and to know that we may converse with him as one man converses with another . . ."[30] As before, Hinckley was illusory, for he failed to give the whole quote. Had he finished Smith's statement, he would have also added, ". . . and that he was once a man like us; yea, that God himself, the Father of us all, dwelt on an earth, the same as Jesus Christ himself did; and I will show it from the Bible."[31]

The God of the Bible loathes the idea of being likened to His creation. In Psalm 50:21 He chided His people for trying to make such a comparison when He declared, "Thou thoughtest that I was altogether such an one as thyself: but I will reprove thee, and set them in order before thine eyes."[32] In Romans 1:22–23, Paul said only fools attempt to change the glory of the incorruptible God into an image made like corruptible man. While pagan religions tend to make their gods in the fashion of some created thing, the God of the Bible will have none of it. In His prohibition of graven images, God eliminated the possibility of imagining a form that they might suppose represented the true God.

Some have used the anthropomorphic language of the Bible to assume God does in fact inhabit a body similar to ours. However, verses that speak of God having arms (Deut. 33:27), hands (2 Chron. 6:4), feet (Ps. 18:9), ears (2 Sam. 22:7), and so on, are never meant to be taken any more literally than those passages that speak of God having wings (Ps. 17:8) or the ability to breathe smoke out of His nostrils and fire from His mouth (2 Sam. 22:9).

NOT OMNIPOTENT

According to Apostle Orson Hyde:

> There are Lords many, and Gods many, for they are called Gods to whom the word of God comes, and the word of God comes to all these kings and priests. But to our branch of the kingdom there is but one God, to whom we all owe the most perfect submission and loyalty; yet our God is just as subject to still higher intelligences, as we should be to him.[33]

It was such reasoning that probably led LDS writer W. Cleon Skousen to conclude that God could stop being God.

> Through modern revelation we learn that the universe is filled with vast numbers of intelligences, and we further learn that Elohim is God simply because all of these intelligences honor and sustain Him as such. ... Since God "acquired" the honor and sustaining influence of "all things" it follows as a corollary that if He should ever do anything to violate the confidence or "sense of justice" of these intelligences, they would promptly withdraw their support, and the "power" of God would disintegrate. ... "He would cease to be God."[34]

While many LDS leaders have taught that their God Elohim is omnipotent (all-powerful), several factors belie this thought. Since Mormonism has reintroduced polytheism to the modern world, the question is, Who among the many gods is the "most powerful"? Some Mormons dodge this dilemma by insisting the word *omnipotent* does not mean "all-powerful" but rather refers to being "unlimited in power." Even this definition does not help solve the problem, since the Mormon God cannot create *ex nihilo,* or out of nothing. The Mormon God's ability to *create* is limited by the fact that he is only able to organize already existing matter. Said Apostle John Widtsoe:

> God, the supreme Power, cannot conceivably originate matter; he can only organize matter. Neither can he destroy matter; he can only disorganize it. . . . The doctrine that God made the earth or man from nothing becomes, therefore, an absurdity.[35]

Although faithful Mormons hope to someday achieve the status of deity, they must concede that they will never rise above the preeminence of Elohim. Even as gods, exalted Mormons will always be subservient to him. In the same way, Elohim will never rise above those gods who preceded him. Contrary to this opinion, the Old Testament is replete with accounts that demonstrate the superior power of the God of Israel. Whether it was Moses versus Pharaoh's magicians or Elijah against the prophets of Baal on Mt. Carmel, God was there to show that His authority reigned supreme. What may be seen as a contest between deities was really nothing of the kind.

The Book of Job contains four chapters in which God personally proclaims His omnipotence to His suffering servant. When He was finished, Job had to admit, "I know that thou canst do every thing, and that no thought can be withholden from thee" (Job 42:2). Unlike the deities worshiped by the pagan world, the God of the Bible does whatever He pleases (Ps. 115:3).[36] With Him all things are possible (Matt. 19:26). The God of Christianity is omnipotent and answers to no one.

The Bible also never hides the fact that the God of both the Jews and Christians is the "God of gods." Five times this expression is used to demonstrate that the God of the Bible is the sovereign and powerful God of creation (Deut. 10:17; Josh. 22:22; Ps. 136:2; Dan. 2:47; 11:36). Although it would be easy for a Mormon to misuse this phrase and try to say it proves the existence of other gods, this idea is not consistent with the many passages of Scripture that insist there is no other God than He Himself (Deut. 4:35, 39; Isa. 45:5–6; 46:9; Mark 12:32). Contrary to pagan belief, God is over anything man might think is a god.

NOT OMNIPRESENT

The God of Mormonism cannot be personally present everywhere because he dwells in a finite body. Brigham Young stated, "Some would have us believe that God is present everywhere. It is not so."[37] According to Mormon theology, no member of the LDS godhead has the ability to be truly omnipresent. Said Apostle James Talmage: "It has been said, therefore, that God is everywhere present; but this does not mean that the actual person of any one member of the Godhead can be physically present in more than one place at one time."[38]

Bruce McConkie explained that as the third member of the godhead, the Holy Ghost is a "Spirit Person" or "Spirit Man" who "can be in only one place at one time" because "of the Man whom [*sic*] he is." McConkie further stated: "Because he is a Spirit Personage, he has power—according to the eternal laws ordained by the Father—to perform essential and unique functions for men. In this dispensation, at least, nothing has been revealed as to his origin or destiny; expressions on these matters are both speculative and fruitless."[39]

Mormon leaders have not always been consistent when it comes to the Holy Ghost/Holy Spirit. Some say the Holy Ghost and Holy Spirit are synonymous terms for the same being, but Apostle John Widtsoe made a clear distinction between the two:

> The Holy Spirit is the agent, means, or influence by which the will, power, and intelligence of God, and the Godhead, personal Beings, may be transmitted throughout space. . . . The Holy Ghost, sometimes called the Comforter, is the third member of the Godhead, and is a personage, distinct from the Holy Spirit. As a personage, the Holy Ghost cannot anymore than the Father and Son be everywhere present in person.[40]

Adding to the confusion is Apostle Parley P. Pratt's idea that the Holy Spirit is a substance or fluid:

Jesus Christ, a little babe like all the rest of us have been, grew to be a man, was filled with a divine substance or fluid, called the Holy Spirit, by which he comprehended and spake the truth in power and authority; and by which he controlled the elements, and imparted health and life to those who were prepared to partake of the same.[41]

Explaining God's omnipresence, Christian scholar R. C. Sproul takes particular notice of the prefix *omni*. He writes:

The "omni" relates not only to the places where God is, but also to how much of Him is in any given place. God is not only present in all places but God is fully present in every place. This is called His immensity. Believers living in New York enjoy the fullness of the presence of God while believers in Moscow enjoy that same presence. His immensity, then, does not refer to His size, but to His ability to be fully present everywhere.[42]

When Solomon dedicated the Jerusalem temple, he fully recognized that such a building could never actually house the person of God. In his dedicatory prayer, Solomon declared God's omnipresence when he proclaimed, "Behold, the heaven and heaven of heavens cannot contain thee" (1 Kings 8:27).[43] In Proverbs 15:3 Solomon expressed both God's omnipresence and omniscience when he stated, "The eyes of the LORD are in every place, beholding the evil and the good." The prophet Jeremiah also extolled God's omnipresence when he wrote Jeremiah 23:23–24: "Am I a God at hand, saith the LORD, and not a God afar off? Can any hide himself in secret places that I shall not see him? saith the LORD."

God's omnipresence is demonstrated by the fact that He has no body. While God is present everywhere, He does not fill space. The concept of a God of spirit is taught ever so precisely in John 4:24, which states that "God is a Spirit."[44] To alleviate this problem, LDS leaders have insisted that this passage was mistranslated. Joseph Smith, in his 1833 Inspired Version of the Bible, actually removed the troubling words.[45] While some Mormons may counter by insisting God *has* a spirit, this passage does not allow for such an interpretation. Since God is Spirit, it stands to reason that He is also invisible (see Col. 1:15; 1 Tim. 1:17; Heb. 11:27).

C O N C L U S I O N

The God of Mormonism:

- Was not always God (once a man)
- Was not the first God
- Organized already-created matter in the creation of the world
- Cannot be in more than one place at once

The God of Christianity:

- Is eternally God
- Is the First Cause of all things
- Created the world *ex nihilo* (out of nothing)
- Is fully present everywhere

Jesus

And virtually all the millions of apostate Christendom have abased themselves before the mythical throne of a mythical Christ.

Apostle Bruce McConkie, *Mormon Doctrine,* 269

On January 1, 2000, the LDS *Church News* published a declaration signed by the First Presidency and Quorum of the Twelve Apostles that testified to their belief in "The Living Christ." The one-page statement mentioned how Jesus was "the first and the last," "the Firstborn of the Father," "the Only Begotten Son in the flesh," "the Redeemer of the world," and "the immortal Son of God." While on the surface the declaration sounded very orthodox, it conspicuously failed to specifically state what the LDS leaders meant by these terms.

THE MYTHICAL JESUS

According to the above quote from Apostle Bruce McConkie, those outside Mormonism believe in a "mythical Christ." Bernard P. Brockbank, a member of the Mormon Seventy, concurred with this assessment: "It is true that many of the Christian churches worship a different Jesus than is worshiped by the Mormons or the Church of Jesus Christ of Latter-day Saints."[1]

Ten years later, Seventy John K. Carmack claimed his church represented the true and historical Jesus. He taught, "The Christ one meets in Matthew, Mark, Luke, John, Acts, and epistles of the New Testament is *basically* the Christ in which Latter-day Saints literally believe."[2] When speaking to a group of Latter-day Saints in Paris, France, in June 1998, President Gordon B. Hinckley responded to those who claimed that Latter-day Saints do not believe in the traditional Christ. Quite candidly, President Hinckley said, "No, I don't. The traditional Christ of whom they speak is not the Christ of whom I speak."[3]

While there are admittedly peripheral issues that Christians might disagree on, it is inconceivable to think that Christians who happen to belong to a different denomination would make such a comment about fellow believers. We cannot imagine, for instance, a Baptist telling a Lutheran, "Our Jesus is *basically* the one Lutherans worship." A Presbyterian would not tell a Methodist that he does not believe in the *traditional Christ.* Nor can we imagine a member from the Assemblies of God telling a Wesleyan that the Christ of the Wesleyan Church is *mythical.*

Clearly the confessions and creeds of such denominations insist that true faith can only be found in the Christ whose attributes are defined by the Bible. This is not to say that heretical views of Christ have not sprung up within various groups or by individuals professing to be Christian. In such cases Christian apologists have been quick to expose the error in the hope that such false teachings concerning Christ would be corrected.

Proper belief in the person of Jesus Christ has always been considered essential to Christian fellowship. History bears out that a biblical view of Christ was imperative if an individual or organization was to be considered part of the Christian fold. As noted above, however, knowledgeable leaders within the Mormon organization have gone on record stating that there is, in fact, a difference when it comes to the Jesus of the LDS faith. The question that must be asked in light of such a confession is, Which Jesus is the true Jesus?

Mormon theology explains that all human beings lived prior to this life in what is called the preexistence. Bruce McConkie stated that Jesus attained the status of a god in the preexistence.

He [Jesus] is the Firstborn of the Father. By obedience and devotion to
the truth he attained that pinnacle of intelligence which ranked him as a
God, as the Lord Omnipotent, while yet in his pre-existent state. . . . Inasmuch, however, as Christ attained Godhood while yet in pre-existence,
he too stood as a God to the other spirits.[4]

In essence, the Mormon Jesus, by becoming a god without having
to live a human life on a previous planet, did something that his own
"father" could not accomplish. According to Mormonism, all humanity must experience a mortal probation in order to prove ourselves
worthy to become gods after death. How could Jesus obtain godhood
in the preexistence when the whole purpose of the mortal probation
is supposedly to test the individual's worthiness to become a god?
Since Elohim had to go through such a process, it could be argued
that Jesus must be more advanced in some respects than the Father.
Unlike the teachings of LDS prophets, there was not a point in time
when the Jesus of the Bible was not God. Christians have historically
defended the doctrine that Christ was, and is, the eternal God.

The Bible very clearly points out that Jesus can be misidentified.
Despite the claim of people who accept the belief that all religions each
have a path to God—a system known as Universalism—a belief in a
false Jesus is just as dangerous as no Jesus at all because faith is only
as good as the object in which it is placed. Indeed, James 2:19 makes
it appear that an intellectual belief in God is not the same as true faith.

Paul certainly admonished the Corinthians for accepting a false version of Christ when he said in 2 Corinthians 11:4, "For if he that cometh
preacheth another Jesus, whom we have not preached, or if ye receive
another spirit, which ye have not received, or another gospel, which
ye have not accepted, ye might well bear with him." He added:

I marvel that ye are so soon removed from him that called you into the
grace of Christ unto another gospel: Which is not another; but there be
some that trouble you, and would pervert the gospel of Christ. But though
we, or an angel from heaven, preach any other gospel unto you than that
which we have preached unto you, let him be accursed. As we said before,
so say I now again, If any man preach any other gospel unto you than that
ye have received, let him be accursed.

                                                           Galatians 1:6–9

Heretical views of Christ have plagued Christianity since its beginning. Because of the importance of the belief in Jesus, early heresies such as Gnosticism,[5] Docetism,[6] Adoptionism,[7] Subordinationism,[8] Modalism,[9] and Arianism,[10] just to name a few, needed the young church's attention. Christian scholar Harold O. J. Brown wrote, "To a degree that is hard for twentieth-century people to grasp, the early church believed that it was absolutely vital to know and accept some very specific statements about the nature and attributes of God and his Son Jesus Christ."[11]

Since how a person believes in Christ can affect his or her eternal destiny, let's consider the Jesus of Mormonism and compare him with the Jesus of biblical Christianity.

JESUS AND THE VIRGIN BIRTH

Since the very beginning, Christ's followers have believed that He was born as a result of a miraculous conception. Matthew 1:18 is very clear about this fact. Mormon leaders have insisted in a belief of the virgin birth, yet they give a description far removed from that held by Christians throughout the centuries. The following quotes verify that several LDS leaders espoused a position regarding the birth of Christ that has never been accepted in Christian circles.

> The Church of Jesus Christ of Latter-day Saints proclaims that Jesus Christ is the Son of God in the most literal sense. The body in which He performed His mission in the flesh was sired by that same Holy Being we worship as God, our Eternal Father. Jesus was not the son of Joseph, nor was He begotten by the Holy Ghost. He is the Son of the Eternal Father![12]

> Thus, God the Father became the literal father of Jesus Christ. Jesus is the only person on earth to be born of a mortal mother and an immortal father.[13]

> The birth of the Saviour was as natural as are the births of our children; it was the result of natural action. He partook of flesh and blood—was begotten of his Father, as we were of our fathers.[14]

> I will say that I was naturally begotten; so was my father, and also my Saviour Jesus Christ. According to the Scriptures, he is the first begotten of his father in the flesh, and there was nothing unnatural about it.[15]

Now, we are told in scriptures that Jesus Christ is the only begotten Son of God in the flesh. Well, now for the benefit of the older ones, how are children begotten? I answer just as Jesus Christ was begotten of his father. . . . Jesus is the only person who had our Heavenly Father as the father of his body.[16]

Christ was Begotten by an Immortal Father in the same way that mortal men are begotten by mortal fathers. . . . And Christ was born into the world as the literal Son of this Holy Being; he was born in the same personal, real, and literal sense that any mortal son is born to a mortal father. There is nothing figurative about his paternity; he was begotten, conceived and born in the normal and natural course of events, for he is the Son of God, and that designation means what it says.[17]

There is no need to spiritualize away the plain meaning of the scriptures. There is nothing figurative or hidden or beyond comprehension in our Lord's coming into mortality. He is the Son of God in the same sense and way that we are the sons of mortal fathers. It is just that simple.[18]

God the Eternal Father, whom we designate by the exalted name-title "Elohim," is the literal Parent of our Lord and Savior Jesus Christ, and of the spirits of the human race. Elohim is the Father in every sense in which Jesus Christ is so designated, and distinctively He is the Father of Spirits. . . . Jesus Christ is the Son of Elohim both as spiritual and bodily offspring; that is to say, Elohim is literally the Father of the spirit of Jesus Christ and also of the body in which Jesus Christ performed His mission in the flesh.[19]

That Child to be born of Mary was begotten of Elohim, the Eternal Father, not in violation of natural law but in accordance with a higher manifestation thereof; and, the offspring from that association of supreme sanctity, celestial Sireship, and pure through mortal maternity, was of right to be called the "Son of the Highest."[20]

[Jesus] was able to make payment because he lived a sinless life and because he was actually, literally, biologically the Son of God in the flesh.[21]

The official doctrine of the Church is that Jesus is the literal offspring of God. He's got 46 chromosomes; 23 came from Mary, 23 came from God the Eternal Father.[22]

Many Latter-day Saints find the above statements to be repulsive; on the other hand, others may be surprised that Christians could be offended by the LDS interpretation. It might be asked, How could a Mormon say Christ was born of a virgin when his leaders have consistently described an act common to the reproductive process? This is accomplished by changing the definition of the phrase "virgin birth."

Since Mormonism teaches that Mary did not have sexual relations with a *mortal* man but instead was impregnated by an *immortal* man (Elohim), many Mormons have no qualms about using this phrase. Bruce McConkie said, "For our present purposes, suffice it to say that our Lord was born of a virgin, which is fitting and proper, and also natural, since the Father of the Child was an Immortal Being."[23]

When one considers that the LDS Church also teaches that every human born on earth is a literal child of God, the above quotes become even more disconcerting. Mormon leaders have maintained that all humans, Mary included, are literally God's spirit children, born in the preexistence via a sexual relationship between Heavenly Father and one of his goddess wives. If Mormon leaders are telling the truth when they say that God physically impregnated Mary, then we have no other recourse than to assume the Jesus of Mormonism was created by way of an incestuous relationship.

THE DIMINISHING OF JESUS

Jesus is said to be humanity's oldest spiritual brother who became a god, according to Seventy Milton R. Hunter, "through consistent effort and continuous obedience to all the Gospel truths and universal laws." That effort, Hunter continues, included Jesus' own baptism:

> Although John recognized Jesus as a perfect man, the Master made it clear that it was absolutely necessary for even the Son of God to be baptized. He—like the least of us—must obey every law of the Gospel if He was to receive all the blessings predicated on obedience.[24]

In a general conference speech, Apostle Russell M. Nelson said Jesus achieved His perfection *after* His resurrection:

That Jesus attained perfection *following* his resurrection is confirmed in the Book of Mormon. It records the visit of the resurrected Lord to the people of ancient America. There he repeated the important injunction previously cited, but with one very significant addition. He said, "I would that ye should be perfect *even as I,* or your Father who is in heaven is perfect" (3 Nephi 12:48). This time he listed himself along with his Father as a perfected personage. Previously, he had not (See Matt. 5:48).[25]

Despite these false teachings, the Bible clearly states that Jesus is God and has been from all eternity. John 1:1–2, 14 clearly state:

In the beginning was the Word, and the Word was with God, and the Word was God. The same was in the beginning with God. . . . And the Word was made flesh, and dwelt among us, (and we beheld his glory, the glory as of the only begotten of the Father), full of grace and truth.[26]

Christianity has historically taught that Jesus, as the very God, took upon Himself the form of a man. This is not to say that at any time His godhood was diminished in any degree after His physical appearance on earth (His incarnation).[27] Jesus was, and is, both divine and human; 100 percent God and 100 percent man. He was conceived through the agency of the Holy Spirit (Matt. 1:18–25; Luke 1:35); He lived a sinless life while subjected to human temptations (John 5:19; Heb. 2:18; 4:15); He died a real death and rose again bodily from the dead to conquer sin (Rom. 5:6–10; 1 Cor. 15:3–4); He will return to judge all humanity (John 5:22); He sent the Holy Spirit to empower the believers (John 14–16; Acts 1:8); He can be prayed to (Acts 7:59);[28] finally, He is deserving to receive honor, love, faith, and worship as the Father (Matt. 10:37; John 5:23; 14:1; Heb. 1:6). At the same time, He shares attributes with the Father because Jesus is also God.

LUCIFER AND JESUS AS BROTHERS

One of the more offensive attributes designated to the Jesus of Mormonism is the claim that Jesus is the spirit-brother of Lucifer. Spencer W. Kimball wrote:

Long before you were born a program was developed by your creators. . . . The principal personalities in this great drama were a Father Elohim, perfect in wisdom, judgment, and person, and two sons, Lucifer and Jehovah.[29]

It was decided that Jesus, not Lucifer, would become the Savior of the earth. According to Seventy Milton R. Hunter:

The appointment of Jesus to be the Savior of the world was contested by one of the other sons of God. He was called Lucifer . . . this spirit-brother of Jesus desperately tried to become the Savior of mankind.[30]

Mormon educator Jess L. Christensen said:

On first hearing, the doctrine that Lucifer and our Lord, Jesus Christ, are brothers may seem surprising to some, especially to those unacquainted with latter-day revelations. But both the scriptures and the prophets affirm that Jesus Christ and Lucifer are indeed offspring of our Heavenly Father and, therefore, spirit brothers. . . . Both Jesus and Lucifer were strong leaders with great knowledge and influence. But as the First-born of the Father, Jesus was Lucifer's older brother.[31]

Ironically, the same passages of the Bible that expound on Christ's eternal godhood also show that Lucifer could not be the brother of Christ. John 1:1–3 tells us that all things (including Lucifer) were made by Jesus, who was, is, and always will be God. Colossians 1:15, the one biblical verse used by Christensen, says, "He (Jesus) is the image of the invisible God, the firstborn of every creature."

However, this verse has nothing to do with Jesus and Satan being brothers. In fact, it shows Christ's deity ("image of the invisible God"). Verses 16–17 show that Christ created all things and that He is before all things, holding them together. Just as a person can look into the mirror to see a reflection, so too is Jesus the exact image of God.[32] The Bible adamantly declares Lucifer to be a creation of Jesus, not in any way the brother of Jesus. Besides, Jesus and Satan are as opposite as light and darkness. Satan merely tries to imitate an angel of light in order to fool as many people as possible (2 Cor. 11:14).

MANY WORLDS, MANY SAVIORS

Problematic also is the fact that the Jesus of Mormonism is but one of many saviors. According to Brigham Young:

> Consequently every earth has its redeemer, and every earth has its tempter; and every earth, and the people thereof, in their turn and time, receive all that we receive, and pass through all the ordeals that we are passing through.[33]

Consider the fact that Young taught the following:

> How many Gods there are, I do not know. But there never was a time when there were not Gods and worlds, and when men were not passing through the same ordeals that we are passing through. That course has been from all eternity, and it is and will be to all eternity.[34]

If such comments were true, we could assume that there are literally millions of saviors on millions of worlds! Another inconsistent aspect of LDS Christology is the idea that Jesus had to "work out" His salvation. Bruce McConkie claimed, "Jesus kept the commandments of his Father and thereby worked out his own salvation, and also set an example as to the way and the means whereby all men may be saved."[35] It is difficult to understand why a being who had become a God before the time of this world would have to work out his own salvation. Such a comment also fails to take into account that only sinners need to be saved in the first place. To say Christ had to do anything toward salvation should rightfully be considered extremely blasphemous by anyone who holds the Bible dear.

THE MARRIAGES OF JESUS

According to the views of some early LDS leaders, Jesus was a polygamist and father. Consider the following quotes:

> The Scripture says that He, the Lord, came walking in the Temple, with His train; I do not know who they were, unless His wives and children.[36]

From the passage in the forty-fifth Psalm, it will be seen that the great Messiah who was the founder of the Christian religion, was a Polygamist. . . . the Messiah chose to take upon himself his seed; and by marrying many honorable wives himself, show to all future generations that he approbated the plurality of Wives under the Christian dispensation, as well as under the dispensations in which His Polygamist ancestors lived.[37]

It will be borne in mind that once on a time, there was a marriage in Cana of Galilee; and on a careful reading of that transaction, it will be discovered that no less a person than Jesus Christ was married on that occasion. If he was never married, his intimacy with Mary and Martha, and the other Mary also whom Jesus loved, must have been highly unbecoming and improper to say the best of it.[38]

The grand reason of the burst of public sentiment in anathemas upon Christ and his disciples, causing his crucifixion, was evidently based upon polygamy, according to the testimony of the philosophers who rose in that age. A belief in the doctrine of a plurality of wives caused the persecution of Jesus and his followers. We might almost think they were "Mormons."[39]

It is doubtful that many modern Mormons would go out of their way to defend the above statements regarding Jesus' polygamy. However, they cannot consistently ignore the notion that Jesus must have been married to at least one person if He had to "work out His own salvation." It would seem necessary that He was married to at least one woman, since marriage is a very important element in the exaltation process.[40]

CONCLUSION

Concerning the Jesus of Mormonism:

- Born of a sexual relationship between God the Father and Mary
- Elder brother of the human race
- Lucifer is his brother
- Reached perfection at some particular point in time

Concerning the Jesus of Christianity:

- Born of the Virgin Mary by being overshadowed by the Holy Spirit
- God in the flesh
- Lucifer, together with all the angels, was created by Jesus and is therefore not Jesus' brother
- Has been eternally perfect

The Trinity

Several church councils, in which men fought for their own theories, foisted upon the Church the incomprehensible and unnatural doctrine of "one in three and three in one." . . . This false doctrine, which has been nurtured through the centuries, is an excellent illustration of philosophical-theological error and nonsense.

Apostle John A. Widtsoe,
Evidences and Reconciliations 1:58

One of the doctrines that Mormon leaders have attacked, probably with more venom than any other, is the doctrine of the Trinity. It has been mocked and slandered despite being the heart and soul of Christian theology. According to the LDS Church magazine *Ensign:*

The Prophet Joseph learned early that the sectarian creeds were confusing in their declarations on the nature of God. They held to the notion of the Trinity as conceived in the Nicene and Athanasian Creeds, developed by councils convened in the early centuries of Christianity to settle theological differences. Those creeds portray God as three personages in one and one in three, "neither confounding the persons, nor dividing the substance"; as being uncreated, incomprehensible, and almighty. From these creeds has grown the current orthodox view held by most Christian denominations that "there is but one living and true God, everlasting, without body, parts, or passions; of infinite power, wisdom, and goodness."[1]

Joseph Smith clearly separated himself from the rest of the Christian world when he proclaimed that he had "always and in all congregations when I have preached on the subject of the Deity, it has been the plurality of Gods." Smith ridiculed the Trinity, saying:

Many men say there is one God; the Father, the Son and the Holy Ghost are only one God. I say that is a strange God anyhow—three in one, and one in three! It is a curious organization. . . . All are to be crammed into one God, according to sectarianism. It would make the biggest God in all the world. He would be a wonderfully big God—he would be a giant or a monster.[2]

Apostle Bruce McConkie wrote:

To those who are bound to defend the mass of confusion in the creeds of Christendom, the concept that the Father, Son, and Holy Ghost are one God is totally incomprehensible. They are baffled by their beliefs, confused by their creeds, unconverted by the incomprehensible. Their only recourse is to glory in the mystery of godliness and to suppose there is something wonderful in worshipping a spirit nothingness that is neither here nor there any more than he exists now or then. The total inability to know God becomes the most basic tenet of their religion and closes the door to that progress which leads to exaltation and Godhood.[3]

Like his predecessors, President Gordon B. Hinckley explained why he also could not believe in the Trinity:

The world wrestles with the question of who God is, and in what form He is found. Some say that the Father and the Son and the Holy Ghost are one. I wonder how they ever arrive at that. How could Jesus have prayed to Himself when he uttered the Lord's Prayer? How could He have met with Himself when He was on the Mount of Transfiguration? No. He is a separate being. God, our Father, is one. Jesus Christ is two. The Holy Ghost is three. And these three are united in purpose and in working together to bring to pass the immortality and eternal life of man.[4]

ONE GOD

The above comments are clearly antithetical to the biblical message. Over and over again the Bible declares that there is only one God. A belief in one Supreme Being was a major point of separation between the religious system of the Jews and their pagan neighbors. This pattern is found throughout the Old Testament. When God rejected King David's offer to build Him a house, the humble king prayed and said, "O LORD, there is none like thee, neither is there any God beside thee, according to all that we have heard with our ears" (1 Chron. 17:20).

The idea that there is only one God is very clear in the New Testament as well. Consider Mark 12:29 when Jesus quoted Deuteronomy 6:4 to an inquiring scribe.[5] In response, the scribe remarked in verse 32, "Well, Master, thou hast said the truth: for there is one God; and there is none other but he." Notice how Jesus responded in verse 34: "And when Jesus saw that he answered discreetly [wisely], he said unto him, Thou art not far from the kingdom of God."

The Mormon may argue that whenever the Bible declares the existence of only one God, it must be speaking of purpose only and that it merely means they agree in all things. Rex E. Lee, who was once the president of Brigham Young University, explained, "Biblical statements that those three are one mean that they are unified in purpose, action, and belief, not that they are one being."[6]

This certainly is a superficial interpretation, for many passages show this *oneness* far surpasses the mere notion of agreement. For example, the Ten Commandments strongly warn, "Thou shalt have no other gods before me" (Exod. 20:3). The Mormon may insist his *worship* does not extend beyond the one he calls Elohim, but context demands that this must also involve his faith (he is not to even believe there are other Gods).

The Book of Isaiah offers perhaps more verses in defense of monotheism than any other. Throughout chapters 43 through 45, this book emphasizes the existence of one God and one God only (see Isa. 43:10; 44:6; 45:5–6, 14, 21–22; 46:9). It is difficult to interpret passages such as Isaiah 43:10 as merely referring to several Gods being one in purpose since it rejects the possibility of other gods existing either before or after the one true God. One would think that even the

God of Mormonism would be aware of the many gods who allegedly exist with him, or for that matter, the god that begat his mortal body. Yet Isaiah 44:8 tells us that the God of the Bible doesn't even know of other gods! Are we to believe in the context of Mormonism that Joseph Smith's God can't remember who his own father was?

A common rebuttal to the Isaiah passages is that these verses speak only of idols. While it is true that idol worship was a problem during the time of Isaiah, the above verses cannot be limited to such an interpretation. Let us assume *idols* are meant in Isaiah 43:10. It could then be understood to read, "Before me there was no *idol* formed, neither shall there be after me."

Are we really expected to believe that idols had not been formed *after* God? If only idols were being referred to in Isaiah 44:8, this passage would read, "Is there an *idol* beside me? yea, there is no idol; I know not any." Does it make sense to conclude that the God of the Bible was unaware that idols existed? Not likely.

Why does the LDS Church reject the historic church's concept of the Trinity? Because not only does the Trinity remove any hope of a Mormon ever achieving godhood, but it also undermines Smith's first vision and subsequent teachings regarding a multiplicity of deities. If it can be demonstrated that the Father, Son, and Holy Ghost/Spirit are God, and at the same time be shown that there exists only one God, it would definitely place the integrity of the first Mormon prophet on the line.

Not only does the Bible provide such a teaching, but the *Book of Mormon* does as well. Were the Nephites practicing polytheists? Alma 11:26–29, which describes a conversation between the prophet Amulek and the wicked lawyer Zeezrom, shows they were not. Before examining this discourse, verse 22 states that Amulek could "say nothing which is contrary to the Spirit of the Lord." With that in mind, Zeezrom and Amulek engage in the following dialogue:

> And Zeezrom said unto him: Thou sayest there is a true and living God?
> And Amulek said: Yea, there is a true and living God.
> Now Zeezrom said: Is there more than one God?
> And he answered, No.

The context revolves around the existence of a "true and living God." Amulek agrees that there is a true and living God, but when asked by Zeezrom if there is more than one (true and living) God, he is told that there is not. With that context in mind, verse 44 goes on to say that the Father, Son, and Holy Spirit "is one Eternal God."

If a Mormon wishes to insist in the existence of more than one God within the godhead, he or she must resolve the dilemma as to which of the three is not true. If the Father, Son, and Holy Ghost are, in fact, three separate Gods, two of them must be false Gods.[7] Even if Mormons insist that this means there is only one God for this world, it still does not relieve them of this difficulty since Mormon theology definitely teaches that Jesus and the Holy Ghost play a prominent role when it comes to *this* world.

Despite the fact that Mormonism technically rejects monotheism, some Mormons have insisted that they are monotheists. For instance, Bruce McConkie wrote:

> Monotheism is the doctrine or belief that there is but one God. If this is properly interpreted to mean that the Father, Son, and Holy Ghost—each of whom is a separate and distinct godly personage—are one God, meaning one Godhead, then true saints are monotheists.[8]

McConkie's definition of monotheism is so flawed that even Mormon apologist Van Hale rejects his conclusion, saying, "It is certainly inaccurate to define Mormon doctrine since the 1840s as monotheistic."[9] McConkie also insisted that "polytheistic concepts are apostate perversions of the original truth about God which was revealed to Adam and the ancient patriarchs. . . . The saints are not polytheists."[10] Perhaps for lack of a better term, the word *henotheism* best describes the LDS position. Henotheism allows for the belief in many gods while only worshiping one of those gods.

THE BASIS FOR THE TRINITY

The doctrine of the Trinity has played an important part in biblical and Christian history. Hebrew scholar Dr. Ronald Youngblood writes:

> God did not reveal himself in clearly defined Trinitarian terms in the OT. To do so would have provided needless temptations to polytheism in the

light of ancient culture. But the OT prepares for the doctrine of the Trinity in several ways: (1) It uses a plural word for God (elohim) with singular verbs (Gen. 1:1 and often). (2) It employs various triadic formulas in references to God (e.g., the three-man visitation in Gen. 18:2, the triple name of the God of the Patriarchs in Exod. 3:15 and often, and the thrice-spoken "Holy" of Isa. 6:3). (3) The "angel of God/the Lord" sometimes refers to God as his sender, sometimes speaks as though he himself were God. (4) Father, Spirit, and Word are all active in creation (Gen. 1:1–3; see also John 1:1–3).[11]

The early Christian church believed that it was absolutely vital to know and accept some very specific statements about the nature and attributes of God. When alternate voices attempted to challenge orthodox positions, the church felt compelled to clearly define its position in answer to the heretical charges being raised. Contrary to Mormon belief, the Trinity was not an invention of the early church; rather, it was a definitive response designed to explain the biblical position of the church. Second-century theologian Irenaeus explained the Trinity this way:

> This, then, is the order of the rule of our faith. . . . God the Father, not made, not material, invisible; one God, the creator of all things: this is the first point of our faith. The second point is this: the Word of God, Son of God, Christ Jesus our Lord, Who was manifested to the prophets according to the form of their prophesying and according to the method of the Father's dispensation; through Whom (i.e. the Word) all things were made. . . . And the third point is: the Holy Spirit, through Whom the prophets prophesied, and the fathers learned the things of God, and the righteous were led into the way of righteousness; Who at the end of the age was poured out in a new way upon mankind in all the earth, renewing man to God.[12]

It would be incorrect to assume that such teachings were the result of later corruption. Clear, definitive statements like the Nicene and Athanasian Creeds were apparently not necessary until orthodoxy was challenged in later years. Essential doctrines were "implicit in Christian faith from the beginning, even though they did not become explicit until considerably later."[13] As for denying the Trinity because it cannot be understood, this does not seem to make sense from the LDS position since most Mormons believe in certain doctrines that they cannot fully understand.

In chapter 1 under the section concerning the self-existence of God, we quoted several LDS leaders who admitted that they could not understand or comprehend the first cause of all things. Apostle John Widtsoe said this doctrine was "mysterious." President Joseph Fielding Smith said humankind has a "limited capacity to understand." Brigham Young boldly stated that it was "as easy for an ant to number the grains of sand on the earth" as it was to understand this teaching. If this is the case, and this doctrine is so hard to comprehend, then why has the doctrine of the Trinity been so often maligned? Our inability to comprehend a teaching is not the basis for its truthfulness. This must be determined by its compatibility with Scripture—the Holy Bible—which is the Christian's source for all truth.

CONCLUSION

The Trinity, according to Mormonism:

- Was an invention of the apostate church
- Cannot be true because it cannot be understood
- Cannot be true because the Father, Son, and Holy Ghost are merely one in purpose

The Trinity, according to Christianity:

- Is a doctrine that came from biblical origins
- Is one of the things about God that is not able to be understood by a finite, created mind
- Is true because there is one God by nature who is evident in three persons

Who Is God?

Using just a few chapters from the Book of Isaiah, a Christian has the opportunity to show the true attributes of God. Allow the Mormon to look these passages up in his or her Bible. Also, be willing to look at the context of each passage, taking as much time as necessary with each point. Remember that this is a sample dialogue, so a Mormon will not necessarily answer in the manner given below. But using these verses can certainly help you show how the Bible and the LDS view of God are incompatible.

> *Christian:* I've heard it said that Mormons believe that "as man is, God once was. As God is, man may become." Would you say that there was a God before Elohim (God the Father)?
>
> *Mormon:* Yes, that has been taught.
>
> *C:* Could we use the Bible to see if this is true?
>
> *M:* Sure.
>
> *C:* Turn with me to Isaiah 43:10. It says here that "before me there was no God formed, neither shall there be after me."
>
> *M:* This only refers to this world. There are no other gods whom we as Latter-day Saints worship except

Elohim. That doesn't mean that there couldn't be other gods.

C: But it doesn't say, "formed in *other worlds* before me." Besides, it says there will be none formed after Him. Doesn't this seem like God is the only one?

M: But He isn't the *only* God, just the God of this world.

C: Would it then be logical to say that God knows about these other gods?

M: Of course.

C: Please turn with me, then, to Isaiah 44:6. It says, "I am the first, and I am the last; and beside me there is no God."

M: Again, this is referring to there not being other gods in this world.

C: But it goes on. Look at verse 8. "Is there a God beside me? yea, there is no God; I know not any." Does God know of other gods beside Himself?

M: It would seem so.

C: But that is the problem. The God of Isaiah makes it clear that He does not know of any other gods. For the Jew as well as the Christian, these chapters certainly mean that God is one (Deut. 6:4) and there is no other. Throughout Isaiah 43–46 the theme is stressed over and over again.

Other verses are Isaiah 45:5–6, 21–22; 46:9. You may also want to include the points that God does not change from a man to a God (Mal. 3:6); rather, He is God from everlasting to everlasting (Ps. 90:2).

Examining the LDS Concept of Humankind

Preexistence and the Second Estate

The Church of Jesus Christ of Latter-day Saints teaches that every person experiences a series of "births." All were born as spirit children of God in a premortal life.

Encyclopedia of Mormonism, volume 1 ("Agency")

Where did I come from? Why am I here? Where am I going? These are questions every thinking human being has asked. The Bible gives much evidence about the final destiny of humankind. However, little is written about our existence before birth. Perhaps this is because there is nothing to talk about, since we did not exist. Mormon leaders, on the other hand, have built an entire doctrine around the idea that, like God, men and women have eternally existed since before the beginning of this world.

PREEXISTENCE AND THE FIRST ESTATE

The LDS doctrine of preexistence is basically the teaching that all men and women had a premortal, spiritual existence with God. According to Apostle Boyd Packer, this doctrine was lost sometime after the death and resurrection of Christ. He also asserted:

> The idea that mortal birth is the beginning is preposterous. There is no way to explain life if you believe that. The notion that life ends with mortal death is ridiculous. There is no way to face life if you believe that. When we understand the doctrine of premortal life, then things fit together and make sense.[1]

Mormon leaders have stated that humans are the literal offspring of Elohim, also known as Heavenly Father, and one of his heavenly wives. This teaching can be traced to the LDS scripture *Pearl of Great Price*. Moses 3:5 records God allegedly saying, "For I, the Lord God, created all things, of which I have spoken, spiritually, before they were naturally upon the face of the earth." Heavenly Father became the God of this earth as a result of his worthiness demonstrated on another planet. As far as the creation of this earth goes, his firstborn spirit son Jesus was aided by "many of the noble and great spirit children of the Father." These included Michael (the preincarnate Adam), Enoch, Noah, Abraham, Moses, Peter, James, John, and even Joseph Smith![2]

It should not be thought that this earth is the only earth ruled by Elohim. Not at all. Apostle Bruce McConkie explained:

> This earth was not the first of the Lord's creations. An infinite number of worlds have come rolling into existence at his command. Each is an *earth;* many are inhabited with his spirit children; each abides the particular law given to it; and each will play its part in the redemption, salvation, and exaltation of that infinite host of the children of an Almighty God.[3]

Lucifer disobeyed God during this preexistent state. Afterwards, according to Seventy Gary J. Coleman:

> During our premortal existence, Satan attempted to alter the plan which Heavenly Father presented in the great council in heaven. His attempt to do so was rejected by the Father and the majority of the hosts of heaven (see Moses 4:1–2; Abr. 3:2728 [sic]). Now, having been cast out of Heavenly Father's presence, Satan and his followers carry out his "cunning

plans which he hath devised to ensnare the hearts of men" (Alma 28:13), "that he might bring [them] into subjection unto him" (12:6).[4]

Lucifer was angry because his plan, which included taking away free agency,[5] was rejected over Jesus' proposal. According to the LDS handbook *Gospel Principles:*

> Because our Heavenly Father chose Jesus Christ to be our Savior, Satan became angry and rebelled. There was war in heaven. Satan and his followers fought against Jesus and his followers. In this great rebellion, Satan and all the spirits who followed him were sent away from the presence of God and cast down from heaven. One-third of the spirits in heaven were punished for following Satan: they were denied the right to receive mortal bodies. Because we are here on earth and have mortal bodies, we know that we chose to follow Jesus Christ and our Heavenly Father. . . . In our premortal life, we chose the right.[6]

Thus, all who are here on earth apparently sided with Jesus. According to Moses 4:4 in the *Pearl of Great Price,* Lucifer "became Satan, yea, even the devil, the father of all lies, to deceive and to blind men, and to lead them captive at his will." Apparently those who were not wise enough to side against Lucifer will never be worthy of receiving a body on earth and will always be spirits, forever doomed to never become gods.

THE SECOND ESTATE: EARTH

According to Mormonism's blueprint, how the spirits acted in the preexistence would determine their position on earth. McConkie wrote:

> The pre-existent life was thus a period—undoubtedly an infinitely long one—of probation, progression, and schooling. The spirit hosts were taught and given experiences in various administrative capacities. Some so exercised their agency and so conformed to law as to become "noble and great"; these were foreordained before their mortal births to perform great missions for the Lord in this life.[7]

Without a body, a spirit could never obtain godhood, which means eternal damnation. So the goal of each spirit would be to leave its

Heavenly Father and Mother and graduate to being born as a human being on an earth to physical parents who were once spirits themselves. This progression to mortality is known as the "Second Estate."

> Our heavenly parents provided us with a celestial home more glorious and beautiful than any place on earth. We were happy there. Yet they knew we could not progress beyond a certain point unless we left them for a time. They wanted us to develop the godlike qualities that they have. To do this, we needed to leave our celestial home to be tested and to gain experience. We needed to choose good over evil. Our spirits needed to be clothed with physical bodies. We would need to leave our physical bodies at death and reunite with them in the Resurrection. Then we would receive immortal bodies like those of our heavenly parents. If we passed our tests, we would receive the fulness of joy that our heavenly parents have received. (See *D&C* 93:30–34.)[8]

Apostle Dallin Oaks added:

> Our understanding of life begins with a council in heaven. There the spirit children of God were taught his eternal plan for their destiny. We had progressed as far as we could without a physical body and an experience in mortality. To realize a fulness of joy, we had to prove our willingness to keep the commandments of God in a circumstance where we had no memory of what preceded our mortal birth. . . . All of the myriads of mortals who have been born on this earth chose the Father's plan and fought for it. Many of us also made covenants with the Father concerning what we would do in mortality. In ways that have not been revealed, our actions in the spirit world influence us in mortality.[9]

According to Apostle George Q. Cannon, those who are Mormon were faithful during their preexistent lives. He wrote:

> We were true in keeping our first estate. The people that are here today stood loyally by God and by Jesus, and they did not flinch. If you had flinched then, you would not be here with the Priesthood upon you. The evidence that you were loyal, that you were true and that you did not waver is to be found in the fact that you have received the Gospel and the everlasting Priesthood.[10]

According to the *Encyclopedia of Mormonism,* when we arrived on this planet, we even looked somewhat like our preexistent bodies:

It is Latter-day Saint doctrine that living things existed as individual spirit beings and possessed varying degrees of intelligence in an active, conscious spirit state before mortal birth and that the spirit continues to live and function in the mortal body. The revelations teach that pre-mortal spirit bodies have general resemblance to their physical counterparts.[11]

This concept played a major role when it came to the size of LDS families. For years Mormons were urged to have as many children as possible in order to make a way for these spirit children to be taught the proper course that would return them to their heavenly parents. Brigham Young explained:

> There are multitudes of pure and holy spirits waiting to take tabernacles, now what is our duty?—To prepare tabernacles for them, to take a course that will not tend to drive those spirits into the families of the wicked, where they will be trained in wickedness, debauchery, and every species of crime. It is the duty of every righteous man and woman to prepare tabernacles for all the spirits they can.[12]

In December 1998 the *Salt Lake Tribune* announced that the LDS Church had issued a new *Handbook of Instructions* that no longer compelled Mormon couples to have as many children as possible.[13] The handbook's two-paragraph entry on birth control reads in part: "The decision as to how many children to have and when to have them is extremely intimate and private and should be left between the couple and the Lord. Church members should not judge one another in this matter."

Apparently the size of a Mormon couple's family was not always considered an intimate and private matter. In the past, church leaders seemed to have little patience for those who would artificially limit the size of their families. President Joseph F. Smith called this "one of the greatest crimes of the world today" and an "evil practice."[14] In a conference message given in October 1947, President David O. McKay included birth control as one of the "insidious and vicious enemies" that would tend to "disintegrate the very foundation of the Christian home."[15]

President Joseph Fielding Smith called birth control "wickedness" because it was an abuse of the marriage covenant. He said that there is

> nothing that should be held in greater sacredness than this covenant by which the spirits of men are clothed with mortal tabernacles. When a man and a woman are married and they agree, or covenant, to limit their offspring to two or three, and practice devices to accomplish this purpose, they are guilty of iniquity which eventually must be punished.[16]

On the same page, Smith offered what could quite possibly, under present circumstances, be an indictment against his own church! He went on to say:

> Unfortunately this evil doctrine is being taught as a virtue by many people who consider themselves cultured and highly educated. It has even crept in among members of the Church and has been advocated in some of the classes within the Church.

Smith clarified what he meant by punishment a few pages later: "Those who wilfully and maliciously design to break this important commandment shall be damned. They cannot have the Spirit of the Lord."[17] He strongly denounced the concept of the small family and likened it to refusing to take on "the responsibilities of family life."

In essence, church leaders today have given sanction to a practice that was once considered an evil and wicked crime. What once was sin in the Mormon Church is now permissible.

PREEXISTENCE AND THE BIBLE

Obviously such teachings are perplexing to the Bible-believing Christian, since the Bible never even hints that people eternally existed or had a literal upbringing by parents before coming into this world. One can only wonder how such a teaching became a part of Mormon thought. Dr. Stephen E. Robinson, a professor at BYU, showed how this teaching could have been borrowed from other groups, including those that most Bible-believing Christians consider to be heretical.

He wrote, "The Gnostics believed in the pre-existence of man and even in his coeternality with God."[18]

Christians do not seek support for a teaching through the example of groups that are pagan or heretical. Mormons, on the other hand, are hard-pressed to find any biblical support for the very idea of preexistence. As a matter of fact, this was not even a teaching during the first few years of the LDS Church's existence. Mormon author Charles R. Harrell writes:

> Spirits or angels mentioned in the Bible as being with God in the first estate, including Lucifer and the spirits who followed him (Isa. 14:12–15; Jude 6; Rev. 12:3–4), were traditionally viewed as being a separate species from humans, not preexistent spirits. Biblical passages used today to support preexistence were interpreted differently when cited by the Saints during the first decade of the Church.[19]

It wasn't until the middle of the 1830s that this teaching was further developed in LDS thought. Many Mormons point to the book of Abraham, found in the LDS scripture *Pearl of Great Price,* for support of preexistence. It reads in part:

> . . . for I rule in the heavens above, and in the earth beneath, in all wisdom and prudence, over all the intelligences thine eyes have seen from the beginning; I came down in the beginning in the midst of all the intelligences thou hast seen. Now the Lord had shown unto me, Abraham, the intelligences that were organized before the world was; and among all these there were many of the noble and great ones; And God saw these souls that they were good, and he stood in the midst of them, and he said: These I will make my rulers; for he stood among those that were spirits, and he saw that they were good; and he said unto me: Abraham, thou art one of them; thou wast chosen before thou wast born.
>
> Abraham 3:21–23

According to Mormonism, Abraham, the man divinely appointed as the "father of many nations," pleased God before the creation of the world, so he was chosen to fulfill God's will in the world. Aside from this *Pearl of Great Price* passage, there are few places Mormons can go to support this important doctrine. In fact, there appears to be only one possible reference to preexistence in the *Book of Mormon,* but this is admittedly a weak correlation.[20] This might be the reason why "the Latter-day Saints did not at first deduce the idea of preexistence from the biblical passages so frequently summoned today to prove it."[21] It also does not appear "in the scriptural or other writings and recorded sermons of Joseph Smith."[22]

Although certain biblical passages have been used to back the teaching, they are taken out of their context to do so. One often-used proof text is Jeremiah 1:5. Christians believe that God is omniscient, knowing everything about each one of us before we were born. The emphasis is on God's foreknowledge ("I knew thee"), not humanity's knowing God.

Another passage used is Job 38:4 where God questions Job and rebukes him for his pride, asking, "Where wast thou when I laid the foundations of the earth?" This is what is known as a rhetorical question. When God formed the world, Job 38:7 says, "The sons of God shouted for joy." If this is really referring to preexistent spirits, as Mormons claim, then Job must have been there as well. However, the whole point of the questions God compels Job to answer is that they are unanswerable, since Job was not there. In effect, God is reminding Job how he wasn't even in existence when the world was created. Just as the clay should not talk back to the potter, so too Job had no business questioning God's work (compare Jer. 18:1–6 with Rom. 9:18–26).

Still another verse used is Ecclesiastes 12:7, which states that "the spirit shall return unto God who gave it." The Mormon who holds to the doctrine of preexistence assumes this is referring to the second leg of a "round trip." This passage, though, merely shows how life exists beyond death. One would have to approach this verse with a preconceived notion of preexistence to draw this conclusion. According to Zechariah 12:1, God gave each person a spirit, so certainly the spirit will return to Him for judgment. It does not imply that we existed before our mortal existence.[23]

The Word of God certainly does not support the LDS concept that all humans are literal children of God.[24] While the Bible does show how all humans are creations of God, becoming a part of His family requires faith in the redemptive work of Jesus Christ. Paul writes in Galatians 3:26, "For ye are all the children of God by faith in Christ Jesus." He also said in Romans 9:8, "That is, They which are the children of the flesh, these are not the children of God: but the children of the promise are counted for the seed."[25]

Until Mormons can show better proof of humanity's eternal existence, Christians are unable to agree with this extrabiblical teaching.

CONCLUSION

The beginnings of humankind and this world, according to Mormonism:

- All people lived with God before this world
- God the Father was aided by His created beings before the creation of the world
- A person's actions in the preexistence affects a person's life on earth
- We knew God and God knew us before our birth
- All humans are the literal sons and daughters of God

The beginnings of humankind and this world, according to Christianity:

- Each person had a beginning that started in this world
- God alone created the world
- With no preexistence, there are no actions before this world
- God foreknew us before our birth
- All Christians become the sons and daughters of God only through faith in Christ

The Fall

Adam fell that men might be; and men are, that they might have joy.

2 Nephi 2:25 in the *Book of Mormon*

While Christianity has always viewed the fall of Adam and Eve in the Garden of Eden[1] as a tragic event, the LDS Church describes it as an essential step toward the completion of humanity's salvation. The act of disobedience by the first man and woman is characterized by Mormons as a fall upward, not downward.

A NECESSARY EVIL?

The joint decision to disobey God by Adam and Eve has been continually commended by LDS leaders throughout Mormonism's existence. Moses 5:10–11 in the LDS scripture *Pearl of Great Price* says:

And in that day Adam blessed God and was filled, and began to prophesy concerning all the families of the earth, saying: Blessed be the name of God, for because of my transgression my eyes are opened, and in this life I shall have joy, and again in the flesh I shall see God. And Eve, his wife, heard all these things and was glad, saying: Were it not for our transgression we never should have had seed, and never should have known good and evil, and the joy of our redemption, and the eternal life which God giveth unto all the obedient.

Apostle James Talmage believed it would have been tragic if Adam had obeyed God's command to abstain from the fruit of the Tree of Knowledge. He taught that

the spirits of God's offspring [in the preexistence] would have remained forever in a state of innocent childhood, sinless through no effort of their own. . . . From Father Adam we have inherited all the ills to which flesh is heir; but such are necessarily incident to a knowledge of good and evil, by the proper use of which knowledge man may become even as the Gods.[2]

President Joseph Fielding Smith concurred when he said:

Let us thank the Lord, when we pray, for Adam. If it had not been for Adam, I would not be here; you would not be here; we would be waiting in the heavens as spirits pleading for somebody . . . to pass through a certain condition that brought upon us mortality.[3]

In essence, a person could say that Adam played just as important a role as does Jesus Christ in the progression of humankind. Without Adam, nobody who existed from Cain and Abel to the generations of today would have been able to receive bodies from the preexistence. The act of transgression by Adam and Eve was an absolute necessity to allow spirit bodies to unite with physical bodies on the planet Earth. Apostle Bruce McConkie explained:

Lehi, whose inspired words are so pointed and clear as to the heaven-directed fall of our first primeval parents, tells us that "if Adam had not transgressed he would not have fallen, but he would have remained in the garden of Eden." (2 Ne. 2:22.) Had this been the case, the billions of mortals who have dwelt on this lowly planet during the past six thousand years would still be spirit beings in the presence of the Lord; they would still be waiting for their mortal probation.[4]

Apostle John Widtsoe said Adam and Eve

chose wisely, in accord with the heavenly law of love for others. . . . It is a thrilling thought that Adam and Eve were not coerced to begin God's work on earth. . . . We, the children of Adam and Eve, may well be proud of our parentage.[5]

Brigham Young University professor Dr. Robert L. Millet wrote:

The Latter-day Saint view of the scenes in Eden is remarkably optimistic when compared to traditional Christian views. We believe that Adam and Eve went into the Garden of Eden to fall, that their actions helped "open the way of the world," and that the Fall was as much a part of the foreordained plan of the Father as was the very Atonement.[6]

Apostle Dallin H. Oaks bluntly stated the following at the fall 1993 general conference:

Some Christians condemn Eve for her act, concluding that she and her daughters are somehow flawed by it. Not the Latter-day Saints! Informed by revelation, we celebrate Eve's act and honor her wisdom and courage in the great episode called the Fall.[7]

Contrary to the LDS concept of the fall, the Bible shows that this event was the result of disobeying God. The Lord made it clear to Adam and Eve that they could eat from any tree in the Garden of Eden *except* the Tree of Knowledge (Gen. 2:16–17). If partaking of the forbidden fruit was necessary to propagate the human race, then it begs the question as to why God would command Adam and Eve to be fruitful and multiply (Gen. 1:28) before turning right around and forbidding them one of the prime ingredients to do so. And if the transgression was positive and it was a blessing to leave Eden, why does Genesis 3:24 say that God had to drive them out?[8]

Genesis 3:3–5 has been used by Mormons to support the idea that Adam and Eve made the right decision. Since the possibility of godhood is considered a Mormon truism, some have said that Satan was telling the truth when he told Eve in verse 5 that she "shall be as gods."

However, is it wise to trust a promise from one who is called the "father of lies"?[9] Consider the following:

- Satan is allowed to appear as a helpful servant as he did to Eve. Second Corinthians 11:14 says, "And no marvel; for Satan himself is transformed into an angel of light." The Greek word for *transform* means to change in appearance, clearly showing that Satan can mask his appearance and be perceived as innocent so that he might be believed.
- Satan does not want good to come to humanity. Mark 4:15 says, "And these are they by the way side, where the word is sown; but when they have heard, Satan cometh immediately, and taketh away the word that was sown in their hearts." Seeing how Job worshiped God, Satan sought to torment him to see if he would curse God. Satan even tempted Jesus in the desert to see if He would sin (Matt. 4:1–11).
- Satan is not someone with whom we can confide and trust. Jesus told Peter, "Behold, Satan hath desired to have you, that he may sift you as wheat" (Luke 22:31). Peter warned all Christians about Satan when he wrote, "Be sober, be vigilant; because your adversary the devil, as a roaring lion, walketh about, seeking whom he may devour" (1 Peter 5:8). James says the devil is to be resisted (James 4:7).
- Satan does not want to see the coming of God's kingdom but rather its downfall. Paul said that Satan "hindered" his work (1 Thess. 2:18). Revelation 12:9 says, "And the great dragon was cast out, that old serpent, called the Devil, and Satan, which deceiveth the whole world." One day he shall pay for his evil deeds (Rev. 20:7–10).

Although Jesus dealt with Satan, defeating the great adversary through His death and resurrection, this created being still seeks to disrupt God's plans. In light of this, we are instructed to be cautious when dealing with this formidable foe. As powerful as the archangel Michael was, Jude 9 says he "durst not bring against [Satan] a railing accusation, but said, The Lord rebuke thee."

It might be argued that Adam and Eve, as the first of the human creation, did not have the advantage of either Scripture or historical precedent to guide them in their decision. While this may be true, this does not discount the fact that Satan blatantly contradicted the direct command of God. That alone should have been sufficient evidence to show how Satan should not be trusted.

SIN VERSUS TRANSGRESSION

To minimize the severity of Adam's disobedience, Mormonism teaches that Adam's act was a *transgression,* not a sin. Joseph Fielding Smith wrote, "This was a transgression of the law, but not a sin in the strict sense, for it was something that Adam and Eve had to do!"[10] Apostle Dallin Oaks attempted to differentiate between transgression and sin during a speech in general conference:

> Some acts, like murder, are crimes because they are inherently wrong. Other acts, like operating without a license, are crimes only because they are legally prohibited. Under these distinctions, the act that produced the Fall was not a sin—inherently wrong—but a transgression—wrong because it was formally prohibited.[11]

If transgression is not sin, as claimed by the LDS authorities, it would seem strange that the apostle John wrote, "Whosoever committeth sin transgresseth also the law: for sin is the transgression of the law" (1 John 3:4). To insist that transgression is not sin certainly goes against the biblical definition. The Bible is saturated with verses proving this.[12] Even Joseph Smith listed transgression and sin in a way that makes them synonymous:

> Verily, verily, I say unto you, if a man marry a wife according to my word, and they are sealed by the Holy Spirit of promise, according to mine appointment, and he or she shall commit any sin or transgression of the new and everlasting covenant whatever, and all manner of blasphemies, and if they commit no murder wherein they shed innocent blood, yet they shall come forth in the first resurrection, and enter into

their exaltation; but they shall be destroyed in the flesh, and shall be delivered unto the buffetings of Satan unto the day of redemption, saith the Lord God.[13]

The apostle Paul plainly stated that death was the result of Adam's *sin* when he wrote in Romans 5:12, 15:

Wherefore, as by one man sin entered into the world, and death by sin; and so death passed upon all men, for that all have sinned. . . . But not as the offense, so also is the free gift. For if through the offence of one many be dead, much more the grace of God, and the gift by grace, which is by one man, Jesus Christ, hath abounded unto many.

Paul compared Adam to Jesus by showing how death came to the world through the former and life through the latter. In verses 18–19, he added:

Therefore as by the offence of one judgment came upon all men to condemnation; even so by the righteousness of one the free gift came upon all men unto justification of life. For as by one man's disobedience many were made sinners, so by the obedience of one shall many be made righteous.

Notice the phrase in verse 19: "by one man's [Adam] disobedience many were made sinners [not merely *transgressors*]." Since becoming a sinner entitles one to death (Rom. 3:23; 6:23), these verses from Romans 5 effectively show that the disobedient act in the Garden of Eden was not a "wise choice."

C O N C L U S I O N

The fall, according to Mormonism:

- Satan told the truth in the Garden of Eden
- Adam and Eve needed to disobey God's command

- Adam and Eve's action in the Garden is merely a transgression, not a sin
- The fall is to be commended as necessary for humankind to attain godhood

The fall, according to Christianity:

- Satan deceived Adam and Eve in the Garden of Eden
- Adam and Eve had the choice to obey or disobey God's command
- Adam and Eve's action in the Garden of Eden is both a transgression and a sin
- The fall made all people become sinners, resulting in physical death and, for some, spiritual death

Apostasy

Nothing less than a complete apostasy from the Christian religion would warrant the establishment of the Church of Jesus Christ of Latter-day Saints.

Seventy B. H. Roberts,
Introduction of *History of the Church* 1:XL

Mormonism was founded on the premise that the authority initially given to the apostles by Jesus Christ was lost until Joseph Smith restored *true* Christianity in 1830. Mormons say that since Christ's church quickly abandoned His principles, the Reformation was not enough. Because, they claim, there was a complete apostasy from the Christian church in the time soon after the death of Jesus' apostles, there was a need for the Mormon Church to exist.

WHERE DID ALL THE CHRISTIANS GO?

The official LDS Church publication *Gospel Principles* states:

One by one, the Apostles were killed. . . . The perfect organization of the Church no longer existed, and confusion resulted. More and more error crept into Church doctrine, and soon the destruction of the Church was complete. The period of time when the true Church no longer existed on earth is called the Great Apostasy.[1]

Claiming that Christ and His apostles predicted the coming apostasy, Rex Lee, the former president of BYU, said:

Both the Savior himself and also the ancient apostles prophesied, however, that this was not to last. The Church would be rocked by apostasy (see Matthew 24:5, 9–12, 23–24), and there would be a falling away (see 2 Thessalonians 2:3). Christ's church, the one he established on a foundation of apostles and prophets, would one day not be found upon the earth. What would remain would be churches that had changed in various ways, both doctrinally and organizationally, from the original church.[2]

When the teenage Joseph Smith began to look for a church in 1820 that possessed the truth, he claimed God told him to not join any of them because

all their creeds were an abomination in his sight; that those professors were all corrupt; that: "they draw near to me with their lips, but their hearts are far from me, they teach for doctrines the commandments of men, having a form of godliness, but they deny the power thereof." He again forbade me to join with any of them.[3]

Speaking at a general conference, Apostle Mark E. Petersen explained the apostasy this way:

Then with his warning these chosen servants of the Lord, these authorities of the early day Church, went forth as commanded by the Lord, and they tasted of the opposition in all things. There was opposition within the Church, and there was opposition out of the Church. Persecution both within and without increased. The spirit of apostasy spread, and finally apostasy overcame the Church. The leaders of the Church were destroyed, and taken out of the ministry. The people were left in darkness, and gross darkness covered their minds, and we had a complete apostasy from the truth.[4]

President Ezra Taft Benson said there was no more Christianity after this time:

With the passing of the Apostles and the loss of the priesthood keys, corrupt doctrines were introduced into the Church. . . . By the second and third centuries, widespread changes had been made in the pure doctrines and ordinances given by the Savior. The Church that Jesus had established and sanctioned was no longer on this earth.[5]

THE PREDICTED "APOSTASY"

The New Testament warned that a time would come when people would turn from the true faith and give heed to "seducing spirits, and doctrines of devils" (1 Tim. 4:1). Writing to the Thessalonian church, Paul said, "Let no man deceive you by any means: for that day [the return of Christ] shall not come, except there come a falling away first" (2 Thess. 2:3).

Jesus Himself warned the fledgling church to be aware of false prophets. He said that these prophets would be like wolves in sheep's clothing, seeking those whom they could devour. False Christs would show great signs and wonders in order to make themselves look authentic in their attempt to deceive the people (Matt. 7:15; 24:24). Peter added that these false prophets would attempt to introduce "damnable heresies" and deny God (2 Peter 2:1). Many zealous LDS members have used these passages to describe what they call "modern Christianity," but in light of all the unbiblical teachings brought forth by LDS teachers, what guarantee can Mormons give that these passages are not talking about them?

While *some* apostasies were certainly predicted,[6] a *complete* apostasy where God's authority fully left the earth was never predicted or implied. In 1 Timothy 4:1–3, Paul said a time would come when *some* would depart from the faith. Paul explained to his protégé that this would take place in the *latter* times. Peter told his readers in 2 Peter 2:1–3 that *many* would follow the pernicious ways of false prophets, but nowhere does he say that *all* would do so.

Many Latter-day Saints seem to overlook what Peter says later in chapter 2. In verse 7, he uses the example of Lot in the city of Sodom to demonstrate God's ability to preserve the righteous in such times. In verse 9, Peter claims that just as He was able to deliver Lot, "the

Lord knoweth how to deliver the godly out of temptations, and to reserve the unjust unto the day of judgment to be punished."

One passage that goes against the complete apostasy theory is Matthew 16:18. It reads, "And I say also unto thee, That thou art Peter, and upon this rock I will build my church; and the gates of hell shall not prevail against it." Because the literal meaning would eliminate the "loss of keys" for the "primitive" Christian church, many Mormons choose to spiritualize this otherwise straightforward verse. For instance, the second volume of the *Encyclopedia of Mormonism* says:

> The Savior's reference to the "gates of hell" (Hades, or the spirit world; Matt. 16:18) indicates, among other things, that God's priesthood power will penetrate hell and redeem the repentant spirits there. Many have been, and many more will yet be, delivered from hell through hearing, repenting, and obeying the gospel of Jesus Christ in the spirit world after the death of the body.[7]

President Harold B. Lee wrote:

> The gates of hell would have prevailed if the gospel had not been taught to the spirits in prison and to those who had not had ample opportunity to receive the gospel here in its fulness. It would have prevailed if there was not a vicarious work for the dead . . . [or] other vicarious work pertaining to the exaltation which those who accept the gospel might receive, both ordinances for the living and for the dead.[8]

Lee also wrote:

> Now, as I think of that plan, so perfect in its conception, it is clear that this plan could not have existed except for revelations of the living God. So we begin to understand what the Lord meant when He said to Peter, ". . . upon this rock I will build my church; and the gates of hell shall not prevail against it." He was speaking of the revelation of the Lord to His authorized servants, and all the forces of hell combined could not prevent it.[9]

While no one will argue that Peter's response was a result of God's intervention,[10] there is no other passage lending support to the idea that the rock in Matthew 16:18 is revelation. However, the New Testament does support the idea that Christ is the rock on which the church is built. In Ephesians 2:20, Paul states that Christ Himself is the cornerstone, a rock or stone placed in the corner of a proposed building on which all the other stones must align. The "apostles and prophets" do not necessarily mean offices, as the LDS Church implies; rather this phrase encompasses the teachings of the prophets (Old Testament) and the apostles (New Testament).

In 1 Corinthians 3:10–11, Paul says that the wise masterbuilder builds on the foundation of Christ Himself. In saying this, he warned others who also build on this foundation to "take heed" how they did so.[11] This conclusion (that Christ is the rock) seems to more adequately explain what Peter said in answer to Christ's question in Matthew 16:15. Peter declared that Jesus was the Christ, the Son of the living God. Because the true church is based on Christ, His sovereign protection would never allow its death; hence, the expression, "the gates of hell [or Hades] would not prevail against it."

JOHN THE APOSTLE AND THE THREE NEPHITES

Despite holding to a complete Christian apostasy, the *Book of Mormon* teaches that three members of the "true church" are still living. In 3 Nephi 28:7, Jesus supposedly granted that three Nephite apostles would remain alive until He came again.[12] This passage reads:

> Ye shall never taste of death; but ye shall live to behold all the doings of the Father unto the children of men, even until all things shall be fulfilled according to the will of the Father, when I shall come in my glory with the powers of heaven.

Mormon scripture also teaches that the apostle John was to remain until Christ's Second Coming. In the introduction to *Doctrine & Covenants* Section 7, it says:

> Revelation given to Joseph Smith the Prophet, and Oliver Cowdery, at Harmony, Pennsylvania, April, 1829, when they inquired through the Urim and Thummin as to whether John, the beloved disciple, tarried in the flesh or had died. The revelation is a translated version of the record made on parchment by John and hidden up by himself.

It should be noted that it is not known whether Joseph Smith ever personally possessed such a parchment,[13] yet Smith commenced to "reveal" that John the Beloved would be given "power over death," and that he "may live and bring souls unto Christ."[14]

Some Latter-day Saints have used Mormon 1:13 in the *Book of Mormon* to say that God took away the three Nephites as a result of the wickedness that prevailed "upon the whole face of the land." Where exactly they were taken is not addressed in the passage, and it would seem to be presumptuous to insist they were somehow taken off the earth in light of the many statements from LDS leaders to the contrary. The following quotes from LDS sources show the teaching of how the three Nephites and John were to physically remain until Christ reappeared:

Book of Mormon witness David Whitmer:
The Three Nephites are at work among the lost tribes and elsewhere. John the Revelator is at work, and I believe the time will come suddenly, before we are prepared for it.[15]

President John Taylor:
Also, John, the revelator, was permitted to live upon the earth until the Savior should come, and the Book of Mormon gives an account of three Nephites, who lived on this American Continent, who asked for the same privilege and it was granted to them.[16]

President Wilford Woodruff:
The first quorum of apostles were all put to death, except John, and we are informed that he still remains on the earth, though his body has doubtless undergone some change. Three of the Nephites, chosen here by the Lord Jesus as his apostles, had the same promise—that they should not taste death until Christ came, and they still remain on the earth in the flesh.[17]

Apostle Franklin Dewey Richards:
And these men that have never tasted death—the three Nephites and the Apostle John—are busy working to bring to pass righteousness and to carry out the purposes of God; it won't be long till we or our generations after us will see them and have fellowship with them.[18]

The thought of a complete apostasy becomes a problem in light of the fact that these men were promised success in making converts. If

John and the Nephites did successfully gain converts to their message, this would seem to deny any such apostasy. In other words, the church really didn't cease to exist. If the word *complete* has any meaning when combined with *apostasy* in the English language, then there should not have been even one of these four individuals who remained through this alleged dark period of church history.

As for the three *Book of Mormon* characters, many Mormons have even testified that they have experienced visitations from these mysterious men.[19] The *Encyclopedia of Mormonism,* however, takes a less serious approach and explains that such tales are examples of LDS folklore:

> LDS stories of the Three Nephites comprise one of the most striking religious legend cycles in the United States. . . . Part of a much larger body of LDS traditional narratives, these stories are not official doctrine and are not published in official literature. . . . As the newly founded Church grew in numbers, an ever-increasing body of stories began circulating among the people, telling of kindly old men, usually thought to be these ancient Nephite disciples, who had appeared to individuals in physical or spiritual distress, helped them solve their problems, and then suddenly disappeared.
>
> Because they span a century and a half of LDS history, these narratives mirror well the changing physical and social environments in which Latter-day Saints have met their tests of faith. For example, in pre–World War II agrarian society, the stories told of Nephites' guiding pioneer trains to water holes, saving a rancher from a blizzard, providing herbal remedies for illnesses, plowing a farmer's field so that he could attend to Church duties, or delivering food to starving missionaries. In the contemporary world, the stories tell of Nephites' leading LDS genealogists to difficult library resources, pulling a young man from a lake after a canoeing accident and administering artificial respiration, stopping to fix a widow's furnace, guiding motorists lost in blizzards, comforting a woman who has lost her husband and daughter in an airplane crash, and pulling missionaries from a flaming freeway crash.[20]

The article adds:

> . . . in telling these stories, Latter-day Saints continue to testify to the validity of Church teachings and to encourage obedience to them. The stories continue to provide the faithful with a sense of security in an unsure world,

persuading them that just as God helped righteous pioneers overcome a hostile physical world, so will he help the faithful endure the evils of urban society. Taken as a whole, then, the stories continue to provide understanding of the hearts and minds of Latter-day Saints and of the beliefs that move them to action.[21]

Such a conclusion is disturbing since the promotion of their faith is based on a lie. If such a practice is deemed to be acceptable, then why was the late LDS Seventy Paul Dunn severely criticized in 1991 when he admitted that his many faith-promoting heroic war stories and sports stories were totally fabricated?

Are John and the "three Nephites" alive today or not? If they are, why do many Mormons want to distance themselves from the reported appearances of these people? If they do not exist, why have so many LDS leaders reported that these men are still alive? And if they were wrong about this issue, on what other issues could the early Mormon leaders have erred?

THE APOSTOLIC CHAIN OF COMMAND

If, as LDS leaders proclaim, the Church of Jesus Christ of Latter-day Saints reflects the practices and beliefs of the "primitive" church, it must be assumed that the early church had a chain of command similar to that found today in Salt Lake City. If this is true, then the apostles must have had a set of checks and balances to ensure that a successor would always be available.

If an apostle was killed or died of natural causes, a godly replacement to carry on the goal of his predecessor would have been picked, much like the system set up today in modern Mormonism. However, if the primitive church did not have this system in place, then the LDS Church leaders have no right to claim they represent the same church as that led by Christ and the biblical apostles.

According to LDS tradition, there were supposedly twelve Nephite apostles existing in the New World simultaneously with the twelve apostles in Palestine.[22] If the office of apostle did not die with the Nephites, who remained alive until the fifth century A.D., then why is the "great" apostasy said to have begun immediately after John, who was the last remaining apostle in the Eastern Hemisphere? While the remaining apostles saw biblical justification to replace Judas's position with another, there is no biblical account that compelled them to do this every time a colleague died. Had this been the practice, it would seem likely that John could not have been the last remaining apostle to be alive; there would have had to have been others who had filled the positions of those who had died.

Some have argued that the New Testament does speak of others who had the title of apostle. Perhaps the LDS conclusion places too much emphasis on this title. In the strictest sense, *apostle* means "one sent forth." With this being the case, numerous people could have rightly held this designation. However, when it came to replacing Judas, the eleven felt that one of the requirements to be an apostle was that the individual had personally seen Christ. It never seemed to be a priority in the Christian church to replace deceased disciples after the account of Matthias in Acts 1:23–26.[23]

If, as the current LDS Church practices today, new apostles should be picked to replace outgoing disciples (through retirement or death), it seems strange that God would have allowed the leaders of His church in Palestine to be so ignorant as to stop replacing martyred apostles. Furthermore, Mormons are often told that God will never allow the leaders of the LDS Church to guide the church into error. This is a teaching that is hammered home on a continual basis. If this is true of the modern Mormon Church, it must have also been true in the apostolic church. If the early church had a prophet like the modern LDS prophet guiding it, how could it ever fall into a state of apostasy? It would make sense that each successor would also be prohibited from allowing the church to fall into such a state.

THE PRIESTHOOD OF THE BELIEVER

If there was no proper authority after the apostles until the time of Joseph Smith, then there must not have been the proper authority on earth to hold the priesthood. So Mormonism teaches that the priesthood also had to be restored. Joseph Smith and Oliver Cowdery claimed to have received the Aaronic priesthood from John the Baptist on 15 May 1829 along the bank of the Susquehanna River, near Harmony, Pennsylvania.

> This ordination gave the two men authority to baptize, and they immediately performed that ordinance for one another in the Susquehanna River. The Prophet Joseph Smith had received no previous revelations authorizing him to baptize; to perform that ordinance properly required specific authorization from God. The return of John to bestow the Aaronic Priesthood confirmed that divine authority had been lost from the earth and that a heavenly visitation was necessary to restore it.[24]

The bishop of a ward serves as the president of the holders of the Aaronic priesthood. Although females are prohibited from holding any priesthood within Mormonism, young LDS men beginning at age twelve are able to hold the Aaronic priesthood.

> Beginning with the reorganization of the priesthood in 1877, the Church established the current practice of ordaining boys to the Aaronic Priesthood during their early teenage years, organizing them at the ward level into priesthood quorums by age group and priesthood office, and advancing them periodically to higher offices and eventually to the higher priesthood. The bishop of each ward presides over the Aaronic Priesthood in the ward. . . . Under the direction of the bishop, someone with proper authority confers the Aaronic Priesthood upon a worthy young man when he is twelve years old, ordaining him to the office of deacon. If he remains faithful and worthy, he is ordained to the office of teacher when he is fourteen years old and is given additional responsibilities. If he continues to remain faithful and worthy, he is ordained to the office of priest in the Aaronic Priesthood when he is sixteen years old, again receiving increased responsibilities. As young men progress in the priesthood, they retain all the rights and duties of lower offices.[25]

The Melchizedek priesthood was also promised to Cowdery and Smith by John the Baptist at the bestowing of the Aaronic priesthood.

> Sometime before June 14, 1829, the Lord instructed Joseph Smith and Oliver Cowdery concerning their ordination as elders, which is a Melchizedek Priesthood office (HC 1:60–61). Furthermore, when Peter, James, and John appeared to Joseph and Oliver, they ordained them also as apostles (D&C 27:12) and committed to them "the keys of the kingdom, and of the dispensation of the fulness of times" (D&C 128:20; cf. 27:13).[26]

Robert J. Matthews makes it a point to link modern Latter-day Saints with ancient Israel, thus granting them the necessary restoration authority. This connection occurs at conversion and baptism into the LDS Church.[27] Bruce McConkie, in no uncertain terms, taught that Mormons are literally the seed of Abraham, thereby lending support to the notion that Mormons can rightfully hold the priesthood. He stated:

> We are literally of the seed of Abraham. Let's just drill it into ourselves! We are literally of the seed of Abraham. We are natural heirs according to the flesh. We are not adopted nor anything else. I don't know how there could be language more express than these revelations, "natural heirs according to the flesh," "the literal seed of the body." You see he [the Lord] just goes out of his way to make it literal. The literal seed of your body has the right to the priesthood and the gospel, and that is us.[28]

Despite this assumption, the Bible clearly shows that neither the Aaronic nor the Melchizedek priesthoods are available for believers today. The Aaronic priesthood was for the priests of the temple, as defined in the books of Moses known as the Pentateuch. The New Testament shows no need for such a priesthood for Christian believers. As far as the Melchizedek priesthood, Hebrews 6:20 says Jesus is the "high priest for ever after the order of Melchisedec." Hebrews 7:24 says that because Jesus lives forever, He holds His priesthood permanently. As for the authority of the Christian, 1 Peter 2:9 says he or she is part of "a chosen generation" and "a royal priesthood." The believer is given the right to be called a child of God. Indeed, when speaking of believers, 1 John 3:2 says that *now* are we the sons of God." First John 5:5 adds that only those who believe "that Jesus is the Son of God" have overcome the world. They, then, are the ones who have been given divine authority.[29]

CONCLUSION

The apostasy, according to Mormonism:

- Christianity died soon after the death of the apostles
- The apostasy continued until Joseph Smith restored the true church in 1830

- Jesus' words in Matthew 16:18 should be taken in a nonliteral sense
- John the apostle and three Nephites never died and are still on earth

The apostasy, according to Christianity:

- There have been true believers in the world since Christ established the Christian church
- There has been no need for a "restoration" of Christianity, and so there is no need for the Mormon Church
- Jesus told His followers that nothing could overcome His presence on this earth
- John the apostle denied the idea that he would remain alive on this earth

Does the LDS Church Have a Role in Christianity Today?

Unless there was a complete apostasy from the Christian faith, there is no need for the LDS religion. This would mean that everything from Joseph Smith and his *Book of Mormon* through the current LDS structure would not be needed. While this topic will not necessarily convince Mormons of their errors, it may help them to see how patently offensive such a belief system is to Christian believers.

Christian: I'm curious as to the meaning of 1 Nephi 14:10 in the *Book of Mormon.* It says that there are only two churches, the "church of the Lamb of God" and the "church of the Devil." It also teaches that those who don't belong to the first church belong to the second church, which is the "mother of abominations" and the "whore of all the earth." Since I do not belong to your church, does this mean that I am a member of Satan's church?

Mormon: I wouldn't say that.

C: Then what does it mean?

M: We believe we have more complete truth than other churches.

C: Was all authority of the Christian gospel lost soon after the death of the apostles?

M: Yes, that's why we needed Joseph Smith to bring us the *Book of Mormon,* which is "Another Testament of Jesus Christ."

C: So, therefore, what authority would you say I have if I don't belong to the restored church?

M: You do not have the authority to participate in temple worship and other important ordinances that allow you to attain the celestial kingdom.

C: I have a problem with this because Jesus clearly promised in Hebrews 13:5 that He would never leave nor forsake us. He also said in the Great Commission, "Lo, I am with you alway, even unto the end of the world" (Matt. 28:20).

M: But the Bible predicted such a great apostasy.

C: If you look closely at the passages talking about apostasy, you will see that a complete falling away from the Christian faith was never taught. Certainly we have had many such fallings away, but there has always been a representation of God's people who have continued to exist. And how do I know these verses are not talking about your church?

M: I'm not sure, but don't you think there have been many changes in doctrines over the years?

C: Actually, the burden of proof is on you as a Mormon to show how these doctrines have changed. When I read the Bible, I see a number of inconsistencies between Mormonism and the revelation given to us by God.

M: For instance . . .

C: For instance, the idea that God would abandon His people and remove His spirit from the world only to return some fourteen centuries later. This also doesn't make sense since your leaders have taught that three Nephite disciples "were given power over death so as to remain on the earth until Jesus comes again" (3 Nephi 28). Also, the apostle John was to have remained as well. Since they were promised to make converts while here on earth, it seems that the church was continuing instead of declining. Since we would assume that these converts were learning under those who apparently had authority, as your church teaches, there could not have been a simultaneous apostasy.

The point should be made that the very existence of the LDS Church is not only offensive to Christians, but it is also not a biblical or logical principle.

PART THREE

Examining the LDS Concept of Scripture

The Bible

Add all this imperfection to the uncertainty of the translation, and who, in his right mind, could, for one moment, suppose the Bible in its present form to be a perfect guide? Who knows that even one verse of the whole Bible has escaped pollution, so as to convey the same sense now that it did in the original?

Apostle Orson Pratt, *The Bible an Insufficient Guide,* 47

The Bible is a perennial best-seller that is accepted by Christians the world over as being the authoritative Word of God. Faithful Christian missionaries throughout the world work full-time translating this book into new languages; in fact, no book has ever been translated into half as many languages. Perhaps the connection between the Bible and Christianity is a reason why the LDS Church began an advertising campaign in the United States in 1997 offering free King James Version Bibles. A person who called the toll-free number would have two neatly dressed Mormon missionaries personally deliver it along with an offer to go through the missionary lessons.

There can be no better way to legitimize a church's existence and make it look like the Christian main-

stream than by showing how the movement accepts the Bible. Historically, LDS leaders have used the Bible in this way, quoting it in
an attempt to support their doctrines on one hand while severely criticizing it on the other.

When Mormons ask us if we have read the *Book of Mormon*—
which we have—we find it interesting when we turn the tables and
ask if they have ever read the Bible. Although many will say they've
read parts, our hearts are saddened because so few have spent much
time doing so, let alone having read the entire Word of God. Could
this lack of biblical interest be a result of the LDS leaders' assertions
that the Bible is not fully trustworthy?

As far as being able to completely trust the Bible, Mormon leaders have taught that the Bible's authority has been diluted over the
years. This pessimism and the need for other scriptures to supercede
the Bible can be traced to the *Book of Mormon* itself. First Nephi
13:28 says, "Wherefore, thou seest that after the book hath gone
forth through the hands of the great and abominable church, that
there are many plain and precious things taken away from the book,
which is the book of the Lamb of God." Second Nephi 29:6 adds,
"Thou fool, that shall say: A Bible, we have got a Bible, and we
need no more Bible. Have ye obtained a Bible save it were by the
Jews?"

LDS leaders have done their fair share to cast doubt on the certainty
of the Bible. Apostle Bruce McConkie insisted:

> The Bible bears true witness of God and his gospel as far as it is trans-
> lated correctly. Many plain and precious things have been deleted, how-
> ever; and the Book of Mormon is the means, provided by divine wisdom,
> to pour forth the gospel word as it was given in perfection to the ancients.
> It has come to preserve and sustain the Bible, not to destroy or dilute its
> message. . . . Satan guided his servants in taking many plain and precious
> things, and many of the covenants of the Lord, from the Bible, so that
> men would stumble and fall and lose their souls. When these truths and
> doctrines and covenants are restored through the Book of Mormon, what
> may we expect from Satan and from his servants? Their natural reac-
> tion—their craft is in danger!—will be to poison the minds of men against
> the Nephite scripture, so they will continue to stumble as they rely on the
> Bible alone.[1]

THE BIBLE—THE CHRISTIAN'S WRITTEN AUTHORITY

According to Christian teaching, God's instructions were handed down through His prophets, apostles, and eyewitnesses. Sixty-six books written by dozens of men over a period of about fifteen hundred years make up this revelation known as the Bible.[2] There is no question that Christians over the centuries consider this collection of books to be extraordinary and, in fact, sacred. Christian theologian A. Berkeley Mickelsen wrote:

> Inspiration means the action of God in the lives and utterances of his chosen servants so that what they declare conveys to men what God wants men to know. The Scriptures are the inspired word of God because they represent all that God deemed it necessary to preserve from the past so that succeeding generations could know the truths he conveyed to men of earlier generations. Because the Bible is an inspired book, it is a unique book. The reason for its inspiration is to bring men into a living encounter with the living God. Hence the Bible came into existence for interaction and reflection—for good hard use.[3]

Although most likely speaking about the Old Testament, Paul wrote in 2 Timothy 3:16–17:

> All scripture is given by inspiration of God, and is profitable for doctrine, for reproof, for correction, for instruction in righteousness: That the man of God may be perfect, throughly furnished unto all good works.

According to this verse, Scripture is useful for:

1. Teaching God's truths and the doctrines we are to believe
2. Rebuking others, such as Jesus' example with Lucifer in Matthew 4:1–11
3. Correcting one another when we stray from God's truth
4. Training for righteousness

The Bible is more than just men's words, for it reveals God's voice to His people. As to how God's written Word was constructed, 2 Peter 1:20–21 gives the process:

Knowing this first, that no prophecy of the scripture is of any private interpretation. For the prophecy came not in old time by the will of man: but
holy men of God spake as they were moved by the Holy Ghost.

The early church gave a stamp of authority to the writings of the
apostles. This is documented in 2 Peter 3:15–16 (emphasis ours):

And account that the longsuffering of our Lord is salvation; even as our
beloved brother Paul also according to the wisdom given unto him hath
written unto you; as also in all his epistles, speaking in them of these things;
in which are some things hard to be understood, which they that are
unlearned and unstable wrest, as they do also the *other scriptures,* unto
their own destruction.

Paul wrote in 1 Thessalonians 2:13 (emphasis ours):

For this cause also thank we God without ceasing, because, when ye
received the word of God which ye heard of us, ye received it not as the
word of men, but as it is in truth, the *word of God,* which effectually work-
eth also in you that believe.

For the Mormon, authority rests not only in written scriptures but
also in *latter-day* or *modern-day* revelation. Apostle Dallin Oaks said:

What makes us different from most other Christians in the way we read and
use the Bible and other scriptures is our belief in continuing revelation. For
us, the scriptures are not the ultimate source of knowledge, but what precedes the ultimate source. The ultimate knowledge comes by revelation.[4]

Even more disconcerting than Mr. Oaks's quote was a letter from the
First Presidency that was printed on page three of the 20 June 1992 LDS
Church News. It read in part, "The most reliable way to measure the
accuracy of any biblical passage is not by comparing different texts, but
by comparison with the Book of Mormon and modern-day revelations."

TRANSMISSION VERSUS TRANSLATION

Those who mistakenly think the Bible cannot be trusted apparently
do not understand how the Bible has been transmitted since the time

of the apostles.⁵ The eighth LDS Article of Faith says the Bible can be trusted only "as far as it is translated correctly." What does this mean? *Translation* means to take words from one language and put them into the words of another. If the Bible were true only as far as it is *translated* correctly, we would certainly agree.

The Bible was written primarily in Hebrew and Koiné Greek. Anytime the words from one language are put into another—whether it is Spanish into English or French into Arabic—there is always the risk of losing something in the translation. It is doubtful that our many modern-day translations were produced by unprincipled people who wanted to keep God's truths hidden. In actuality, quite the opposite is true. The motivation behind a new translation is, in most cases, to give a clearer understanding of what God wants to reveal to His people. Granted, some translations do a better job at achieving this goal than others.

However, does Article Eight correctly state the problem the LDS Church has with the Bible? Some Mormons have recognized that the word *translated* as used in the Articles of Faith is not entirely correct. Knowledgeable Mormons who have studied the methods of translating languages admit that the transmission, not the translation, of the biblical texts concerns them.

Transmission refers to how the manuscripts were copied and handed down through the centuries. A number of Mormons contend that the manuscripts were corrupted throughout the years, saying that unscrupulous people had purposely left out "many plain and precious truths" with some inserting their own erroneous philosophies. However, this is an argument from silence, since these same detractors cannot produce any untainted manuscripts against which to measure the "tainted" ones.

Some Mormons believe that the King James Version Bible was a translation of another Bible translation. This, in turn, was a translation of another translation, all the way down to Jerome's Latin Vulgate. Nothing could be further from the truth. The translators of the King James Version state their methods in their dedication: "Out of the Original Sacred Tongues, together with comparing of the labours, both in our own, and other foreign Languages, of many worthy men who went before us, there should be one more exact Translation of the holy Scriptures in the *English Tongue*."

Although translations will differ, a good translation will go back to the most accurate manuscripts and then attempt to put the words of the Bible into an understandable language for the audience it addresses.

Two translators of any written piece will differ in the choice of words, verb tense, and style. But if two good Spanish translators independently translate this morning's paper, you would have to say that the basic message would be the same despite their numerous differences. There is no such thing as a *perfect* translation. The LDS Church leaders must certainly be aware of this, since their translators have often had to revise not only their English edition of the *Book of Mormon* but several foreign editions as well.[6]

HOW DO WE KNOW ANYTHING IS TRUE?

Before Latter-day Saints unduly criticize the accuracy of the Bible,[7] perhaps they should first consider the following:

1. How do we know if James 1:5, the verse that Joseph Smith used to draw him to the "Sacred Grove," was indeed correct? For that matter, how can anyone trust other proof texts used to support Mormonism? It would seem reasonable that whatever test for accuracy that could be applied to James 1:5 could also be applied to every other Bible verse as well.
2. If the LDS Church has a prophet who has direct communication with God, then it would seem plausible for him to fix these alleged errors. After all, *D&C* 107:92 states that one of the "gifts of God which he bestows upon the head of the church" is the role of translator.[8] If the God of Mormonism was able to help Smith translate the *Book of Mormon* from the golden plates, he could also be able to help the prophet with these alleged errors. Although the LDS Church does not officially publish the Joseph Smith Translation as a bound volume, Smith's corrections are included as footnotes and endnotes in the LDS-published version of the King James Bible.[9] Many Mormons are unaware that Joseph Smith failed to "correct" many of the so-called problematic verses.

3. If Mormons want to make a great deal about the small percentage of questionable material in the Bible—none of which affects essential doctrine—then do they also have a problem with the many changes made to the *Book of Mormon* over the years?[10]

CONCLUSION

The Bible, according to Mormonism:

- It is true only as far as it does not disagree with Mormon doctrine
- It is the only book of the four LDS scriptures that is accepted with limitations
- It is filled with alleged contradictions
- It cannot be trusted by itself

The Bible, according to Christianity:

- It is the Word of God that is reliable for the modern Christian
- It is the only Scripture fully inspired by God
- The context of a passage and the rest of the Bible must be considered when interpreting supposed contradictions
- It can be fully trusted

The *Book of Mormon*

Take away the Book of Mormon and the revelations, and where is our religion? We have none.

President Joseph Smith,
Teachings of the Prophet Joseph Smith, 71

In 1987 LDS President Ezra Taft Benson urged his followers to flood the earth with the *Book of Mormon.* Through several vigorous campaigns, the LDS Church has been successful at giving away millions of copies of a book touted as "Another Testament of Jesus Christ." "Read this book and pray about it" is the common challenge made by the missionaries who go door-to-door propagating their faith.[1] After all, the *Book of Mormon* was rated by one magazine's readers as the eighth most influential book in the United States.[2] What is this book all about? And what makes it so special to the Latter-day Saint?

THE PREEMINENT BOOK

In 1823 Joseph Smith claimed to have been visited by an angel named Moroni. This heavenly being told

him about buried gold plates that contained a record of ancient inhabitants of the American continent. Smith would not be allowed to
retrieve the gold record for another four years. In 1827 Smith claimed
that he went to a small hill not far from his New York home and dug
up the record spoken of by the angel. He reported:

> These records were engraven on plates which had the appearance of gold,
> each plate was six inches wide and eight inches long, and not quite so thick
> as common tin. They were filled with engravings, in Egyptian characters,
> and bound together in a volume as the leaves of a book, with three rings
> running through the whole. The volume was something near six inches in
> thickness, a part of which was sealed. The characters on the unsealed part
> were small, and beautifully engraved. The whole book exhibited many
> marks of antiquity in its construction, and much skill in the art of engrav-
> ing. With the records was found a curious instrument, which the ancients
> called "Urim and Thummim," which consisted of two transparent stones
> set in the rim of a bow fastened to a breast plate. Through the medium of
> the Urim and Thummim I translated the record by the gift and power of
> God.[3]

This "translation" became the *Book of Mormon,* which is said to
contain the story of primarily two groups of people who came to the
Americas. The first group was known as the Jaredites. The following
is a description of their history:

> This particular people left the Tower of Babel at the time of the confusion
> of tongues. Their prophet-leaders were led to the ocean, where they con-
> structed eight peculiar barges. These were driven by the wind across the
> waters to America, where the Jaredites became a large and powerful nation.
> After many centuries, wickedness and wars led to a final war of annihi-
> lation. During that final war, Ether, a prophet of God, wrote their history
> and spiritual experiences on twenty-four gold plates, perhaps relying on
> earlier Jaredite records.[4]

The second group arrived in the Americas approximately six hundred years before the birth of Christ. Lehi, a Jewish prophet from
Jerusalem, claimed that God told him to flee the city prior to the Baby-
lonian captivity. He fled with his wife, Sariah, and their four sons:
Laman, Lemuel, Sam, and Nephi. Also joining Lehi were Zoram, Ish-

mael, and Ishmael's family. They sailed across the ocean, landed in the Western Hemisphere, and commenced to build cities and a large civilization. After Lehi's death, some of the people accepted Nephi as their leader, while the rest gave allegiance to Laman.

The *Book of Mormon* narrative describes how these two groups were known as Nephites and Lamanites. Much of the story tells about the hatred between the two groups and the wars they fought. It also records Jesus' appearance to these civilizations after He was resurrected from the dead in Palestine. By the fifth century A.D., the Lamanites had completely annihilated the Nephite people at the battle of Hill Cumorah.

According to Mormon belief, the descendants of the Lamanites are the American Indians. Moroni, who was the son of Mormon, was the last living Nephite. He buried the record of his people in the Hill Cumorah, which is located near present-day Palmyra in upstate New York. This record on gold plates was later discovered and translated into the *Book of Mormon* by Joseph Smith.

Both former and contemporary Mormon authorities and scholars have upheld the prominent place the *Book of Mormon* has in the Latter-day Saints religion. Asserting the supremacy of the *Book of Mormon,* Apostle Bruce McConkie bluntly stated:

> Almost all of the doctrines of the gospel are taught in the Book of Mormon *with much greater clarity and perfection* than those same doctrines are revealed in the Bible. Anyone who will place in parallel columns the teachings of these two great books on such subjects as the atonement, plan of salvation, gathering of Israel, baptism, gifts of the Spirit, miracles, revelation, faith, charity, (or any of a hundred other subjects), will find conclusive proof of the *superiority* of Book of Mormon teachings.[5]

Ezra Taft Benson agreed, adding in a 1978 address, "There will be more people saved in the kingdom of God—ten thousand times over— because of the Book of Mormon than there will be because of the Bible."[6]

"TRANSLATING" THE *BOOK OF MORMON*

Many paintings depict Joseph Smith leaning over in a prayerful position while he was translating the gold plates; however, testimony from his contemporaries provides another picture as to how the "Reformed Egyptian" language was translated into English. David Whitmer, one of the "three witnesses" whose name is found in every edition of the *Book of Mormon,* described the method in which Joseph Smith translated the plates into English:

> I will now give you a description of the manner in which the Book of Mormon was translated. Joseph Smith would put the seer stone into a hat, and put his face in the hat, drawing it closely around his face to exclude the light; and in the darkness the spiritual light would shine. A piece of something resembling parchment would appear, and on that appeared the writing. One character at a time would appear, and under it was the interpretation in English. Brother Joseph would read off the English to Oliver Cowdery, who was his principle scribe, and when it was written down and repeated to Brother Joseph to see if it was correct, then it would disappear, and another character with the interpretation would appear. Thus the Book of Mormon was translated by the gift and power of God, and not by any power of man.[7]

Martin Harris, also one of the three witnesses mentioned in the *Book of Mormon,* gave a similar account:

> By aid of the Seer Stone, sentences would appear and were read by the Prophet and written by Martin, and when finished he would say "written"; and if correctly written, the sentence would disappear and another appear in its place; but if not written correctly it remained until corrected, so that the translation was just as it was engraven on the plates, precisely in the language then used.[8]

Joseph Smith's brother, William Smith, concurred with the above statements, although he refers to the stones as the Urim and Thummim:[9]

> The manner in which this was done was by looking into the Urim and Thummim, which was placed in a hat to exclude the light, (the plates lying near by covered up), and reading off the translation, which appeared in the stone by the power of God.[10]

Despite these and other eyewitness accounts, President Joseph Fielding Smith denies that such a rock was used:

While the statement has been made by some writers that the Prophet Joseph Smith used a seer stone part of the time in his translating of the record, and information points to the fact that he did have in his possession such a stone, yet there is no authentic statement in the history of the Church which states that the use of such a stone was made in that translation. The information is all hearsay, and personally, I do not believe that this stone was used for this purpose.[11]

THE *BOOK OF MORMON* WITNESSES: WHAT ABOUT CREDIBILITY?

An introductory page found in every copy of the *Book of Mormon* lists the two combined testimonies made by eleven men who belonged to five families: Cowdery, Whitmer, Harris, Page, and Smith. Their testimonies are said to verify the story of the *Book of Mormon*. Without the witness of these men, we would have to rely on Smith's word alone that what he translated was real.

As far as the eight men who signed a short statement called "The Testimony of the Eight Witnesses," four belonged to the Whitmer family and three were from Joseph Smith's immediate family (his father and two brothers). The eighth person was Hiram Page who, interestingly enough, was married to a Whitmer. While eight witnesses may sound like a strong testimonial support to Smith's story, only three families are represented. Besides Smith's own family, the other witnesses were close friends of the LDS prophet.

Oliver Cowdery, David Whitmer, and Martin Harris were three of Smith's most trusted men who signed "The Testimony of the Three Witnesses," another statement testifying to the authenticity of the *Book of Mormon*. Many Mormons do not realize the dubious background of these men. Former LDS historian D. Michael Quinn wrote that folk magic and seer stone divination were quite popular among the *Book of Mormon* witnesses:

The Three Witnesses to the Book of Mormon were also involved in folk magic. Oliver Cowdery was a rodsman before he met Smith in 1829 and was soon authorized by divine revelation to continue the revelatory use of his "rod of nature." David Whitmer revered Smith's use of a seer stone, may have possessed one of his own, and authorized a later spokesman for his own religious organization to obtain revelations through a stone. Martin Harris endorsed Smith's use of a seer stone for divination and treasure seeking, and participated in treasure digging himself after the discovery of the gold plates. Of the remaining Eight Witnesses, John Whitmer possessed a seer stone which his descendants preserved, his brothers Christian, Jacob, and Peter were included in their pastor's accusation of magic belief, and Hiram Page, their brother-in-law, had a stone for revelations.[12]

In 1838 Cowdery was excommunicated from the Mormon Church after he accused Smith of adultery, lying, and teaching false doctrines. The Mormon founder classified Cowdery as one who was "too mean to mention." Cowdery charged Smith with having an affair with a woman named Fanny Alger.[13]

After his excommunication, Cowdery was accused of a number of crimes, including "denying the faith," "persecuting the brethren," "urging on vexatious lawsuits," "falsely insinuating [Joseph Smith] was guilty of adultery," and dishonesty.[14] Cowdery later joined a church whose denomination (Methodist) had been supposedly condemned by God.[15] He is said to have returned to the LDS Church in 1848 and died two years later at the young age of forty-three.

David Whitmer claimed that none of the three witnesses ever denied the truthfulness of the *Book of Mormon*. However, Whitmer did believe Joseph Smith was a fallen prophet when he wrote:

Many of the Latter Day Saints believe that it was impossible for Brother Joseph to have fallen. I will give you some evidence upon this matter which I suppose you will certainly accept, showing that Brother Joseph belonged to the class of men who could fall into error and blindness. From the following you will see that Brother Joseph belonged to the weakest class—the class that were very liable to fall. . . . All of you who believe the revelations of Joseph Smith as if they were from the mouth of God. You should have acknowledged belief in the errors of Joseph Smith, and not tried to hide them when there is so much evidence that he did go into error and blindness. . . . I am doing God's will in bringing the truth to light concerning the errors of Brother Joseph. They will see that it is necessary, as he is the man who introduced many doctrines of error into the Church of Christ; and his errors must be made manifest and the truth brought to light, in order that all Latter Day Saints shall cease to put their trust in this man, believing his doctrines as if they were from the mouth of God.[16]

Whitmer—whom Smith called a "dumb ass" and "mean man," saying "Satan deceiveth [Whitmer]"[17]—believed Joseph Smith intentionally changed the very revelations that God had supposedly given him.[18] Believing that God told him to leave the Mormon faith, Whitmer walked away and never returned. He wrote:

> If you believe my testimony to the Book of Mormon; if you believe that God spake to us three witnesses by his own voice, then I tell you that in June, 1838, God spake to me again by his own voice from the heavens, and told me to "separate myself from among the Latter Day Saints, for as they sought to do unto me, so should it be done unto them."[19]

Toward the end of his life, Whitmer joined an offshoot of Mormonism called the Church of Christ, a group that accepted the *Book of Mormon*.[20] Meanwhile, the third signer, Martin Harris, upset the Mormon founder when he declared that "Joseph drank too much liquor when he was translating the Book of Mormon" and that he knew more than Smith did.[21] Smith retaliated for Harris's many antics by twice referring to him as a "wicked man" in Mormon scripture.[22] It was for these sins that Harris was supposedly commanded by Christ Himself to repent.[23] Harris expressed his worship to God in unique ways. Regarding this, Smith said:

> Martin Harris having boasted to the brethren that he could handle snakes with perfect safety, while fooling with a black snake with his bare feet, he received a bite on his left foot. The fact was communicated to me, and I took occasion to reprove him, and exhort the brethren never to trifle with the promises of God.[24]

Harris left the Mormon movement and joined several other groups, among them the Shakers and the Strangites.[25] While Harris eventually returned to the LDS Church, he apparently never found peace. He told one early Mormon writer that he "never believed that the Brighamite branch of the Mormon church, nor the Josephite church, was right, because in his opinion, God had rejected them." As to why he went to the LDS temple in Salt Lake City, he apparently was curious to discover "what was going on in there."[26]

Regarding their testimony to the *Book of Mormon,* each of these three "witnesses" had questionable qualifications since, as Joseph Smith said, they all fell into error.[27] They were gullible, and their credibility was stained with cases of counterfeiting, dowsing, false prophecies, money digging, and lying. Even their testimony claiming to have "seen the plates" is suspicious. For instance, John Gilbert, who assisted E. B. Grandin in printing the *Book of Mormon,* personally asked Martin Harris if he had actually seen the plates with his "naked eyes." Gilbert remembered:

> Martin was in the office when I finished setting up the testimony of the three witnesses. . . . I said to him, "Martin, did you see those plates with your naked eyes?" Martin looked down for an instant, raised his eyes up, and said, "No, I saw them with a spiritual eye."[28]

Marvin S. Hill, an instructor at BYU, wrote:

> . . . there is a possibility that the witnesses saw the plates in vision only. . . . There is testimony from several independent interviewers, all non-Mormon, that Martin Harris and David Whitmer said they saw the plates with their "spiritual eyes" only. . . . This is contradicted, however, by statements like that of David Whitmer in the Saints Herald in 1882, "these hands handled the plates, these eyes saw the angel." But Z. H. Gurley elicited from Whitmer a not so positive response to the question, "did you touch them?" His answer was, "We did not touch nor handle the plates." . . . Stephen Burnett quotes Martin Harris that "the eight witnesses never saw them. . . ." Yet John Whitmer told Wilhelm Poulson . . . that he saw the plates when they were not covered, and he turned the leaves.[29]

HISTORICAL PROBLEMS WITH THE *BOOK OF MORMON*

Across the street from Temple Square in Salt Lake City is a museum owned by the Mormon Church where numerous artifacts dating back to the early years of the church are displayed. Museum pieces include tools owned by Brigham Young, handwritten manuscripts from the *Book of Mormon,* a replica of the Nauvoo Sunstone, and even the gun Joseph Smith used to shoot three people during his last moments at Carthage Jail. One thing not in this museum is any artifact that can be clearly traced to the cultures mentioned in the *Book of Mormon.* While Mormon leaders have insisted that virtually millions of Jaredites, Nephites, and Lamanites existed during the *Book of Mormon* era, the LDS Church has no tangible evidence to support this claim.[30]

In order to find archaeological evidence, knowing where to dig would be paramount. Unfortunately, there is no official position within the LDS Church as to where the alleged lands of the *Book of Mormon* should be. The *Book of Mormon* lands are probably most commonly believed to be in the Central American area. One of the biggest supporters for this location is the Foundation for Ancient Research and Mormon Studies (FARMS). Many of its members have staunchly defended the idea that Central America is the location for places mentioned in the *Book of Mormon.*

In 1991 FARMS conducted a tour to Central America offering Latter-day Saints the opportunity to see what they believe to be the lands of the *Book of Mormon.* However, a flyer advertising the tour shows that such sites are only speculative. Take the following examples into account: Lake Atitlan, a *good candidate for* the waters of Mormon; Oaxaca and the ruins of Monte Alban, a *probable* site for the Jaredite land of Moron, Tuxtla Gutierrez, and San Critobal Las Casas, *thought to be* the land of Zarahemla; Grijalva River, *possibly* the river Sidon; Villahermosa and La Venta Park, *likely remnants* of the Jaredite civilization, Lake Catemaco, and the Tuxtla Mountains, *thought to be* the Hill Cumorah region. We commend FARMS for its honesty in admitting that there are no definitive *Book of Mormon* sites; unfortunately many zealous Latter-day Saints continue to tell people that the *Book of Mormon* has both historical and archaeological support.

The Central American theory has not been without its critics. Probably one of the more vocal critics of this view was Joseph Fielding Smith, who wrote:

> Within recent years there has arisen among certain students of the *Book of Mormon* a *theory* to the effect that within the period covered by the *Book of Mormon,* the Nephites and Lamanites were confined almost

entirely within the borders of the territory comprising Central America and the southern portion of Mexico—the isthmus of Tehauntepec probably being the "narrow neck" of land spoken of in the *Book of Mormon* rather than the isthmus of Panama. . . . In the face of this evidence coming from the Prophet Joseph Smith, Oliver Cowdery, and David Whitmer, we cannot say that the Nephites and Lamanites did not possess the territory of the United States and that the Hill Cumorah is in Central America. Neither can we say that the great struggle which resulted in the destruction of the Nephites took place in Central America.[31]

Smith also said:

It must be conceded that this description fits perfectly the land of Cumorah in New York, as it has been known since the visitation of Moroni to the Prophet Joseph Smith, for the hill is in the proximity of the Great Lakes and also in the land of many rivers and fountains. Moreover, the Prophet Joseph Smith himself is on record, definitely declaring the present hill called Cumorah to be the exact hill spoken of in the *Book of Mormon*. . . . It is difficult for a reasonable person to believe that such men as Oliver Cowdery, Brigham Young, Parley P. Pratt, Orson Pratt, David Whitmer, and many others, could speak frequently of the Spot where the Prophet Joseph Smith obtained the plates as the Hill Cumorah, and not be corrected by the Prophet, if that were not the fact. That they did speak of this hill in the days of the Prophet in this definite manner is an established record of history.[32]

Apostle James Talmage also placed the Nephite people in North America when he wrote:

At that time North America was inhabited by two great peoples, the Nephites and the Lamanites, each named after an early leader, and both originally of one family stock. Except for brief periods of comparative peace the two nations lived in a state of hostility due to Lamanite aggression.[33]

President Ezra Taft Benson insisted that not only did the alleged Nephites live in the area of the United States, but that Adam and the "Jaredites"[34] lived there as well.

Consider how very fortunate we are to be living in this land of America. The destiny of this country was forged long before the earth was even created. . . . This was the place of three former civilizations: that of Adam, that of the Jaredites, and that of the Nephites.[35]

Despite the above comments, many modern LDS scholars have since abandoned the idea that the *Book of Mormon* lands include areas of North America. In doing so they have claimed that such leaders as those above were misinformed.[36] For instance, Dr. John Sorenson, a retired BYU anthropology professor and a former board member for FARMS, stated:

> A very common view is that the entire Western Hemisphere was involved and that Nephites and Lamanites were everywhere until the final destruc-tion of the Nephites in New York, and then only Lamanites were left and those were the Indians. Now, it does little for our satisfaction in under-standing the scripture to take that simpleminded view. It simply is not true. The reason I say it is not true is because when we examine the Book of Mormon, which, after all, is the authority on the Nephites when we exam-ine the Book of Mormon text, and try to learn everything about it where and when then we find that the Nephites lived in a very small land. Not quite as small as Palestine, but small nevertheless, a few hundred miles in length and a hundred or two hundred miles across. Not thousands of miles, not the whole Western Hemisphere. If that were so if the whole hemisphere were the scene then the Book of Mormon text, its own state-ments about itself, and its scene would be wrong.[37]

If there is any misunderstanding, it would seem that the blame should be laid at the feet of Jesus Himself. A message from the First Presidency in 1930 stated:

> Jesus Christ, referring to the time when he would manifest himself in the latter days, declared that whereas he manifested himself to his own peo-ple in the meridian of time and they rejected him, in the latter days he would come first to the Gentiles, and then to the house of Israel. He says: "And behold, this people (the Nephites) will I establish in this land, (Amer-ica) and it shall be a new Jerusalem."[38]

In a declaration made by the First Presidency on 1 May 1911 and printed in the *Deseret News* a few days later, President Joseph F. Smith and his counselors Anthon Lund and John Henry Smith stated that it was Moroni himself who claimed to have "ministered to a people called Nephites, a branch of the house of Israel, formerly inhabiting *this land.*"[39] Conflicting information of this sort must certainly be confusing to the Latter-day Saint, especially since there is, for example, an LDS Church marker located north of Gallatin, Missouri, stating how a Nephite altar once existed near the place Joseph Smith called Adam-ondi-Ahman. If the Nephites were relegated to an area in Central America, how did one of their altars appear as far north as the state of Missouri?

While most LDS scholars would feel that there is historical and scientific value in the *Book of Mormon,* we have found no scientist or historian outside the Mormon faith who would support such a notion. On 25 August 1984 Dr. John Carlson addressed a Sunstone Symposium in Salt Lake City where he noted, "The Book of Mormon itself has not made a significant contribution to New World archaeology. Ask any New World archaeologist." When asked on 16 June 1999 if he had changed this position, he said, "No, I have not changed my opinion and would stand by what I said."

Dr. Carlson, who now serves as the director for the Center for Archaeoastronomy at the University of Maryland, did note that "interest in the Book of Mormon by believers has stimulated interest in the ancient Americas and promoted archaeological research." While he stated that much of this research is good and unbiased, "there are also plenty of examples of highly biased research designed to support the Book of Mormon."[40]

Dr. Michael Coe, a non-Mormon professor emeritus of anthropology at Yale University, is an expert in the early history of Mesoamerica.[41] He wrote a paper in 1973 that discussed the lack of historical evidence in the *Book of Mormon.* Said Coe:

> Mormon archaeologists over the years have almost unanimously accepted the Book of Mormon as an accurate, historical account of the New World peoples between about 2000 B.C. and A.D. 421. They believe that Smith could translate hieroglyphs, whether "Reformed Egyptian" or ancient American. . . . Let me now state uncategorically that as far as I know there is not one professionally trained archaeologist, who is not a Mormon, who sees any scientific justification for believing the foregoing to be true, and I would like to state that there are quite a few Mormon archaeologists who

join this group. . . . The bare facts of the matter are that nothing, absolutely nothing, has ever shown up in any New World excavation which would suggest to a dispassionate observer that the Book of Mormon, as claimed by Joseph Smith, is a historical document relating to the history of the early migrants to our hemisphere.[42]

With a hint of sarcasm, Coe concluded with these suggestions:

Forget the so-far fruitless quest for the Jaredites, Nephites, Mulekites, and the lands of Zarahemla and Bountiful: there is no more chance of finding them than of discovering the ruins of the bottomless pit described in the book of Revelations. . . . Continue the praiseworthy excavations in Mexico, remembering that little or nothing pertaining to the Book of Mormon will ever result from them.[43]

Despite the fact that many experts in the field of anthropology concur with Coe's 1973 assessment, some Mormons have tried to set it aside by claiming that his comments are outdated. Did new evidence cause him to change his position since 1973? We wrote Coe in 1993 to see if he still believed twenty years later what he had written in 1973. He responded:

I haven't changed my views about the Book of Mormon since my 1973 article. I have seen no archaeological evidence before or since that date which would convince me that it is anything but a fanciful creation by an unusually gifted individual living in upstate New York in the early 19th century.[44]

Mormon apologist L. Ara Norwood claims that the analysis by Coe (and any other non-LDS scholar, for that matter) should be rejected because he is not Mormon. He writes:

So we have a non-Latter-day Saint archaeologist who does not believe in the supernatural claims of the coming forth of the Book of Mormon due to the lack of "scientific evidence"? Is that significant? If a non-Latter-day Saint individual were to come to believe in the supernatural/spiritual claims of the Book of Mormon, would not that person then in all likelihood join the Latter-day Saint church?[45]

Norwood seems to miss the point. Coe is not basing his conclusion on the *spiritual* significance of the *Book of Mormon* but on the lack of *historical* significance.

Another point to consider is that the LDS Church has a history of being very sensitive about its scholars disseminating information that is anything less than faith promoting. In the world of Mormonism, image plays a major role, and many scholars have been disciplined for exposing information that can be damaging to that image.

It should also be noted that not all LDS scholars view FARMS as the final authority. In a paper printed in *Dialogue: A Journal of Mormon Thought,* Dr. Stephen Thompson, who at the time served as a research assistant in the department of Egyptology at Brown University, commented on the lack of freedom allowed to church-employed scholars:

> . . . the church has shown that the intellectual freedom of its employees is considerably circumscribed. . . . Perhaps through no fault of their own, the work of many FARMS researchers does not qualify as "critical" because they lack the essential ingredient of freedom.[46]

Mormon archaeologists may argue that they just need more time to discover pertinent artifacts that will help to validate the *Book of Mormon.* However, biblical archaeologists have not had much of a head start over their Mormon counterparts. According to Jack Meinhart, an associate editor of the magazine *Biblical Archaeology Review,* archaeology as a science is not much more than a century old. The golden ages of biblical archaeology occurred between the 1920s and World War II and the decades of the 1960s and 1970s. Certainly people found things in the biblical lands before then, but interpreting what they were and extracting legitimate information has come more recently.

Truly serious research in the biblical lands has been going on only since the nineteenth century, and the vast majority of what we know today wasn't discovered until the twentieth century. And despite all of the evidence that has been uncovered, some have estimated that 90 percent of the evidence in the biblical lands is still buried in the sands.[47] Until *Book of Mormon* evidence moves beyond the realm of faith, it can be rightly classified as a myth, legend, or story without any basis in historical fact.

"FULNESS OF THE EVERLASTING GOSPEL"

One of Mormonism's primary arguments against the Bible is that "many plain and precious truths" have been taken away from it. To make up for this, the LDS Church presents the *Book of Mormon* to the world. According to Ezra Taft Benson:

> The Book of Mormon is a second witness to Jesus Christ because it contains the plain and precious truths of His gospel. Within this sacred record is the fulness of the gospel of Jesus Christ; in other words, the Lord's requirements for salvation. . . . Not all truths are of equal value, nor are all scriptures of the same worth. What better way to nourish the spirit than to frequently feast from the book which the Prophet Joseph Smith said would get a man "nearer to God by abiding by its precepts than by any other book."[48]

Benson's comment says two things. First, he says that "the plain and precious truths" apparently not found in the Bible are found in the "sacred record" of the *Book of Mormon.* Second, he claims that "the Lord's requirements for salvation" can be found there as well. In other words, whatever is necessary in order to achieve complete salvation should be found in the pages of the *Book of Mormon.* Benson echoes Joseph Smith, who said, "I told the brethren that the Book of Mormon was the most correct of any book on earth, and the keystone of our religion, and a man would get nearer to God by abiding by its precepts, than by any other book."[49] Can these comments be substantiated?

WHERE ARE THE PRECEPTS?

Several Mormon leaders have equated getting nearer to God with exaltation. For instance, at the 1902 general conference, Apostle Matthias F. Cowley said:

> As we live near to God in all respects, so shall we be entitled to the companionship and, according to our faithfulness, a greater measure of the Holy Spirit, that will give us a better understanding of the things of God,

qualify us to live nearer unto God, and consequently to secure unto ourselves a greater exaltation in His presence.[50]

If, in fact, getting nearer to God is the same as exaltation, the *Book
of Mormon* should contain everything Latter-day Saints need to guide
them into the presence of God. According to the LDS Church handbook *Gospel Principles,* "There are specific ordinances we must have
received to be exalted." These are (with italicized portions not found
whatsoever in *Book of Mormon* teaching):

1. We must be baptized and confirmed a member of the Church of Jesus
   Christ.
2. We must receive the laying on of hands for the gift of the Holy Ghost.
3. *We must receive the temple endowment.*
4. *We must be married for time and eternity.*

In addition to receiving the required ordinances, the Lord commands all
of us to

1. Love and worship God.
2. Love our neighbor.
3. Repent of our wrongdoings.
4. Live the law of chastity.
5. *Pay honest tithes and offerings.*
6. Be honest in our dealings with others and with the Lord.
7. Speak the truth always.
8. *Obey the Word of Wisdom.*
9. *Search out our kindred dead and perform the saving ordinances of the
   gospel for them.*
10. Keep the Sabbath day holy.
11. Attend our Church meetings as regularly as possible to renew our bap-
    tismal covenants by partaking of the sacrament.
12. Love our family members and strengthen them in the ways of the Lord.
13. Have family and individual prayers every day.
14. Honor our parents.
15. Teach the gospel to others by word and example.
16. Study the scriptures.
17. Listen to and obey the inspired words of the prophets of the Lord.
18. Receive the Holy Ghost and learn to follow his direction in our indi-
    vidual lives.[51]

Numerous requirements not mentioned at all in the *Book of Mormon* must be met. This book does not mention temple endowments, marriage for time and eternity, the necessity of paying tithes, the Word of Wisdom, or baptism for the dead as prerequisites to exaltation. Since this is the case, how can it honestly be said that "the Lord's requirements for salvation" are found completely within its pages? According to Mormonism, without the aforementioned requirements, the best a person could hope for would be the terrestrial kingdom. In addition, the *Book of Mormon* does not discuss other important LDS doctrines. These are:

- The Mormon Church organization, on which its leaders place so much emphasis, cannot be found in the *Book of Mormon.*
- The Mormon so-called "Melchizedek Priesthood order" cannot be found in the *Book of Mormon.*
- The Mormon so-called "Aaronic Priesthood order" cannot be found in the *Book of Mormon.*
- The Mormon doctrine of the plurality of gods cannot be found in the *Book of Mormon.*
- The Mormon doctrine that God is an exalted man cannot be found in the *Book of Mormon.*
- The Mormon doctrine that people may become gods cannot be found in the *Book of Mormon.*
- The Mormon doctrine of the "three degrees of glory" cannot be found in the *Book of Mormon.*
- The Mormon doctrine of the plurality of wives cannot be found in the *Book of Mormon.*
- The Mormon doctrine of "preexistence" cannot be found in the *Book of Mormon.*
- The Mormon doctrine of "eternal progression" cannot be found in the *Book of Mormon.*
- The Mormon doctrine of a "Heavenly Mother" cannot be found in the *Book of Mormon.*
- The Mormon doctrine of a "temporary hell" cannot be found in the *Book of Mormon.*[52]

In all actuality, there is no evidence to suggest that the Nephites mentioned in the *Book of Mormon* believed or practiced what modern-day Mormons believe and practice. When presented with this information, some Mormons feel the words *fulness* and *gospel* are being misunderstood. Dr. Daniel Peterson, a BYU professor of ancient scripture, explained:

> In its most basic sense, the word [gospel] does not refer to all of the ordinances and all of the specific doctrines held by the Latter-day Saints, but represents a six-point formula including repentance, baptism, the Holy Ghost, faith, endurance to the end, and eternal life. These teachings are clearly set out in the Book of Mormon. . . . But there is no need for these doctrines to be explicitly discussed in the Book of Mormon, for the Nephite record itself repeatedly teaches that, after the believer has come to Christ and received the Holy Ghost, important further revelations will follow.[53]

While Peterson is entitled to his opinion, this definition does not concur with Bruce McConkie, who wrote:

> The gospel of Jesus Christ is the plan of salvation. It embraces all of the laws, principles, doctrines, rites, ordinances, acts, powers, authorities, and keys necessary to save and exalt men in the highest heaven hereafter. It is the covenant of salvation which the Lord makes with men on earth.[54]

Many people are under the impression that, by reading the *Book of Mormon,* they will get a better understanding of LDS Church doctrines. But this is not so; the reader actually becomes victim to the proverbial "bait and switch" scheme. Indeed, the *Book of Mormon* does not live up to its billing.

CONCLUSION

The problems with the *Book of Mormon* include:

- Dubious means of translation
- No historical or scientific support
- Witnesses who lack credibility
- Missing essential doctrines that define Mormonism

The *Doctrine and Covenants* and the *Pearl of Great Price*

I wish that every honest soul in this world would read the Book of Mormon; would read the Doctrine and Covenants, the Pearl of Great Price, besides reading the Bible. What a glorious privilege is ours. The so-called Christian world, divided and subdivided maintains that the Bible contains all of the word of God. To them the Lord has never given a revelation. According to its teachings nothing has come from the heavens by way of counsel and advice or revelation, comparable to that which we find in what they are pleased to call the canon of scripture.

President Joseph Fielding Smith,
Conference Report, October 1950, 10

Besides the *Book of Mormon,* Mormonism has two additional books in what is known as the standard works of the LDS Church. These are the *Doctrine and Covenants (D&C)* and the *Pearl of Great Price.* Many important and unique doctrines come from the pages of the *Doctrine and Covenants,* which is mainly the teachings of Joseph Smith plus several added declarations given to Mormon prophets, such as the abolishment of polygamy and allowing blacks to hold the LDS priesthood.

The *Pearl of Great Price,* meanwhile, is composed primarily of two smaller works, the Book of Moses and the Book of Abraham. The Book of Moses is "an extract from the translation of the Bible as revealed to Joseph Smith the Prophet, June 1830–February 1831." The Book of Abraham was allegedly translated from an Egyptian papyrus that Smith obtained in 1835. The *Pearl of Great Price* includes thirteen articles of faith, a brief history of Smith, and extracts from the Book of Matthew that were revised by Joseph Smith in his "translation" of the Bible.

THE *DOCTRINE AND COVENANTS:* A MODERN-DAY REVELATION?

According to the explanatory introduction to the *Doctrine and Covenants:*

> The Doctrine and Covenants is a collection of divine revelations and inspired declarations. . . . Although most of the sections are directed to members of The Church of Jesus Christ of Latter-day Saints, the messages, warnings, and exhortations are for the benefit of all mankind. . . . [It] is unique because it is not a translation of an ancient document, but is of modern origin and was given of God through his chosen prophets for the restoration of his holy work and the establishment of the kingdom of God on the earth in these days.[1]

President Ezra Taft Benson taught that the *D&C* "brings men to Christ" as it

> is the binding link between the Book of Mormon and the continuing work of the Restoration through the Prophet Joseph Smith and his successors. . . . The Book of Mormon is the "keystone" of our religion, and the Doctrine and Covenants is the capstone, with continuing latter-day revelation.[2]

The *D&C* was first put together as the *Book of Commandments:*

> By the fall of 1831, Joseph Smith had recorded seventy or more revelations, most of which contained instructions to Church members. In a spe-

cial conference held November 1, 1831, in Hiram, Ohio, the Church decided to publish a selection of these revelations, or "commandments." . . . Shortly after the unsuccessful 1833 effort to print the Book of Commandments was stopped, plans were made to publish the revelations in Kirtland, Ohio. Renamed the *Doctrine and Covenants of the Church of the Latter Day Saints,* the book was presented to, and accepted by, the members of the Church in an August 1835 conference as the word of God.[3]

Some of the more important doctrines and events recorded in the *D&C* include:

- the claim in 1:30 that there is only one true church
- words of the angel Moroni to Smith in 1823 (Section 2)
- an explanation of how Smith needed to repent for having lost the first 116 pages of the "Book of Lehi" (which was supposed to be a part of the *Book of Mormon*) to Martin Harris's wife and that he was not to retranslate these pages because wicked men sought to destroy Smith and the Mormon movement (Sections 3, 10)
- the assertion that the apostle John continues to live until today (Section 7)
- the way God wanted His church organized (Section 20)
- the establishment of Smith as the church's "seer, translator, prophet, apostle, and elder" (given on the first day of the church's existence, 6 April 1830, Section 21)
- the need to be rebaptized, no matter in which church a person had been previously baptized (Section 22)
- how only Smith could receive revelations, and that Hiram Page, one of the *Book of Mormon*'s eight witnesses, was receiving false revelations from Satan (Section 28)
- how Independence, Missouri, was to be the place for the City of Zion and the first LDS temple (Section 57)
- the way the devil and sons of perdition fell, how all receive some type of salvation, and the three kingdoms of "heaven" (Section 76)
- New Jerusalem would be built in Missouri (Section 84)

- the Word of Wisdom, a health code that, when obeyed, brings "temporal and spiritual blessings" (Section 89)[4]
- only the descendants of Aaron are to hold Aaronic priesthood (Section 107)[5]
- the name of Jesus was returned to "The Church of Jesus Christ of Latter-day Saints," previously named the "Church of the Latter-day Saints" (Section 115)
- Spring Hill in Daviess County, Missouri, is named by God as "Adam-ondi-Ahman" because "it is the place where Adam shall come to visit his people" (Section 116)
- Baptisms for the dead should be performed in LDS temples (Sections 124, 127, 128)
- God has a body of flesh and bone and, along with Jesus, may make appearances to men (Section 130)
- celestial marriage is required to achieve godhood and continue one's family into eternity (Sections 131–32)
- plural marriage (polygamy) is allowed (Section 132)
- the "martyrdom" of Smith and his brother Hyrum (Section 135)
- the plans for the "Camp of Israel" to head west were made in 1847 in order to search for a new place to reside (Section 136)
- the doctrines of salvation for the dead and how all children are saved in the celestial kingdom (Section 137)
- a vision sixth LDS President Joseph F. Smith had in 1918, including Christ's visit to the spirits of the dead while His body was in the tomb (Section 138)
- the 1890 "Manifesto" officially overturning the practice of polygamy (Official Declaration 1)
- the 1978 revelation declaring all worthy male members eligible to hold the Mormon priesthood (Official Declaration 2)

FALSE PROPHECIES FOUND IN THE *DOCTRINE AND COVENANTS*

Although there are several questionable predictions made in the *Doctrine and Covenants,* two that seem to stand out from the rest come from sections 84 and 87. *D&C* 84 predicts the establishment of the New Jerusalem and the building of a temple in Independence, Missouri. Verses 4 and 5 say:

> Verily this is the word of the Lord, that the city New Jerusalem shall be built by the gathering of the saints, beginning at this place, even the place of the temple, which temple shall be reared in this generation. For verily this generation shall not all pass away until an house shall be built unto the Lord, and a cloud shall rest upon it, which cloud shall be even the glory of the Lord, which shall fill the house.

The writings from those who lived at the time of Smith's revelation show that the Mormons were anticipating the imminent construction of this building. Despite the fact that the Saints were forced to leave the area around a year after the prediction was given, they still hoped to return and see the prophecy come to fruition. Apostle Orson Pratt referred to this prophecy in 1870:

> I hope this, because God promised in the year 1832 that we should, before the generation then living had passed away, return and build up the City of Zion in Jackson County; that we should return and build up the temple of the Most High where we formerly laid the corner stone. . . . We believe in these promises as much as we believe in any promise ever uttered by the mouth of Jehovah. The Latter-day Saints just as much expect to receive a fulfilment of that promise during the generation that was in existence in 1832 as they expect that the sun will rise and set to-morrow. Why? Because God cannot lie. He will fulfil all His promises. He has spoken, it must come to pass.[6]

As late as 1901, President Lorenzo Snow said, "Many of you will be living in Jackson County, and there you will be assisting in building the temple."[7] However, another prophet, Joseph Fielding Smith, later conceded that the prophecy could not come to pass in the way many earlier Saints had believed it would. He wrote:

> It may be reasonable to assume that in giving this revelation to the Prophet the Lord did have in mind the generation of people who would still be living within the one hundred years from the time of the announcement of the revelation, and that they would enjoy the blessings of the temple, and

a glorious cloud would rest upon it. It is also reasonable to believe that no soul living in 1832, is still living in mortality on the earth.[8]

Mormon historian Richard S. Van Wagoner noted that Smith's "prophetic failures" regarding Zion and the return of Christ led Sidney Rigdon, Smith's right-hand man, to eventually lose faith in the LDS prophet.[9] Meanwhile, *D&C* 87 is a "revelation and prophecy on war, given through Joseph Smith the Prophet, December 25, 1832." The first four verses say:

> Verily, thus saith the Lord concerning the wars that will shortly come to pass, beginning at the rebellion of South Carolina, which will eventually terminate in the death and misery of many souls; and the time will come that war will be poured out upon all nations, beginning at this place. For behold, the Southern States shall be divided against the Northern States, and the Southern States will call on other nations, even the nation of Great Britain, as it is called, and they shall also call upon other nations, in order to defend themselves against other nations; and then war shall be poured out upon all nations. And it shall come to pass, after many days, slaves shall rise up against their masters, who shall be marshaled and disciplined for war.

If this is supposed to be a prophecy about the Civil War, as many Mormons claim it to be, then Smith's prediction has numerous flaws. It is true that the Southern states did call on other nations for support, including Great Britain, during the Civil War. However, Great Britain's role during the war was merely as a supplier, never as a fighting force. Since this was the case, Great Britain never had to "call upon other nations, in order to defend themselves against other nations." In addition, the "War Between the States" was basically just that and not an international conflict. Smith was wrong when he said that "war shall be poured out upon all nations."

It should be noted that Smith's prediction was not all that unique. One month prior to the alleged revelation, the newspaper *Painesville Telegraph* printed a story in which it predicted the secession of South Carolina and an eventual War Between the States. South Carolina had been making such threats for some time, and many felt it was only a matter of time before South Carolina would act on its threat.

D&C 87:8 says the day of the Lord would come quickly, and many LDS leaders preached sermons during the Civil War anticipating the desolation of the United States. When that did not happen, Smith's prophecy on war was given a broader interpretation. For instance, Apostle James E. Talmage believed World War I was a partial fulfillment of Smith's prophecy:

> A careful study of the Revelation and Prophecy on War, given, as stated, through the Prophet Joseph Smith, December 25, 1832, makes plain that the conflict between North and South in America was to be, as now we know it to have been, but the beginning of a new era of strife and bloodshed. The Lord's words were definite in predicting wars "beginning at the rebellion of South Carolina"; and declared further: "And the time will come that war will be poured out upon all nations, beginning at this place." The great World War, 1914–1918, embroiled, directly or indirectly, every nation of the earth; and recovery from the effects of that stupendous conflict is beyond the horizon of human vision.[10]

In a 4 October 1981 general conference speech, Ezra Taft Benson said this prophecy dealt with "world wars":

> This war would be the beginning of world wars which would eventually involve all nations and result in the death and misery of many souls. Specifically, he said that the great Civil War would begin with a rebellion in South Carolina (see D&C 87). This prophecy was published to the world in 1851.[11]

One has to drastically revise history to draw the conclusion that World War I and/or World War II had anything to do with the rebellion beginning at South Carolina. While Smith's prediction was published in the *Pearl of Great Price* in 1851, the *Pearl of Great Price* did not become part of the standard works until 1880. Smith's prophecy on war did not become a part of the *D&C* until 1876, more than a decade after the Civil War had ended.[12]

THE *PEARL OF GREAT PRICE*

According to the introductory note found at the beginning of this LDS scripture:

> The Pearl of Great Price is a selection of choice materials touching many significant aspects of the faith and doctrine. . . . These items were produced by the Prophet Joseph Smith and were published in the Church periodicals of his day.

Apostle Franklin D. Richards put the first collection of materials together in 1851. Over the years revisions were made, including sections that were taken out of the *Pearl of Great Price* in 1979 and moved to the *D&C* (Sections 137 and 138). According to Bruce McConkie, the *Pearl of Great Price* has five sections:

1. Selections from the Book of Moses. This is an extract from the Book of Genesis of Joseph Smith's translation of the Bible.
2. Joseph Smith—Matthew. A one-chapter reinterpretation of Matthew 23:39 and chapter 24.
3. Joseph Smith—History. This includes "excerpts from Joseph Smith's official testimony and history, which he prepared in 1838 . . ."
4. The Articles of Faith. Written by Smith and originally known as the Wentworth Letter, these are the thirteen major points of LDS doctrine.
5. The Book of Abraham. Joseph Smith took Egyptian papyri and *translated* them, publishing this serially in the *Times and Seasons* beginning in 1842. It is said to contain "priceless information about the gospel, pre-existence, the nature of Deity, the creation, and priesthood, information which is not otherwise available in any other revelation now extant."[13]

THE HISTORY OF THE BOOK OF ABRAHAM

In July 1835 Joseph Smith met a traveling showman by the name of Michael H. Chandler who was displaying four Egyptian mummies in Kirtland, Ohio. Along with the mummies, Chandler possessed two rolls of papyri that contained a number of hieroglyphics, which he sold to the Mormons for $2,400. The next day, Smith proclaimed that the manuscripts were actually written by none other than two Old Testament patriarchs: "I commenced the translation of some of the characters or hieroglyphics, and much to our joy found that one of the rolls contained the writings of Abraham, another the writings of Joseph of Egypt, etc."[14]

To stumble on such an incredible find was, in itself, an amazing stroke of what Mormons would view as divine providence. Imagine for a moment what a find this would be if, in fact, Smith had really discovered the writings of Abraham and Joseph. They would be priceless. In fact, they would be the only autograph manuscripts of biblical personalities currently available. If authentic, the Book of Abraham would predate the Book of Genesis by about five hundred years.

TRUTH OR FICTION?

Few people in 1835 could have been considered experts in the field of Egyptology. The famous Rosetta Stone, currently on display at the British Museum in London, was discovered accidentally in 1799 by Napoleon's army in Egypt. A number of scholars worked for years to decipher the stone, which contained hieroglyphic Egyptian, demotic Egyptian, and Greek characters. Finally, J. F. Champollion announced his results in 1822, and the mystery of the Egyptian language came to an end. The fact that Joseph Smith was not an expert in hieroglyphics has led some LDS scholars to speculate that he translated the manuscript by divine inspiration.

> Probably no one in the United States in 1835 could interpret Egyptian hieroglyphics through ordinary translation techniques. When he translated the gold plates of the Book of Mormon from the "reformed Egyptian" text (1827–1829), the Prophet stated that he did it "by the gift and power of God." Likewise, it was principally divine inspiration rather than his knowledge of languages that produced the English text of the Book of Abraham. His precise methodology remains unknown.[15]

Of the two papyri, Smith chose to focus on the one he claimed was written by Abraham. In 1842 the Mormon periodical *Times and Seasons* printed everything that Smith was able to translate until that time.[16] Circumstances would prohibit him from translating the rest of the Book of Abraham papyrus or the other papyrus that he called the Book of

Joseph. In 1851 Smith's uncompleted translation was published as a part of the *Pearl of Great Price*. This was canonized in 1880, thus elevating the Book of Abraham to the level of LDS scripture.

THE REDISCOVERED PAGAN PAPYRI

For more than a century, the actual papyri from which Smith translated were believed to be lost. Thus, just like the *Book of Mormon,* nobody could go back to the original manuscripts to see what he had translated. They had originally remained the property of Emma Smith, Joseph's widow, following his death in 1844. According to LDS historian William E. Berrett, Emma sold the manuscripts to a museum in St. Louis. The papyri eventually found their way to the Chicago Museum. When the Great Chicago Fire occurred in 1871, it was assumed that the manuscripts were destroyed along with the museum.

In 1967 interest in the Book of Abraham again surfaced when the papyri Smith used in 1835 were found in the Metropolitan Museum of Art in New York. These were eventually given back to the LDS Church. With the manuscript of the Book of Abraham now available, scholars could investigate the actual Egyptian that Smith translated.

If Joseph Smith was indeed a prophet inspired by God who had the ability to translate the Book of Abraham, here was the perfect opportunity to prove it. Instead of *proving* Smith to be a true prophet, however, Egyptologists agree that Smith's "translation" was taken from a papyrus known as the Book of Breathings, a funerary papyrus dating around the time of Christ, long after the Egyptian dynasty when Abraham lived. It is, in fact, of pagan origin and has nothing to do with Abraham.

Smith's papyrus was both torn and attached to a backing that held it in place. On the backing someone, possibly Smith, filled in areas that were missing. An examination of Joseph Smith's Facsimile No. 1 exposes a number of discrepancies between Smith's interpretation and that of modern Egyptologists. Smith claimed that the facsimile portrays Abraham lying on an altar. Standing next to him is the idolatrous priest Elkanah who holds a knife in his hand. Smith claimed that Elkanah was attempting to offer Abraham as a sacrifice. Below the altar are figures that Smith describes as idolatrous gods. Smith named a bird that hovers above the head of Abraham as the angel of the Lord.

Dr. Richard A. Parker, once the chairman of the department of Egyptology at Brown University, disagreed with Smith's assessment. He claimed:

> This is a well-known scene from the Osiris mysteries, with Anubis, the jackal-headed god, on the left ministering to the dead Osiris on the bier. The pencilled(?) restoration is incorrect. Anubis should be jackal-headed. The left arm of Osiris is in reality lying at his side under him. The apparent upper hand is part of the wing of a second bird which is hovering over the erect phallus of Osiris (now broken away). The second bird is Isis and she is magically impregnated by the dead Osiris and then later gives birth to Horus who avenges his father and takes over his inheritance. The complete bird represents Nephthys, sister to Osiris and Isis. Beneath the bier are the four canopic jars with heads representative of the four sons of Horus, human-headed Imseti, baboon-headed Hapy, jackal-headed Duamutef and falcon-headed Kebehsenuf.[17]

Other problems develop when Facsimile No. 2 is considered. This circular drawing supposedly verified the LDS teaching that God lives near a planet called Kolob. Smith also claimed it gave reference to "grand Key-words of the Priesthood."[18] According to Egyptologist Stephen E. Thompson:

> Facsimile 2 is a drawing of an Egyptian funerary amulet known as a hypocephalus, which was placed under the head of the mummy and was intended to protect the head of the deceased, provide him with the sun's life-giving warmth, and to make it possible for him to join the sun god Re in his celestial boat, and thereby insure his continued, pleasant existence in the next life.[19]

Thompson goes on to say:

> Concerning Joseph Smith's interpretations of the figures in this facsimile, it has been stated that "his explanations, are, in general, reasonable in light of modern Egyptological knowledge." A comparison of Smith's interpretations with current Egyptological scholarship shows that this statement is also incorrect.[20]

DOUBTS ABOUT THE 1967 DISCOVERY

Because of the vast evidence that shows Smith did not know how to translate Egyptian, some LDS apologists have tried to raise doubts about the 1967 papyri discovered in New York. Was this the same papyri that Smith had in his possession? BYU professor Daniel Peterson wrote:

> Critics have long attempted to make a case against the Book of Abraham. They argue that some ancient texts do not support the book. They point to the fragments of the Joseph Smith papyri that we now possess and claim that since the contents of these papyri bear little obvious relationship to the book of Abraham, the book is a fraud; but Hugh Nibley has made an exhaustive study of these claims and has shown that the papyri we now have were probably not the ones from which Joseph Smith translated the book of Abraham.[21]

Christian researcher Charles Larson challenges this claim:

> And there could be no question that the Metropolitan papyri were indeed none other than the ones which Joseph Smith had once purchased and used. The reverse sides of the paper to which they were glued contained such things as architectural drawings of a temple and maps of the Kirtland, Ohio area.[22]

Indeed, we know of no official LDS Church pronouncement that denies the authenticity of these documents.

It is obvious why the Mormon Church needs to maintain the Book of Abraham as authentic. As B. H. Roberts noted:

> . . . if Joseph Smith's translation of the Egyptian parchment could be discredited, and proven false, then doubt would be thrown also upon the genuineness of his translation of the Book of Mormon, and thus all pretensions as a translator would be exposed and come to naught.[23]

If Smith were unable to properly translate a common piece of Egyptian funerary papyrus, it would be doubtful that he had the translating ability to decipher the "Reformed Egyptian" supposedly contained in the *Book of Mormon*. The discovery of the papyri that Smith used for the Book of Abraham puts serious doubt on Smith's translating ability and his claim to being a prophet.

CONCLUSION

The *Doctrine and Covenants:*

- Contains 138 sections, most of which include modern-day revelations given to Joseph Smith
- Also contains two declarations: (1) Declaration 1, known as the Manifesto, that officially abolished polygamy, and (2) Declaration 2 that allowed all worthy male members to hold the LDS priesthood

The *Pearl of Great Price:*

- Contains five sections, including the history of Joseph Smith and some of his "retranslation" of the Bible
- The Book of Abraham has a questionable history, showing that Joseph Smith was unable to accurately translate Egyptian into English

Why Should I Accept the *Book of Mormon* as Coming from God?

Mormons are told that the *Book of Mormon* is a monumental work concerning the appearance of Jesus in the Americas. But Christians wonder what is in this book that is so important. In opening up a conversation with Mormons, it is crucial for us to begin by understanding how much weight they put on their own personal testimony for validating the truthfulness of this book. To even suggest that the *Book of Mormon* is not divine could be quite upsetting to them, but it is an issue that they need to be able to defend.

Mormon: I believe the *Book of Mormon* is the word of God.
Christian: How do you know that?
 M: I prayed about it, and the Holy Ghost bore witness to me that it was true.
 C: How do you know it was the Holy Ghost?
 M: I just do.
 C: So your belief in the *Book of Mormon* is based solely on a subjective feeling?
 M: I don't need the wisdom of man to know that the book is true.

C: The only way to know if your feeling is absolutely true is if your feelings have never betrayed you. Have you ever had a feeling that was wrong?

M: Sure.

C: So there is a possibility that your feeling could be wrong when it comes to the *Book of Mormon?*

M: Perhaps, but I don't think so.

C: Have you ever objectively examined the *Book of Mormon?* Have you checked it for historical accuracy? Have you checked it against archaeological evidence?

M: I just know within my heart that it is true.

C: Yes, but Jeremiah 17:9 tells us that the human heart is "deceitful above all things, and desperately wicked." Besides, Joseph Smith once said that a person "would get nearer to God by abiding by its precepts, than by any other book." Could you please tell me what those precepts are that I can't find in any other book? What makes the *Book of Mormon* so unique?

M: It teaches about faith, repentance, and baptism.

C: But these are also taught in the Bible. Why do I need the *Book of Mormon* for these?

M: It teaches these things with much more clarity.

C: Could you support that?

M: I'm sure I could if I had the time.

C: Doesn't your faith teach that, in order to get nearer to God, you must receive the temple endowment, be married for time and eternity, obey the Word of Wisdom, and pay an honest tithe? Are these mentioned in the *Book of Mormon?*

M: Well, no, I don't think so.

C: So what you're telling me is that I really can't get nearer to God by just following the precepts as found in the *Book of Mormon.* If Smith was misleading in this statement, how can I trust his other statements?

Examining the LDS Concept of Salvation

The Atonement

Forgiveness is available because Christ the Lord sweat great drops of blood in Gethsemane as he bore the incalculable weight of the sins of all who ever had or ever would repent.

Apostle Bruce McConkie,
The Promised Messiah, 337

Jesus Christ paid a tremendous price when He sacrificed His life at the hands of the Romans and the Jewish leaders. There is no question about the costly nature of this unselfish act. While Christians and Mormons would both accept the atonement of Christ, they disagree as to what this sacrifice actually accomplished and even, for some, where it took place.

THE ATONEMENT ACCORDING TO MORMONISM

Mormon leaders have taught that the atonement of Jesus Christ releases the "human family" from the consequences of Adam's fall and allows a general resurrection from the dead. It also makes available the forgiveness of personal sins on the condition of repentance.

The universal, infinite, and unconditional aspects of the Atonement of Jesus Christ are several. They include his ransom for Adam's original transgression so that no member of the human family is held responsible for that sin. Another universal gift is the resurrection from the dead of every man, woman, and child who lives, has ever lived, or ever will live, on the earth.[1]

And not only was this vicarious atonement made to cover the transgression of Adam, but it was made to reach also to the individual sins of men, that they might not suffer if they would accept the gospel.[2]

Mormon leaders have taught that this atoning sacrifice began in the Garden of Gethsemane. This teaching is drawn from two passages within the LDS standard works. Mosiah 3:7 in the *Book of Mormon* gives a description of Christ's suffering similar to what the biblical Gospels say He experienced in the Garden of Gethsemane:

And lo, he shall suffer temptations, and pain of body, hunger, thirst, and fatigue, even more than man can suffer, except it be unto death; for behold, blood cometh from every pore, so great shall be his anguish for the wickedness and the abominations of his people.

D&C 19:15–19 adds:

Therefore I command you to repent—repent, lest I smite you by the rod of my mouth, and by my wrath, and by my anger, and your sufferings be sore—how sore you know not, how exquisite you know not, yea, how hard to bear you know not. For behold, I, God, have suffered these things for all, that they might not suffer if they would repent; but if they would not repent they must suffer even as I; which suffering caused myself, even God, the greatest of all, to tremble because of pain, and to bleed at every pore, and to suffer both body and spirit—and would that I might not drink the bitter cup, and shrink—nevertheless, glory be to the Father, and I partook and finished my preparations unto the children of men.

While he acknowledged that Jesus would eventually go to the cross, President Ezra Taft Benson concluded that it was in the Garden where Jesus took on Himself the sins of the world:

[Christ] suffered as only God could suffer, bearing our griefs, carrying our sorrows, being wounded for our transgressions, voluntarily submitting Himself to the iniquity of us all, just as Isaiah prophesied (see Isaiah 53:4–6). It was in Gethsemane that Jesus took on Himself the sins of the world, in Gethsemane that His pain was equivalent to the cumulative burden of all men, in Gethsemane that He descended below all things so that all could repent and come to Him.[3]

Apostle Bruce McConkie wrote:

And as he came out of the Garden, delivering himself voluntarily into the hands of wicked men, the victory had been won. There remained yet the shame and the pain of his arrest, his trials, and his cross. But all these were overshadowed by the agonies and sufferings in Gethsemane. It was on the cross that he "suffered death in the flesh," even as many have suffered agonizing deaths, but it was in Gethsemane that "he suffered the pain of all men, that all men might repent and come unto him." . . . Jesus took upon himself the sins of all men when he suffered and sweat great drops of blood from every pore in Gethsemane. It was then that his suffering causing himself, even God, to suffer both body and spirit in a way which is totally beyond mortal comprehension.[4]

According to Mormon teaching, then, while the blood shed on Calvary's cross completed the atonement, the Garden of Gethsemane is the place where the efficacious atonement took place. McConkie stated it plainly:

Where and under what circumstances was the atoning sacrifice of the Son of God made? Was it on the Cross of Calvary or in the Garden of Gethsemane? It is to the Cross of Christ that most Christians look when centering their attention upon the infinite and eternal atonement. And certainly the sacrifice of our Lord was completed when he was lifted up by men; also, that part of his life and suffering is more dramatic and, perhaps, more soul stirring. But in reality the pain and suffering, the triumph and grandeur, of the atonement took place primarily in Gethsemane.[5]

If Mormons doubt that their church emphasizes the importance of Gethsemane today, consider what the *Encyclopedia of Mormonism* says in more than one article about this doctrine:

This spiritual anguish of plumbing the depths of human suffering and sorrow was experienced primarily in the Garden of Gethsemane. It was there that he was "in an agony" and "prayed more earnestly." It was there that his sweat was "as it were great drops of blood falling down to the ground" (Luke 22:44) for he bled "at every pore" (D&C 19:18). It was there that he began the final March to Calvary. . . . Jesus suffered most in Gethsemane during his Atonement. . . . First, he was able, in Gethsemane, in some majestic but incomprehensible manner, to assume the burdens and effects of the sins of all mankind and, in doing so, to engage suffering and anguish beyond what a mere mortal could endure. . . . In Gethsemane, Christ took upon himself the burden of the sins of the world and suffered for them in a way that is incomprehensible to mortals.[6]

In light of all these statements showing the importance of Gethsemane, it should be mentioned that the Bible refers to this garden only twice. While LDS commentators point to the sweating of "great drops of blood," the New Testament says nothing about this phenomenon having any role in the atonement. Yet not all LDS leaders have held that Jesus' greatest agony took place in this garden. For example, President Lorenzo Snow stated that Jesus' suffering in the garden was a result of knowing He was about to face the cross:

> . . . the time approached that He was to pass through the severest affliction that any mortal ever did pass through, He undoubtedly had seen persons nailed to the cross, because that method of execution was common at that time, and He understood the torture that such persons experienced for hours. He went by Himself in the garden and prayed to His Father, if it were possible, that that cup might pass from Him; and His feelings were such that He sweat great drops of blood, and in His agony there was an angel sent to give Him comfort and strength.[7]

President Joseph Fielding Smith, however, refuted this notion:

> A great many people have an idea that when he was on the cross, and nails were driven into his hands and feet, that was his great suffering. His great suffering was before he ever was placed upon the cross. It was in the Garden of Gethsemane that the blood oozed from the pores of his body: "Which suffering caused myself, even God, the greatest of all, to tremble because of pain, and to bleed at every pore, and to suffer both body and spirit—and would that I might not drink the bitter cup, and shrink." That was not when he was on the cross; that was in the garden. That is where he bled from every pore in his body.[8]

CHRISTIANITY'S DEFINITION OF ATONEMENT

The atonement is the act of bringing people together with God by means of a sacrifice. Since all men and women are inherently sinful by nature as well as action,[9] Philippians 2:7 reports that Christ made Himself of no reputation by taking "the form of a servant." He was made in human likeness and humbled Himself, becoming "obedient unto death, even the death of the cross" (v. 8). Hebrews 2:17 says this was done in order that He might make "reconciliation for the sins of the people."

Since Matthew 1:21 says that Jesus would come to "save his people from their sins," no other conclusion can be made except that only God's personal intervention would be able to overcome humanity's sinful condition. If our personal merit could satisfy the penalty of sin, then such an atonement would not be necessary, as Galatians 2:21 says.

In Old Testament times, redemption was demonstrated through the ceremonial sacrifice. God made it clear that forgiveness would be provided only through the death of an innocent substitute that represented the payment for the penalty of sin. Sacrifices were made in the Jerusalem temple on a daily basis for the sins of individuals; however, the people of Israel celebrated the Day of Atonement, or Yom Kippur, once a year. On this sacred day, the Jewish high priest would offer sacrifice for Israel as a nation, which sought reconciliation with the God whom they had offended.

Still, the mere act itself of killing an animal for one's sins did not appease God. Through numerous examples, the Bible states that redemption was based on an individual's faith in what the sacrifice represented. This faith would lead to the obvious act of repentance, thereby making the sacrifice efficacious. God had no pleasure in sacrifice without these two important elements.

This principle can be seen in the example of Cain and Abel. Genesis 4:3–5 says that both Cain and Abel offered sacrifices to the Lord, "but unto Cain and to his offering he had not respect." The writer of Hebrews explained that Abel's sacrifice was accepted because, unlike Cain's, it was offered in righteous faith (Heb. 11:4). Since the wages of sin is death (both physical and spiritual), the repentant sinner sees the sacrifice as a vicarious substitute. The animal was symbolically taking on itself the penalty due sinful people. Christian theologian Leon Morris explains:

> Nobody who came thoughtfully to God by the way of sacrifice could be in any doubt but that sin was a serious matter. It could not be put aside by a lighthearted wave of the hand but required the shedding of blood. . . . No-one who came to God by the way of offering the best in his flock would put a low value on the privilege of such an approach. He would realize, as many of us today do not, that the service of God must cost us something.[10]

Unfortunately, as time went on, many Jews offered sacrifice out of mere protocol, not by faith. To many the significance of what the sacrifice represented was lost in legalistic attitudes. The New Testament Book of Hebrews explains that the animal sacrificial system typified what Christ would do when He would voluntarily pay the price of sin through His own death. Morris adds:

> The high priest could do no more than enter the Holy of Holies himself. He could not take anyone with him. And he could enter only on the one day in the year. The fullest exercise of his ministry with all the solemnity at his command obtained only a very limited access: access on one day for him only. The people must forever be content with access by proxy. But in Hebrews there is emphasis on two wonderful truths: Christ secured access into the very presence of God in heaven (as we have just seen, Heb. 9:11–12, 24) and access not for himself only but for all his people as well. . . . Because Christ's blood was shed, all who believe in him have access into the very holiest of all.[11]

Another Christian theologian, A. W. Tozer, wrote:

> The theme of bloodguiltiness is a recurring theme in the Bible and here we have two concepts. The Old Testament picture is that of the blood of murdered Abel crying out for justice; the New Testament picture is that of the blood of Jesus Christ the Savior and mediator crying from the throne of God for mercy![12]

To be sure, Christians throughout the centuries have seen the atonement of Christ as God's way of reconciling sinful humanity to Himself. Through the sacrifice of God's Son, those who were once ene-mies of God can now know that the barrier that separated them from their Creator has been removed. So powerful is this sacrificial act that believers can be assured that *all* their sins—past, present, and future—are now forgiven. Colossians 2:13–14 reads:

> And you, being dead in your sins and the uncircumcision of your flesh, hath he quickened together with him, having forgiven you all trespasses; blotting out the handwriting of ordinances that was against us, which was contrary to us, and took it out of the way, nailing it to his cross.

Christians have long maintained that this glorious act of sacrifice took place on Golgotha Hill, known as the Place of the Skull. This area outside the walls of Jerusalem was reserved for the execution of prisoners, both political and criminal. It was here that God Himself was subject to the humiliating death of a common criminal.

THE CROSS, NOT THE GARDEN

By emphasizing the Garden of Gethsemane, LDS leaders miss a significant point regarding the atonement. The expiation of sin (mak-ing amends for wrongdoing) was not based on the substitute's per-spiration; rather, it was based on his expiration. Christ's atonement for the sins of the believer was accomplished in His death, not in the short time that He spent in the Garden.

In his letter to the Corinthians, Paul stressed that Christ's death was of primary importance in the atonement. In 1 Corinthians 15:3 he wrote, "I delivered unto you *first of all* . . . that Christ *died* for our sins." Throughout the New Testament, the *death* of Christ is emphasized. Referring to Christ's reconciliation, Paul told the Christians in Rome:

> But God commendeth his love toward us, in that, while we were yet sin-ners, Christ died for us. . . . For if, when we were enemies, we were rec-onciled to God by the death of his Son, much more, being reconciled, we shall be saved by his life (Rom. 5:8, 10).

Meanwhile, Hebrews 9:22 states that there is no remission of sins without the shedding (not sweating) of blood. According to verse 26,

Christ came in order to do away with sin by His own sacrifice. Referring to this passage, Leon Morris writes:

> Animal sacrifice can never produce a purification valid in heaven. But Christ's sacrifice can. . . . The sacrifice of himself means an infinitely better sacrifice than any that was possible under the Levitical system.
>
> That is one point that this author emphasizes. Another is the finality of Christ's atoning sacrifice. Repeatedly he tells us that Christ offered himself "once and for all" or the like. Believers have been made holy "through the sacrifice of the body of Jesus Christ once for all" (Heb. 10:10); he "offered for all time one sacrifice for sins" (verse 12); "by one sacrifice he has made perfect for ever those who are being made holy" (verse 14). And he removes decisively the possibility of any further offering by saying that, when sins have been forgiven (as they have been through what Christ has done), "there is no longer any sacrifice for sin" (Heb. 10:18). The utter finality of Christ's sacrifice is an important truth.[13]

The sacrifice spoken of was the death that Jesus suffered. The cross—not the Garden of Gethsemane—is given preeminence, as the following texts attest:

> But God forbid that I should glory, save in *the cross* of our Lord Jesus Christ, by whom the world is crucified unto me, and I unto the world (Gal. 6:14, emphasis added).

> And that he might reconcile both unto God in one body *by the cross,* having slain the enmity thereby (Eph. 2:16, emphasis added).

> And being found in fashion as a man, he humbled himself, and became obedient unto death, even the death of *the cross* (Phil. 2:8, emphasis added).

> And, having made peace *through the blood of his cross,* by him to reconcile all things unto himself; by him, I say, whether they be things in earth, or things in heaven (Col. 1:20, emphasis added).

> Blotting out the handwriting of ordinances that was against us, which was contrary to us, and took it out of the way, *nailing it to his cross* (Col. 2:14, emphasis added).

> Looking unto Jesus the author and finisher of our faith; who for the joy that was set before him *endured the cross,* despising the shame, and is set down at the right hand of the throne of God (Heb. 12:2, emphasis added).

Indeed, Paul gloried in the cross, not the garden, for it was on the cross that Jesus provided for the Christian's future salvation.

AT THE CROSS WHERE I FIRST SAW THE LIGHT

While LDS leaders sometimes mention Christ's death on the cross, the implication is that this method of execution was only a necessary evil so that the resurrection could take place. During a conference speech in 1953, Marion Romney, a member of the First Presidency under David O. McKay, stated:

> Jesus then went into the Garden of Gethsemane. There he suffered most. He suffered greatly on the cross, of course, but other men had died by crucifixion; in fact, a man hung on either side of him as he died on the cross. But no man, nor set of men, nor all men put together, ever suffered what the Redeemer suffered in the garden. He went there to pray and suffer.[14]

No doubt this is but one of several reasons why crosses cannot be found on LDS buildings. Certainly in the mind of the Latter-day Saint, the significance of the cross is not nearly as important as it is to the evangelical Christian. President Joseph Fielding Smith wrote:

> However, to bow down before a cross or to look upon it as an emblem to be revered because of the fact that our Savior died upon a cross is repugnant to members of The Church of Jesus Christ of Latter-day Saints. . . . To many, like the writer, such a custom is repugnant and contrary to the true worship of our Redeemer. Why should we bow down before a cross or use it as a symbol? Because our Savior died on the cross, the wearing of crosses is to most Latter-day Saints in very poor taste and inconsistent to our worship. . . . We may be definitely sure that if our Lord had been killed with a dagger or with a sword, it would have been very strange indeed if religious people of this day would have graced such a weapon by wearing it and adoring it because it was by such a means that our Lord was put to death.[15]

For those who teach that there is atonement available in the blood of Christ, Bruce McConkie, writing in an LDS Church tract, exclaimed:

> Christians speak often of the blood of Christ and its cleansing power. Much that is believed and taught on this subject, however, is such utter nonsense

and so palpably false that to believe it is to lose one's salvation. For instance, many believe or pretend to believe that if we confess Christ with our lips and avow that we accept him as our personal Savior, we are thereby saved. They say that his blood, without any other act than mere belief, makes us clean.[16]

Obviously these Mormons have missed the point of the atonement of Christ. It was at the cross of Christ that the death of God's own Son was given in payment for the believer's sins. For more than a century Christians have revered the hymn "At the Cross" for the way it portrays the importance of the atonement. Its chorus is:

> At the cross, at the cross, where I first saw the light,
> And the burden of my heart rolled away (rolled away),
> It was there by faith I received my sight,
> And now I am happy all the day.[17]

Christians realize that salvation is a result of what Jesus did for them on the cross. The blood shed at Calvary is satisfactory for all sin. In effect, Jesus (as the Righteous One) bore all of His people's sins so that they could be forgiven, once and for all. To even insinuate that this took place in the Garden of Gethsemane is a foreign concept to the Christian.

People can find true freedom in Christ only when they grasp the essential concept of the atonement and what Jesus has already done for them. We who hold the Bible dear to our hearts have no choice but to concur with Paul as he declared in 1 Corinthians 1:18: "The preaching of the cross [not the Garden] is to them that perish foolishness; but unto us which are saved it is the power of God."

C O N C L U S I O N

The atonement, according to Mormonism:

- provides everyone with a general resurrection and cancellation of the consequences of Adam's transgression
- took place primarily in the Garden of Gethsemane

- was possible before Christ had died and was raised
- is not complete unless the individual demonstrates total obedience

The atonement, according to Christianity:

- provides for the salvation of only those who have faith in Christ
- took place on the cross alone
- was possible only after Christ's death
- is complete for the believer by the grace of God

Grace and Works

One of the most fallacious doctrines originated by Satan and propounded by man is that man is saved alone by the grace of God; that belief in Jesus Christ alone is all that is needed for salvation.

President Spencer Kimball,
The Miracle of Forgiveness, 206

Many Christians have become understandably confused when their Mormon acquaintances tell them how salvation comes by "grace coupled with gospel obedience."[1] The problem lies in the fact that Mormon leaders have redefined the word *salvation* and given it a split definition that is certainly not taught by the Bible.

According to LDS teaching, salvation by grace is synonymous with mere resurrection from the dead, which is given to the entire human race born on this earth and other planets. According to Apostle Bruce McConkie, this is called "unconditional or general salvation." "The mere fact of resurrection," he said, "is called salvation by grace alone."[2]

Mormonism has taught that humanity is inherently good. President John Taylor affirmed, "In fact, as the President [Brigham Young] stated here not long ago, it is not natural for men to be evil."[3] Rex Lee, a former president of BYU, said general salvation comes to everyone regardless of whether or not they are obedient to Mormonism's teachings.

> Many aspects of God's grace are unconditional. For instance, one free gift of salvation is resurrection and immortality, given by Jesus Christ to all people who have lived on this earth. This gift is not affected by anything we do here. Everyone, from the most righteous to the most wretched, will be resurrected and will live forever in the next life. . . . By breaking the bands of death, Jesus Christ overcame death, and all will live again. In this respect, we are saved by grace unconditionally.[4]

On the other hand, "conditional or individual salvation," otherwise known as exaltation or godhood, goes far beyond a mere resurrection from the dead. McConkie explained:

> Salvation in its true and full meaning is synonymous with *exaltation* or *eternal life* and consists in gaining an inheritance in the highest of the three heavens within the celestial kingdom. . . . Salvation in the celestial kingdom of God, however, is not salvation by grace alone. Rather, it is salvation by grace coupled with obedience to the laws and ordinances of the gospel.[5]

Unlike resurrection from the dead, exaltation requires a concerted effort on the part of the individual to live according to all of the commandments. It means keeping all the commandments as instructed by the LDS Church for a person's entire life.

MORMONISM'S ATTACK ON THE DOCTRINE OF SALVATION BY GRACE

Most Mormons have the mind-set that they need to do something in order to achieve this exalted state. Second Nephi 25:23 in the *Book of Mormon* clearly teaches this when it says that "it is by grace that we are saved, *after all we can do*" (emphasis ours). It is not uncommon for numerous Latter-day Saints to stereotype the evangelical Christian church as teaching that works are not important.[6]

McConkie reflected this misrepresented idea when he said that salvation by grace alone was the second greatest heresy of Christianity.[7] He said it is "[a] soul-destroying doctrine [that] has the obvious effect of lessening the determination of an individual to conform to all of the laws and ordinances of the gospel."[8] Apostle LeGrand Richards felt "this false doctrine would relieve man from the responsibility of his acts other than to confess a belief in God, and would teach man that no matter how great the sin, a confession would bring him complete forgiveness and salvation."[9] Apostle James Talmage said "redemption from personal sins can only be obtained through obedience to the requirements of the gospel, and a life of good works. . . . The sectarian dogma of justification by faith alone has exercised an influence for evil" and was a "pernicious doctrine."[10]

The message sent by LDS leadership has come through loud and clear to much of its membership. For instance, Richard R. Hopkins, a Mormon lawyer, wrote:

> In the Mormon viewpoint, these two doctrines are the landmarks of the Great Apostasy, prophesied by Christ and His Apostles from the beginning. They are monuments to the influence of Greek philosophy on the early Christian Church. The fact that Christendom has come to regard them as the fundamental characteristics of Christ's Church is a bit like finding the tenets of Nazi Germany proclaimed as the cornerstone of Judaism two thousand years from now! . . . The need for Evangelicals to reconsider their teachings on the points noted in this book is critical. If their misconceptions about the Gospel, for example, are not corrected, many more well-meaning Christians will find themselves swallowed by the tide of evildoing that inexorably engulfs all who embrace the notion that Man can be saved without obedience to God. Already, some of the best and brightest Evangelical leaders have fallen prey to serious sin because of this false teaching.[11]

CELESTIAL LAW—CAN IT BE LIVED?

While they may admit that they must obey all of God's commandments, many Mormons find it offensive when they are accused of believing that works are required for salvation. If there is any confu-

sion as to whether eternal life must be earned, it must be stressed that
LDS leaders have taught just that. For instance, Apostle Francis Lyman
clearly stated:

> *All* the requirements of the Lord must be accomplished if we would attain
> to all that is to be obtained in the celestial kingdom of our Father. And
> every Latter-day Saint has started out for that—the obtaining of eternal
> life, and the greatest degree of glory that can be obtained in the celestial
> kingdom. Then to obtain this I say that the *full and perfect law* of the Father
> *must* be observed. We are to be rewarded for our works. We must *earn*
> what we obtain.[12]

Is this possible to accomplish? Joseph Fielding Smith sounded pes-
simistic regarding the chances of many LDS entering this glory when
he said "that if we save one-half of the Latter-day Saints, that is, with
an exaltation in the celestial kingdom of God, we will be doing well."[13]
Brigham Young pointed out that "if we obey this law, preserve it invi-
olate, live according to it, we shall be prepared to enjoy the blessings
of a celestial kingdom."[14] Another LDS president, John Taylor, wrote,
"One thing we do know; one thing is clearly told us, and that is if we
are not governed by the celestial law and cannot abide a celestial law,
we cannot inherit a celestial kingdom."[15]

What exactly is "celestial law"? Apostle Orson Whitney described
it in the following manner:

> It does not mean any one thing; it means all things. It is the fullness of
> obedience: it is living by every word that proceeds from the mouth of God.
> If today, you are keeping those commandments that are now in force, you
> are living a celestial law, and your chances are good for celestial glory.
> Amen.[16]

Notice how Whitney describes this concept. Celestial law involves
fully obeying every word that proceeds from God's mouth. It is neither partial obedience to every word nor full obedience to portions of
God's words. Instead, it is *fullness* of obedience to *all* of God's words.
Brigham Young said:

> "Will everybody be damned except the Latter-day Saints?" "Yes," said
> Joseph, "and many of them, unless they take a different course from what

they are now taking." Who will be saved in the celestial kingdom, and go into the presence of the Father and Son? *Those only who observe the whole law,* who keep the commandments of God—those who walk in newness of life, observe *all* his precepts and do his will.[17]

President John Taylor wrote:

We are told that if we cannot abide the law of the celestial kingdom we cannot inherit a celestial glory. Is not that doctrine? Yes. "But," says one, "are not we all going into the celestial kingdom?" I think not, unless we turn round and mend our ways very materially. It is only those who can abide a celestial glory and obey a celestial law that will be prepared to enter a celestial kingdom.[18]

Obeying the celestial law is "implicit and complete obedience to the commandments of God,"[19] which is the same as "perfect obedience, to the will of God."[20] The blessings of exaltation can only be obtained when a person has "unwavering faith, repentance, and complete obedience to the gospel of Jesus Christ."[21] And just who can accomplish this? Certainly most Latter-day Saints must seriously doubt they will ever achieve their desired goal. Quite frankly, no person except Jesus Christ has been able to accomplish such a feat. For any Mormon to think he or she can, in fact, consistently obey every law commanded by God is to demonstrate the epitome of prideful arrogance.[22] To such a person comes the condemnation of the *Book of Mormon:*

Have ye walked, keeping yourselves blameless before God? Could ye say, if ye were called to die at this time, within yourselves, that ye have been sufficiently humble? That your garments have been cleansed and made white through the blood of Christ, who will come to redeem his people from their sins? Behold, are ye stripped of pride? I say unto you, if ye are not ye are not prepared to meet God. Behold ye must prepare quickly; for the kingdom of heaven is soon at hand, and such an one hath not eternal life.[23]

Most Mormons must surely realize their shortcomings and how they are not keeping the whole law, no matter how good their intentions. The prospect of having to keep all of the commandments must weigh heavily on the thinking Latter-day Saint. Despite the smiles many Mormons wear, it should not be assumed that all is spiritually well in their personal lives. Strapped with the heavy requirement of perfection placed on them by their faith, such a countenance may hide deep-seated feelings of guilt and failure. Because of the unreasonable demand put on them, these people may live their daily lives with the guilt of never being good enough for celestial exaltation. Some have even given up trying.[24]

"I CAN DO IT LATER"

Some Latter-day Saints have felt that moral lapses in obedience can be overcome in the next life. Such thinking undermines the LDS concept of a mortal probation, which is the short time on this earth "linking the eternity past with the eternity future." Joseph Fielding Smith claimed this life would determine a person's destiny:

> It would either give to those who received it the blessing of eternal life, which is the greatest gift of God, and thus qualify them for godhood as sons and daughters of our Eternal Father, or, if they rebelled and refused to comply with the laws and ordinances which were provided for their salvation, it would deny them the great gift and they would be assigned, after the resurrection, to some inferior sphere according to their works. *This life is the most vital period in our eternal existence.*[25]

Bruce McConkie wrote:

> One of the great purposes of this mortal probation is to test and try men, to see if they will keep the commandments and walk in the light no matter what environmental enticements beckon them away from the straight and narrow path.[26]

The aforementioned quotes harmonize with the *Book of Mormon:*

> For behold, this life is the time for men to prepare to meet God; yea, behold the day of this life is the day for men to perform their labors. And now, as I said unto you before, as ye have had so many witnesses, therefore, I beseech of you that ye do not procrastinate the day of your repentance until the end; for after this day of life, which is given us to prepare for

eternity, behold, if we do not improve our time while in this life, then cometh the night of darkness wherein there can be no labor performed.[27]

Kimball clearly stated:

Only as we overcome shall we become perfect and move toward godhood. As I have indicated previously, the time to do this is *now,* in mortality. Someone once said: "A fellow who is planning to reform is one step behind. He ought to quit planning and get on with the job. *Today* is the day."[28]

He also said:

Because men are prone to postpone action and ignore directions, the Lord has repeatedly given strict injunctions and issued solemn warnings. Again and again in different phraseology and throughout the centuries the Lord has reminded man so that he could never have excuse. And the burden of the prophetic warning has been that *the time to act is now, in this mortal life.* One cannot with impunity delay his compliance with God's commandments.[29]

"THAT IS WHY WE HAVE REPENTANCE"

When Mormons are confronted with the fact that they cannot keep all of the commandments, many find refuge in their ability to repent. Repentance, they say, erases the transgression and makes everything all right. Repentance of personal sins might sound like the logical remedy, except that repentance is a verbal admission of a violation of God's law or laws. To be sure, many of the same leaders who insist that complete obedience is the requirement for exaltation have also spoken on the need to repent. This appears to be inconsistent, since it is in keeping the law that one is exalted, not admitting you broke it. Some might argue that repentance is a part of celestial law. If that is so, are Mormons keeping the law when they admit they broke it?

Furthermore, how do Mormons know that their repentance is the kind that merits forgiveness? Spencer Kimball said that the "repentance which merits forgiveness" is the kind in which

the former transgressor must have reached a "point of no return" to sin wherein there is not merely a renunciation but also a deep abhorrence of the sin—where the sin becomes most distasteful to him and where the desire or urge to sin is cleared out of his life.[30]

While penitent people should understand the seriousness of their sin, we doubt that any human has the ability to clear the desire or urge to sin out of their life. If this is what is really required to achieve forgiveness, no Mormon will ever receive it, because all humans struggle with their sin nature. Kimball said the only way Mormons can know if they have total forgiveness of sins is if they are "living all the commandments." Kimball also declared that those who thought frequent repentance was a means of getting right with God must "straighten out their thinking." He taught:

> To return to sin is most destructive to the morale of the individual and gives Satan another handhold on his victim. Those who feel that they can sin and be forgiven and then return to sin and be forgiven again and again must straighten out their thinking. Each previously forgiven sin is added to the new one and the whole gets to be a heavy load. Thus when a man has made up his mind to change his life, there must be no turning back. Any reversal, even in a small degree, is greatly to his detriment.[31]

ACHIEVING PERFECTION

Mormon leaders have certainly given mixed signals as to whether or not perfection is necessary for exaltation. Speaking at the spring general conference in 1989, Apostle Marvin J. Ashton stated,

> We need to come to terms with our desire to reach perfection and our frustration when our accomplishments or our behaviors are less than perfect. I feel that one of the great myths we would do well to dispel is that we've come to earth to perfect ourselves, and nothing short of that will do. If I understand the teachings of the prophets of this dispensation correctly, we will not become perfect in this life, though we can make significant strides toward that goal.[32]

Where did this "myth" come from? Perhaps its genesis can be found in the teachings of a number of LDS leaders who have utilized

Matthew 5:48 as a rallying cry for personal perfection. Using this verse as a springboard, Spencer Kimball declared:

> This progress toward eternal life is a matter of achieving perfection. Living all the commandments guarantees total forgiveness of sins and assures one of exaltation through that perfection which comes by complying with the formula the Lord gave us. In his Sermon on the Mount he made the command to all men: "Be ye therefore perfect, even as your Father which is in heaven is perfect." (Matt. 5:48). Being perfect means to triumph over sin. This is a mandate from the Lord. He is just and wise and kind. He would never require anything from his children which was not for their benefit and which was not attainable. Perfection therefore is an achievable goal.[33]

In the October 1999 general conference, President Gordon Hinckley also used Matthew 5:48 but seemed to draw a different conclusion:

> Jesus said, "Be ye therefore perfect, even as your Father which is in heaven is perfect" (Matt. 5:48). That is the great crowning example of excellence. May each of us have a rich and wonderful life moving in that direction. We will not become perfect in a day or a month or a year. We will not accomplish it in a lifetime, but we can keep trying, starting with our more obvious weaknesses and gradually converting them to strengths as we go forward with our lives.[34]

It is interesting that in the same conference where Hinckley made the above remarks, another LDS general authority, Apostle Henry B. Eyring, paraphrased 1 Nephi 3:7 by saying, "God gives no commandments to the children of men save He prepares for them to obey."[35] If Mormons believe personal perfection is what Jesus is stressing, it would seem logical that Mormons should be able to achieve it.

Much of the confusion the Mormons have on this issue is due to the fact that their leaders have badly misinterpreted this passage. Jesus was not at all addressing the subject of personal or even sinless perfection. The context points to a consistency of behavior toward believers and unbelievers alike. While it is common for some to repay evil deeds done them in a vengeful manner, Jesus was saying that His disciples should take the high road and repay evil with good. As Jesus said, even Gentiles do good to those who treat them well (Matt. 5:44–47). Christians should go beyond this expected response and treat favorably even those who treat them badly. Granted, this is not easy.

"BUT I'M TRYING!"

As noted in the October 1999 general conference speech by President Hinckley, the faithful Latter-day Saint must "keep trying" to attain perfection and obey all of the laws of God. If it is impossible to be perfect, then it is wrong for the LDS Church to demand complete obedience to all of the laws of God in order to receive exaltation. It would be better and even more honest for Mormons to merely promise to do their best to keep God's commands. BYU professor Stephen E. Robinson, a popular LDS speaker and author, admits that the phrase "keeping the commandments" is a troublesome expression for Latter-day Saints, "particularly when they talk to non-Latter-day Saints."[36] In an attempt to clarify what he feels is the LDS position, he writes:

> We generally say "keeping the commandments" when what we really mean is "trying real hard to keep the commandments and succeeding most of the time." Defined in this way, the phrase describes the attempts at obedience that the new covenant requires as our token of "good faith." Defined in this way, "keeping the commandments" is both possible and necessary; that is, trying to keep the commandments, doing the best we can at it, is a requirement of the gospel covenant, even though succeeding right now in keeping all of the commandments all of the time is not.[37]

Apostle Russell M. Nelson said trying *was* good enough. He stated, "Meanwhile, brothers and sisters, let us *do the best we can* and *try* to improve each day. When our imperfections appear, we can keep *trying* to correct them."[38] This opinion flatly contradicts Kimball's assessment:

> It is normal for children to try. They fall and get up numerous times before they can be certain of their footing. But adults, who have gone through these learning periods, must determine what they will do, then proceed to do it. To "try" is weak. To "do the best I can" is not strong. We must always do better than we can.[39]

This comment took on a much stronger meaning when Kimball related a hypothetical dialogue between an army officer and a soldier to show that trying is "not sufficient" if exaltation is to be achieved:

> An army officer called a soldier to him and ordered him to take a message to another officer. The soldier saluted and said, "I'll try, sir! I'll try!" To this the officer responded: "I don't want you to try, I want you to deliver this message." The soldier, somewhat embarrassed, now replied: "I'll do the best I can, sir." At this the officer, now disgusted, rejoined with some vigor: "I don't want you to try and I don't want you to 'do the best you can.' I want you to deliver this message." Now the young soldier, straightening to his full height, approached the matter magnificently, as he thought, when he saluted again and said: "I'll do it or die, sir." To this the now irate officer responded: "I don't want you to die, and I don't want you merely to do the best you can, and I don't want you to try. Now, the request is a reasonable one; the message is important; the distance is not far; you are able-bodied; you can do what I have ordered. Now get out of here and accomplish your mission."[40]

Kimball's kick-in-the-tail pep talk hardly allows for failure. When Mormons insist they are trying, it is usually in the context of failing to succeed. Kimball's analogy does not allow for this possibility. There certainly appears to be some theological schizophrenia among LDS leaders when it comes to this subject. On the one hand, members are told that they must "be ye perfect," but on the other, they are told they cannot ever achieve perfection. Some leaders say complete obedience is the requirement for exaltation, while others declare that partial obedience will suffice. At one point they are told trying is *insufficient,* but then they are taught that trying *is satisfactory.* How are Mormons to decipher the true teaching? And how can they know when they have done enough?

CHRISTIANITY'S UNDERSTANDING OF SALVATION

Within the context of salvation, we find three aspects that need to be understood. These are justification, sanctification, and glorification.

JUSTIFICATION

When people accept Jesus Christ as their Lord and Savior, a miraculous event occurs. They become justified before the living God and are thereby declared guiltless, allowing them to be identified with Christ from the point of conversion to eternity future. It comes not by a person's own works but by God's working in that person. Acts 13:39 says, "And by him all that believe are justified from all things, from which ye could not be justified by the law of Moses." Romans 3:28 and 5:1 add, "Therefore we conclude that a man is justified by faith without the deeds of the law. . . . Therefore being justified by faith, we have peace with God through our Lord Jesus Christ."

Christian theologian Leon Morris wrote:

> Justification then means the according of the status of being in the right. Sin has put us in the wrong with God and justification is the process whereby we are reckoned as right. In one way or another all religions must face the ultimate question: "How can man, who is a sinner, ever be right with a God who is just?" Most religions answer, in some form, "By human effort." Man committed the sin, so man must do what is required to put things right and undo the effects of his sin. It is the great teaching of the New Testament that we are justified, not by what we do, but by what Christ has done. Paul puts it simply when he says that we are "justified by his blood" (Rom. 5:9). He links our justification directly with the death of Jesus.[41]

Since we are unable to comply with all of God's standards (Rom. 3:23; Gen. 8:21; Ps 51:5, 58:3; Eccles. 9:3; Jer. 17:9), we deserve death because all good works by themselves are like "filthy rags" in the sight of God (Rom. 6:23; Isa. 64:6). But God Himself has provided the way through faith to allow believers to experience the fellowship of God and become righteous in His sight.

BELIEF EQUALS SALVATION

One of the toughest concepts for anyone, especially Mormons, to understand is that faith, not works, justifies a person before God. A good example of justification by faith is the story of the Philippian jailer in Acts 16. Paul and Silas were incarcerated in Philippi when a miraculous earthquake opened their jail cell door. When the jailer saw that all of the prison cells were open as well, he prepared to commit suicide only to be stopped by Paul, who told him not to fear because no one had escaped.

Seeing this to be true, the frightened jailer asked Paul, "What must I do to be saved?" (v. 30). If Paul had been a good Mormon living in modern times, his response might have been, "Believe that Joseph Smith was a prophet of God and that the *Book of Mormon* is the Word of God. Join the true church, don't drink coffee or tea, pay a full tithe, receive the Melchizedek priesthood, be baptized for your dead relatives, perform your endowments, and make sure you are married for time and eternity. Do these, along with following the whole law, and thou shalt be saved."

Instead, Paul and Silas merely answered, "Believe on the Lord Jesus Christ, and thou shalt be saved, and thy house" (v. 31). It is important to note that Paul made no reference to following any set of rules or rigid standards. Rather, his message was simply, "Believe . . . and thou shalt be saved."

As stated earlier in this chapter, the word *salvation* has two different meanings according to LDS theology. "Salvation by grace," known as unconditional or general salvation, is a free gift provided by Christ to everyone on this earth. This salvation allows each person the ability to be resurrected. On the other hand, conditional or individual salvation (exaltation) is the right to go to the highest level within the celestial kingdom.

So to which salvation was Paul referring when he spoke to the Philippian jailer? He certainly could not have been speaking of general salvation ("Believe and thou wilt be *resurrected*"), since everyone receives this regardless of belief. On the other hand, Paul could not have been referring to individual exaltation ("Believe and thou wilt be *exalted*"), since perpetual good works and strict adherence to celestial law are the only ways to achieve this, according to Mormonism.

The New Testament is replete with examples of how belief alone, not one's works, justifies a person before God. For instance, Jesus said in John 5:24, "Verily, verily, I say unto you, He that heareth my word, and believeth on him that sent me, hath everlasting life." He

"SALVATION" ACCORDING TO MORMONISM

Acts 16:31: "And they said, Believe on the Lord Jesus Christ, and thou shalt be saved, and thy house."

Read Acts 16:31

Which definition of *saved* did Paul mean in this passage?

General Resurrection	*Individual Exaltation*
"Believe . . . and thou shalt be resurrected . . ."	"Believe . . . and thou shalt be exalted . . ."

But this definition can't be correct because . . .

General Resurrection comes to all mankind "by grace alone without obedience to gospel law"	Exaltation comes only to those "with gospel obedience" and continued good works to the end of life

also said in John 6:47, "Verily, verily, I say unto you, He that believeth on me hath everlasting life."

Paul clearly communicated this truth in Ephesians 2:8–9 when he said faith, not works, justifies a person before God. He also declared in Titus 3:5–6, "Not by works of righteousness which we have done, but according to his mercy he saved us, by the washing of regeneration, and renewing of the Holy Ghost; which he shed on us abundantly through Jesus Christ our Saviour."

Christian theologian F. F. Bruce explained:

If there is to be any salvation for either Jews or Gentiles, then, it must be based not on ethical achievement but on the grace of God. What Jews and Gentiles need alike, in fact, is to have their records blotted out by an act of divine amnesty and to have the assurance of acceptance by God for no merit of their own but by his spontaneous mercy. For this need God has made provision in Christ. Thanks to his redemptive work, men may find themselves "in the clear" before God. . . . The benefits of the atonement thus procured may be appropriated by faith—and only by faith.[42]

Several other terms used by Christians can be easily misunderstood by Mormons. These terms are related to the justification process.

REDEMPTION

Redemption is the deliverance from sin in its guilt, defilement, power, and liability through Christ's sacrifice. Believers can find comfort in the fact that God does not keep track of their sins. Certainly the psalmist knew this when he stated in Psalm 130:3, "If thou, LORD, shouldest mark iniquities, O Lord, who shall stand?" (see also Isa. 43:25; Jer. 31:34; Heb. 8:12). Galatians 3:13 clearly states, "Christ hath redeemed us from the curse of the law, being made a curse for us." First Peter 1:18–19 says,

> Forasmuch as ye know that ye were not redeemed with corruptible things, as silver and gold, from your vain conversation received by tradition from your fathers; but with the precious blood of Christ, as of a lamb without blemish and without spot.

Referring to this passage, Leon Morris commented:

> "Your sin," he seems to be saying, "is a very serious matter. It set you in opposition to God and handed you over to eternal condemnation. From that situation there was no escape. You were hopelessly, irrevocably lost. There is no ransom from such a situation. And then, incredibly, unbelievably, a ransom was found. It meant a heavy price, the price of the death of the wonderful Son of God. But that price was paid and you have been redeemed. Never take your redemption for granted. Never count it a common, ordinary thing. It is the most incredible thing that has ever happened. But it did happen. Accept it, then, with gratitude and with awe. Live your life in reverent fear."[43]

GRACE

It has been said that *grace* stands for "*G*od's *R*iches (or Righteousness) *A*t *C*hrist's *E*xpense." Grace is unmerited favor from God provided to those who believe (Rom. 12:3, 6). Again there is nothing we can do on our own to achieve this. Romans 5:2 and 20 say:

> By whom also we have access by faith into this grace wherein we stand, and rejoice in hope of the glory of God. . . . Moreover the law entered, that the offence might abound. But where sin abounded, grace did much more abound.

Romans 11:5–6 adds:

> Even so then at this present time also there is a remnant according to the election of grace. And if by grace, then is it no more of works: otherwise grace is no more grace. But if it be of works, then is it no more grace: otherwise work is no more work.

Morris wrote:

> It is not at all unlikely that at first the Christians did not realize the full significance of the cross. But in time they came to see that the crucifixion is rightly understood only when it is seen as God's great saving act. It is the means God used to deal with the problem of human sin. The Christians came to emphasize that the way of salvation is not the way of law, as devout Jews held. It is the way of grace. People do not merit salvation but receive it as a free gift from God on the basis of what Christ's death accomplished.[44]

IMPUTATION

Suppose you received a bank statement informing you that you had one million dollars in your account, even though you had never deposited this amount. Imagine if someone had deposited this in your name! In the same way, Christianity has taught that imputation is the righteousness of God credited to a person's account based on belief in Jesus. Since a person's works cannot do this, it was necessary that Christ impute His righteousness to the believer. In Romans 4:6–7 Paul stated that God imputes this righteousness apart from works. Paul continued this thought in Romans 4:20–24 when he said that Abraham

> staggered not at the promise of God through unbelief; but was strong in faith, giving glory to God; and being fully persuaded that, what he had promised, he was able also to perform. And therefore it was imputed to him for righteousness. Now it was not written for his sake alone, that it was imputed to him; but for us also, to whom it shall be imputed, if we believe on him that raised up Jesus our Lord from the dead.

FORGIVENESS

The complete putting away of sin and its consequences with no strings attached summarizes forgiveness. This occurs at the time of belief when a person is redeemed from the penalty of sin. The believer's sins are permanently covered. Ephesians 4:32 reiterates that "God for Christ's sake hath forgiven you." Paul added in Ephesians 1:7, "In whom we have redemption through his blood, the forgiveness of sins, according to the riches of his grace." John declared in 1 John 2:12 that the believer's "sins are forgiven you for his name's sake." Morris commented:

> The blood of animal sacrifices could never cope with the problems of man, made in God's image as he is. But the blood of Christ can and does. Our Day of Atonement was the day of the cross. Jesus "suffered outside the city gate to make the people holy through his own blood" (Heb. 13:12).[45]

SANCTIFICATION

While justification—which took place in an instantaneous moment and is good forevermore—is a past event in the Christian's life, sanctification has its roots in conversion and will continue to blossom throughout the rest of the believer's life. Sanctification is synonymous with holiness and means to be set apart for God.

First Corinthians 6:11 says, "And such were some of you: but ye are washed, but ye are sanctified, but ye are justified in the name of the Lord Jesus, and by the Spirit of our God." Hebrews 10:10 and 14 read, "By the which will we are sanctified through the offering of the body of Jesus Christ once for all. . . . For by one offering he hath perfected for ever them that are sanctified."

On profession of faith, believers are immediately qualified to dwell with the Father. This does not say that new believers will always do what is right. They are still human beings fraught with human frailties and defects. However, because the Lord has begun a new work in them, their desires and outlook will be different. Because of the indwelling presence of the Holy Spirit in the believer's life, the fruit of the Spirit as described in Galatians 5:22–23 should become more evident while the "works of the flesh" as described in the previous three verses diminish.

The Christian needs to realize that the sanctification process is what Paul was describing in Philippians 2:12 when he implored the believers to "work out your own salvation with fear and trembling."[46] Although Paul declared in Ephesians 2:10 that the believer was created *unto* good works, he was very clear to also point out in the previous two verses that it is faith and faith alone, not works, that justifies the believer. According to Romans 3:28, "Therefore we conclude that a man is justified by faith without the deeds of the law."

Paul says almost the exact same thing in Galatians 2:16 and 21:

> Knowing that a man is not justified by the works of the law, but by the faith of Jesus Christ, even we have believed in Jesus Christ, that we might be justified by the faith of Christ, and not by the works of the law: for by the works of the law shall no flesh be justified. . . . I do not frustrate the grace of God: for if righteousness come by the law, then Christ is dead in vain.

On this issue Leon Morris wrote:

> The cross is the making of a new covenant, but this means that we are to live as the people of God. It is the perfect sacrifice, but we are to present our bodies as living sacrifices. If Christ died for us, we are to live for him. . . . And this means we have a great privilege. We must neither neglect it nor use it carelessly. Christ our Passover has been offered for us so that we, the church, constitute the people of God, and so that we should cleanse out every evil thing. Passover warns us against complacency. The Lamb of God brings us back to the thought of the perfect sacrifice with all that that means.[47]

Many Mormons are quick to point to James 2:14–26 in an attempt to show how works are more important than faith. If it's just faith that's needed for "salvation," the argument goes, then it would seem reasonable that Christians could do whatever they wished (i.e., murder, commit adultery, steal) and still call themselves Christians. Those who hold this position miss the point of the entire gospel message.

Never has the Christian church taught that the believer has the license to break God's commands. Paul clearly instructed in Romans 6:15, "What then? shall we sin, because we are not under the law, but under grace? God forbid." As far as James 2:14–26 is concerned, it is important to understand the context of this passage. Written by the half brother of Jesus to explain how good works *are* important, James never taught that we receive salvation through our works. Rather, his point was to show how good works should accompany a valid salvation. Like a butterfly that has shed its chrysalis, so, too, does the believer begin to be "transformed by the renewing of your mind" and display good fruit because of the dramatic life change (Rom. 12:2; 2 Cor. 5:17; Gal. 5:22–23). Concerning this good fruit, F. F. Bruce wrote, "As an apple-tree does not produce apples by Act of Parliament, but because it is its nature so to do, so the character of Christ cannot be produced in his people by rules and regulations; it must be the fruit of his Spirit within them."[48]

Although it is true that a doctrine can be misapplied, it is a dreadful mistake to suppose that it is false merely because it can be abused. Should good works be minimized merely because groups like the Pharisees took them to a legalistic extreme? Obviously not! Jesus reserved His harshest words for those who felt their good works made them righteous in God's sight, calling the legalistic Pharisees vipers, whitewashed tombs, and hypocrites (Matt. 23:27, 33). These rebukes, however, were not meant to take away the importance of righteous actions. When we accept the love of God as offered through belief in His Son, our response is to obey our Creator and Sustainer. The more we learn about God's love for us, the more we want to reciprocate by demonstrating our love for Him through service. Christian preacher Vance Havner summarized the role works play in the believer's life when he said, "We hear these days about 'cheap grace.' It doesn't mean much to be a Christian. But salvation is the costliest item on earth. It cost our Lord everything to provide it and it costs us everything to possess it."[49]

GLORIFICATION

Not only does salvation have a past tense (justification/sanctification) and a present tense (sanctification), but it also implies a future tense as well. The believer has a future hope of reigning with Christ in glory. This will not be completely fulfilled until the believer arrives in heaven.

However, the idea of glorification is such a certainty that it can be counted on. Paul speaks of this as a "done deal" in Romans 8:30:

"Moreover whom he did predestinate, them he also called: and whom he called, them he also justified: and whom he justified, them *he also glorified*" (emphasis added). He also said in 1 Thessalonians 3:13 that this event takes place when the believer sees Christ. Philippians 3:12–14 shows how the believer's work is not complete until he or she is in the presence of the Redeemer:

> Not as though I had already attained, either were already perfect: but I follow after, if that I may apprehend that for which also I am apprehended of Christ Jesus. Brethren, I count not myself to have apprehended: but this one thing I do, forgetting those things which are behind, and reaching forth unto those things which are before, I press toward the mark for the prize of the high calling of God in Christ Jesus.

As Christians, we can be eternally grateful to God that we "may know that [we] have eternal life" (1 John 5:13). What a glorious promise! What a glorious hope!

C O N C L U S I O N

Grace and works, according to Mormonism:

- The grace of God provides for resurrection from the dead
- Works are necessary for a person to achieve exaltation, or godhood
- Salvation by grace alone is a pernicious doctrine
- Perfection is an achievable goal

Grace and works, according to Christianity:

- Grace is provided free to those who believe
- Works are the result of saving faith
- Salvation by grace alone is a biblical concept
- Nobody is able to live up to the whole law, which is why grace is needed

TWELVE

Heaven and Hell

From a revelation given in 1832 we learn that three great kingdoms or degrees of glory are established, known as the Celestial, the Terrestrial, and the Telestial. Far below the last and least of these, is the state of eternal punishment prepared for the sons of Perdition.

Apostle James E. Talmage, *Articles of Faith,* 405

The question "What happens to people when they die?" is probably the foremost topic of every religion in the world. Every faith has its paradise, a "Nirvana" of pleasure and delight. Most religions also have their hells, a place of torture and suffering (whether temporal or eternal) that, as depicted by Dante Alighieri's *The Divine Comedy—Inferno,* is saved for the wicked.

Jesus warned the people of His day about how terrible hell is, yet He also comforted His followers by explaining that He was reserving them rooms in a great mansion. Historically, the Christian church has asserted that believers will enjoy eternal happiness in the presence of God, while those who don't have faith and reject God will be eternally separated from Him and exposed to the torments of hell. Mormonism has a much different version of these two final states, and it is to this topic that we now turn.

THE FINAL STATES ACCORDING TO MORMONISM

Mormonism teaches that a person is destined for one of six places after death. These are:

- Outer darkness: located outside the three "kingdoms," this place of torment is reserved for those who were not given mortal bodies (Satan and his demons) and the extremely wicked, including apostate Mormons.
- Telestial kingdom: the lowest level of the three heavens where the wicked of the world will spend eternity.
- Terrestrial kingdom: the second level, this is where honorable people will be, including "lukewarm" Mormons.
- Celestial kingdom: this kingdom actually consists of three separate levels, with the top level being the place where the Mormon hopes to be exalted.

Depending on a person's actions and attitudes on earth, almost all people will end up in one of the three kingdom levels. President Joseph Fielding Smith explained:

> The Lord will judge each individual case and will assign transgressor to that degree to which each is entitled according to his works. If a man only merits a place in the telestial, that will be his reward; if it should be the terrestrial, then he shall be admitted to that kingdom. In order to enter the celestial a man must be true and faithful to the end, observing all things which the Lord has commanded, otherwise he shall be assigned to some other kingdom, or to outer darkness if his sins so merit.[1]

Once an individual is assigned to a particular "glory," he or she is there permanently. President Spencer W. Kimball taught:

> No progression between kingdoms. After a person has been assigned to his place in the kingdom, either in the telestial, the terrestrial, or the celestial, or to his exaltation, he will never advance from his assigned glory to another glory. That is eternal! That is why we must make our decisions early in life and why it is imperative that such decisions be right.[2]

To understand how they arrived at such a conclusion, we need to examine the biblical proof texts the Latter-day Saints use. A passage they often cite to support their view is 1 Corinthians 15:40, which says, "There are also celestial bodies, and bodies terrestrial: but the glory of the celestial is one, and the glory of the terrestrial is another." In light of verse 41, many scholars believe that Paul was referring to heavenly bodies such as the moon, sun, and stars. The references to terrestrial bodies seems to further explain what he wrote in verse 39 when he spoke of the flesh of men, beasts, fishes, and birds. One thing for sure, there is no mention of "bodies telestial." But this did not stop Joseph Smith from inserting this term into his *Inspired Version* of the Bible, which is also known as the Joseph Smith Translation (JST).[3] His version, however, is the only one to contain the word *telestial,* and there is no ancient manuscript that supports Smith's change to the text. He clearly included this word to bolster his erroneous doctrine.

Another Bible passage many Latter-day Saints like to use to support the idea of three degrees of glory is 2 Corinthians 12:2–4:

> I knew a man in Christ above fourteen years ago, (whether in the body, I cannot tell; or whether out of the body, I cannot tell: God knoweth;) such a one caught up to the third heaven. And I knew such a man, (whether in the body, or out of the body, I cannot tell: God knoweth;) how that he was caught up into paradise, and heard unspeakable words, which it is not lawful for a man to utter.

Using these passages to validate the idea of three kingdoms making up heaven ignores the Jewish tradition Paul would have known. According to that tradition, *paradise* was the abode of God, the place of eternal joy for God's people. However, Jewish custom never viewed a first or second heaven as alternative eternal destinations. Rather, these referred to the atmospheric heaven (the sky) and the galactic heaven (the universe).[4]

OUTER DARKNESS: RESERVED FOR THE SONS OF PERDITION

Outer darkness has been depicted a number of ways in LDS theology. In a generic sense it describes the situation of any man or woman who was not qualified to live eternally in the presence of the Father. In a more specific sense, outer darkness is a type of holding tank for the souls of the wicked, who will remain here until the end of the millennium when they will be resurrected and judged. Those with crimes not including murder or apostasy will be allowed entrance into the telestial kingdom, which is the lowest of the kingdoms of glory.[5] Those who fail to prove themselves worthy of a telestial reward will return again to outer darkness, this time for eternity. George Q. Cannon, a member of the First Presidency, wrote:

> Those who are unfaithful, those who will listen to Satan, who will lend a willing ear to his blandishments and to his allurements, when they go from this state of existence, they go into a condition where they are subject to his power. They will dwell in darkness, and according to their sins their punishment will be. Some will be consigned to "outer darkness," where there is weeping and wailing and gnashing of teeth; and they will remain in that condition until they will be visited by some servant of God to unlock the prison doors to them and to preach to them again the Gospel of salvation, through repentance and faith in the Lord Jesus Christ. . . .
> They will remain in that condition, according to the enormity of their offenses, until punishment will be meted out to them sufficiently to bring them to a condition that they will receive the Gospel of salvation. That Gospel which is taught to us will be taught to them, and they will have an opportunity of obeying it in their damned condition and through repentance will receive salvation.[6]

On this same subject Bruce McConkie explained:

> When the wicked depart this life, they are "cast out into outer darkness," into hell, where "they have no part nor portion of the Spirit of the Lord," where they are spiritually dead. (Alma 40:13–14.) They remain spiritually dead in hell until the day of their resurrection (*D&C* 76:103–112), until "death and hell" deliver up the dead which are in them, so that they may be judged according to their works.[7]

As mentioned earlier, for many the reprieve from outer darkness will be short-lived. Following the judgment, those who come from outer darkness and are deemed not worthy enough for entrance into the telestial kingdom will be returned. McConkie taught: "After their resurrection, the great majority of those who have suffered in hell will pass into the telestial kingdom; the balance, cursed as sons of perdition, will be consigned to partake of endless wo with the devil and his angels."[8]

While many Mormons do not like the concept of an eternal punishment that includes "hellfire," it is apparent that outer darkness is a place that is anything but pleasant. According to Joseph Fielding Smith:

> The extent of this punishment none will ever know except those who partake of it. That it is the most severe punishment that can be meted out to man is apparent. Outer darkness is something which cannot be described, except that we know that it is to be placed beyond the benign and comforting influence of the Spirit of God—banished entirely from his presence.[9]

Many Mormons find the Christian view of hell (eternal punishment with no second chances) to be both unfair and offensive. They ask, How can a God of love send His own children into such punishment? This complaint seems strange since it is taught in Mormonism that the devil and his demons are also God's spirit children, cast out of Elohim's presence following the "war in heaven." If Mormonism is true, then one-third of God's children who were cast out of heaven in the preexistence will automatically end up in hell and eternal torment. How is this any more "fair"?

THE TELESTIAL KINGDOM: THE LOWEST LEVEL OF GLORY

Mormon leaders have taught that some of the wicked of this world will eventually rise from outer darkness and be allowed to spend eternity in the telestial kingdom. Joseph Fielding Smith said these would include the unclean, liars, sorcerers, adulterers, and those who have broken their covenants.[10] McConkie added blasphemers and the proud to this list.[11] Although *D&C* 76:81–84 describes this state as "hell," it does not compare to the horrors of hell described in the Bible. Seventy B. H. Roberts said:

> But even of the least of the three grand divisions, the telestial kingdom, it is said that it "surpasses all understanding"; and that even its inhabitants, the last to be redeemed, and even then deprived of the personal presence

of God and the Christ, shall nevertheless receive the ministration of angels and the Holy Ghost, for they are to be accounted "heirs of salvation." How infinitely more glorious, then, must be the higher kingdoms of God and the Christ![12]

To think that the inhabitants of this state will be "heirs of salvation" is completely foreign to the Bible. In fact, many of the attributes given to those who will be sent to the telestial kingdom are exactly the same as those who will be cast into the lake of fire mentioned in Revelation 21:8: "But the fearful, and unbelieving, and the abominable, and murderers, and whoremongers, and sorcerers, and idolaters, and all liars, shall have their part in the lake which burneth with fire and brimstone: which is the second death."

Note that the unbelieving, sorcerers, liars, and whoremongers (sexually immoral) are together lumped with murderers in the lake of fire. Revelation 20:10 clearly states that the punishment here will be a permanent torment that will last "day and night for ever and ever." It is inconceivable that such a fate could ever be considered having anything to do with "salvation."

THE TERRESTRIAL KINGDOM: A PLACE WHERE CHRIST'S PRESENCE REIGNS

For those whose "righteousness" will enable them to escape both outer darkness and the telestial kingdom, the next level up is a terrestrial kingdom where residents will receive more benefits than their telestial counterparts. Here is a description from the *Encyclopedia of Mormonism:*

The inhabitants of the Terrestrial Kingdom are described as the honorable people of the earth who received a testimony of Jesus but were not sufficiently valiant in that testimony to obey all the principles and ordinances of the gospel (*D&C* 76:71–80). Also, those of "the heathen nations" who "died without law," who are honorable but who do not accept the fulness of the gospel in the postearthly spirit world, are candidates for the terrestrial glory (*D&C* 45:54; 76:72). In the hereafter, they receive the presence of the Son, but not the fulness of the Father. The glory of the Terrestrial

Kingdom differs from the celestial as the light we see from the moon differs from that of the sun in glory. There is no mention of different degrees or levels in the Terrestrial Kingdom, but it is reasonable that there, as in the celestial and telestial kingdoms, individuals will differ from one another in glory.[13]

Those who enter here are not wicked enough for the telestial kingdom, but at the same time they are not good enough for the celestial. According to Spencer Kimball:

Lukewarm Saints get terrestrial glory. The terrestrial kingdom will not be enjoyed by the very wicked, for they shall obtain only the telestial. Neither will the terrestrial be given to the valiant, the faithful, the perfected, for they will go into the celestial kingdom prepared for those who live the celestial laws. But into the terrestrial will go those who do not measure up to the celestial. Speaking of one category of terrestrial people, the Lord says: "These are they who are not valiant in the testimony of Jesus; wherefore, they obtain not the crown over the kingdom of our God."[14]

While this will be a comfortable state and will have the presence of Jesus Christ, the presence of Heavenly Father will be missing. This glory, which "differs from the celestial glory as the light of the moon differs from the light of the sun," will be inherited by those "who are honorable men of the earth, who were blinded by the craftiness of men . . . (and) who are not valiant in the testimony of Jesus, therefore they obtain not the crown over the kingdom of God."[15] Joseph Fielding Smith further explained:

Those who were honorable men who will be permitted to go to the terrestrial kingdom will be blessed with ministrations from the celestial kingdom. They will be privileged with visitations from Jesus Christ but will be denied the presence of the Father. Thus we learn that our Eternal Father will do all that he can for the inhabitants of the earth according to their works. The inhabitants of the telestial and terrestrial kingdoms will be given a measure of salvation, but not the fulness. They will be redeemed from the power of Satan after they have paid the penalty of their transgressions and have learned to be obedient to divine law.[16]

CELESTIAL KINGDOM: THE ULTIMATE GOAL

It is the goal of every sincere Latter-day Saint to gain entrance into the celestial kingdom. Here faithful Mormons hope to eternally reside with their family, and Mormon males become gods of their newly inherited worlds.

Latter-day Saints believe that life is more secure and more joyous when it is experienced in the sacred relationships of the eternal family. Those who maintain such worthy relationships on earth will live as families in the Celestial Kingdom following the resurrection. Thus, a person who lives a righteous life in mortality and who has entered into an eternal marriage may look forward to an association in the postmortal world with a worthy spouse, and with those who were earthly children, fathers, mothers, brothers, and sisters.[17]

Unlike the other kingdoms previously discussed, the celestial is where God the Father dwells and where those who achieve such a status are granted privileges and abilities the other kingdoms do not afford. However, there are different levels within this kingdom. According to Bruce McConkie:

"In the celestial glory there are three heavens or degrees." The highest of these is reserved for those who gain eternal life. All others are damned in the sense that their progress is limited. There are restrictions placed upon them; they have reached the "end of [their] kingdom"; they "cannot have an increase." (*D&C* 131:1, 4.)[18]

This highest level is known as the Church of the Firstborn. It is here where a person can truly experience eternal life known as exaltation, or godhood. Joseph Fielding Smith admitted that many Mormons would never see this state:

Those who gain exaltation in the celestial kingdom are those who are members of the Church of the Firstborn; in other words, those who keep *all* the commandments of the Lord. There will be many who are members of the Church of Jesus Christ of Latter-day Saints who shall *never* become members of the Church of the Firstborn.[19]

Theoretically, those who reach the celestial kingdom but were not faithful in all things will be prohibited from enjoying the pleasures of godhood. These include angels, which in LDS theology are ministering servants who were not qualified to become gods. Brigham Young stated:

> Angels are those beings who have been on an earth like this, and have passed through the same ordeals that we are now passing through. . . . They are persons who have lived upon an earth, but did not magnify the Priesthood in that high degree that many others have done who have become Gods, even the sons of God. Human beings that pertain to this world, who do not magnify or are not capable of magnifying their high calling in the Priesthood and receive crowns of glory, immortality, and eternal lives, will also, when they again receive their bodies, become angels and will receive a glory.[20]

While angels have a place in the celestial kingdom, they play a subservient role.[21] The Bible, however, does not teach that people become angels. Angels are a distinct creation of God. They are not beings who have undergone some sort of spiritual development or physical evolution. Psalm 148:2 and 5 state that God created angels as angels: "Praise ye him, all his angels: praise ye him, all his hosts. . . . Let them praise the name of the *Lord*: for he commanded, and they were created."

To most Latter-day Saints, to strive to be an angel is like finding satisfaction in brass when it is possible to obtain gold. Godhood is the anticipated reward, not servitude as an angel.

ETERNAL INCREASE

Like their Heavenly Father before them, worthy Mormons are taught to hope for celestial exaltation and the reward of godhood. Like the millions of gods who have preceded them, the Mormon couple will then commence with their eternal quest of populating their kingdoms through what is known as "eternal increase." Apostle James Talmage explained:

> Great and glorious as is the boon of Redemption from the grave, greater and more glorious as are the conditions prescribed for the soul's Salva-

tion, the revealed Gospel of Jesus Christ provides yet more transcendent blessings in the plan for Exaltation, whereby resurrected man may advance from one stage of relative perfection to another, with powers of eternal increase and never ending progression.[22]

Eternal increase includes the ability to procreate throughout eternity. Just as the Mormon God continually populates his earth, so it is taught that Mormon males and their goddess wives will have the ability to populate the worlds they will inherit. Because procreation plays such a large part in the LDS concept of salvation, it is imperative that marriage relationships formed here on earth be carried on into eternity. To marry and bear children is of the utmost importance to the Latter-day Saint, said President Joseph Fielding Smith:

When young people marry and refuse to fulfill this commandment given in the beginning of the world—and just as much in force today—they rob themselves of the greatest eternal blessing. If the love of the world and the wicked practices of the world mean more to a man and a woman than to keep the commandment of the Lord in this respect, then they shut themselves off from the eternal blessing of increase. Those who wilfully and maliciously design to break this important commandment shall be damned. They cannot have the Spirit of the Lord.[23]

Much of the LDS outlook on true salvation centers on the desires of the Mormon individual and not on Jesus Christ. Rather than the picture portrayed in the Book of Revelation, where God's saints pay rightful homage to the One who redeemed them, the Mormon heavenly system is more focused on personal power, gain, and sex. Apostle Orson Pratt taught that each Mormon male who achieves godhood would have the ability to multiply forever and ever.

As soon as each God has begotten many millions of male and female spirits, and his Heavenly inheritance becomes too small, to comfortably accommodate his great family, he, in connection with his sons, organizes a new world, after a similar order to the one which we now inhabit, where he sends both the male and female spirits to inhabit tabernacles of flesh and bones.[24]

Pratt went on to say on the same page that "the inhabitants of each world are required to reverence, adore, and worship their own personal father who dwells in the Heaven which they formerly inhabited."[25] Thus, Mormonism's heaven revolves around personal adoration and eternal sexual relations. As one member of the LDS Church put it to us, "If I had the choice between building a family (which is my greatest joy today) and sitting by a river singing praises to Jesus, I think you can guess what I would choose."[26]

WE ARE NOT ALONE

Since the Latter-day Saint male is following the same "path" to godhood as Elohim, he is really doing nothing more than repeating a process started by an infinite number of gods aeons ago. The "exalted" Mormon male, like all gods before him, will supposedly go on to populate his world, just as the God of Mormonism populates this one. In turn, he will receive worship of his offspring just as Elohim receives worship. Apostle Orson Pratt explained:

> If we should take a million of worlds like this and number their particles, we should find that there are more Gods than there are particles of matter in those worlds. . . . One world has a personal God or Father, and the inhabitants thereof worship the atributes [sic] of that God, another world has another, and they worship His attributes, and besides Him there is no other.[27]

If a human-turned-god has the ability to procreate throughout eternity and organize a new world when the former is full, are we to assume that Elohim, the God of planet Earth, has other planets to take care of somewhere in the galaxy? Apparently so, according to Joseph Fielding Smith: "We are not the only people that the Lord has created. *We have brothers and sisters on other earths. They look like us because they, too, are the children of God* and were created in his image, for they are also his offspring."[28]

Apostle Neal Maxwell stated:

> We do not know how many inhabited worlds there are, or where they are. But certainly we are not alone. This is a universe of spiritual order, in which "Kolob is set nigh unto the throne of God, to govern all those planets which belong to the same order as that upon which thou standest."[29]

HEAVEN ON EARTH?

What if Mormonism is true and people can become gods and god-desses of their own planets? What will this heavenly state be like? Those who are righteous will be able to rule their own worlds. Each world will be filled with children, repeating the process of Heavenly Father and his family.[30] And sin will be introduced into this world as demonstrated by the words of Brigham Young:

> Sin is upon every earth that ever was created, and if it was not so, I would like some philosophers to let us know how people can be exalted to become sons of God, and enjoy a fulness of glory with the Redeemer. Consequently every earth has its redeemer, and every earth has its tempter; and every earth, and the people thereof, in their turn and time, receive all that we receive, and pass through all the ordeals that we are passing through.[31]

If Young was telling the truth, then every earth ever created, including that earth that a faithful Mormon hopes to eventually inherit, is predestined to be infected with sin. Every Mormon couple who obtains exaltation has no choice but to look forward to the day when one of their own children will serve as a tempter and cause one-third of the other family members to rebel and fall into sin. Thus it will be necessary to sacrifice another one of their sons as a redeemer in order to shed his blood for the sins of the rest of the family. As Young said, "all the ordeals that we are passing through"—such as sorrow, failure, and death—will be experienced again and again.

All of us have seen the effects of a fallen race, and the view is very unpleasant. We hear of places like Auschwitz, Rwanda, Tiananmen Square, and Kosovo. Such names flash horrible pictures of the dead, in some cases tens of thousands of them, slaughtered as a result of human depravity. Historical figures like Adolf Hitler, Joseph Stalin, Idi Amin, Pol Pot, and Mao Tse-tung prove there is no limit to man's inhumanity to man. This time, however, the Mormon as "God" will be in charge of the mess. This hardly sounds like a blissful, peaceful state!

THE FINAL STATES ACCORDING TO THE BIBLE

When it comes to heaven, the Bible provides few details. Perhaps with our sin-tainted minds, such a wondrous concept would be difficult to grasp. Probably the greatest description of heaven is found in Revelation 21. The apostle John describes a heavenly city whose walls are adorned with precious stones, gates made of pearl, and streets made of pure gold, transparent like glass. In reality, it is not the description of the walls, the gates, or the streets that places the Christian in awe. Heaven is heaven because it is where Jesus, the Savior and Redeemer, lives. He gives light to all abiding in His presence. Throughout eternity those whose names are written in the Book of Life will dwell with the Lamb who gave His life for them. Their communion with Christ will remain forever constant, unbroken, and unmolested by earthly distractions and satanic deceptions.

Revelation 21:4 says heaven is a place where God Himself will wipe away every tear from the eyes of the believer; death, sorrow, crying, and pain will forever be a thing of the past. Our minds cannot imagine the greatness of this abode. As Paul wrote in 1 Corinthians 2:9, "Eye hath not seen, nor ear heard, neither have entered into the heart of man, the things which God hath prepared for them that love him." All of the redeemed believers represent God's family. Second Corinthians 6:16 says, "As God hath said, I will dwell in them, and walk in them; and I will be their God, and they shall be my people." According to Revelation 19:6, believers will join the angels in praise to their God and King.

Not everyone makes it to this wonderful state. Those who, for whatever reason, reject God's gift of salvation on this earth will exist in a place of endless torment. They will be unable to ever experience the joy of God's eternal presence. This holds true for those who were deluded into thinking that they were not as "bad" as others were. They will forever learn that people were never expected to compare themselves with others of the fallen race but rather see themselves in light of God's holiness and perfection. Only the blindness of sin keeps a person from crying out, "I am undone!" (see Isa. 6:5). Only a people ignorant of God's righteousness can think that they can establish their own righteousness and thereby meet the standard of God's absolute perfection.

How disappointed they will be to hear the words found in Matthew 25:41: "Depart from me, ye cursed, into everlasting fire, prepared for the devil and his angels." Some like to think that a loving God would never punish unbelievers in such a manner. That conclusion, though, fails to take into account that it was Christ Himself who made such a pronouncement! To assume otherwise is to accuse Jesus of a terrible deception amounting to nothing more than a cruel and dishonest scare tactic.

The fact is that Jesus referred to hell on numerous occasions throughout the Gospels. For instance, Matthew 10:28 says, "And fear not them which kill the body, but are not able to kill the soul: but rather fear him which is able to destroy both soul and body in hell." Jesus said in Matthew 18:9 that "if thine eye offend thee, pluck it out, and cast it from thee: it is better for thee to enter into life with one eye, rather than having two eyes to be cast into hell fire." In addition, He warned His followers in Luke 12:5 to "fear him, which after he hath killed hath power to cast into hell."

In all the above passages, the word used to describe hell is *Gehenna*. In using this word, Jesus vividly illustrated the everlasting burnings of hell by comparing it to the perpetual fires in the valley of Hinnom just south of Jerusalem. In this valley was the city garbage dump, a heap of refuse that burned continually; hence His phrase found twice in Mark 9:43–45, "The fire that shall never be quenched."

That all will be judged is a biblical fact. Acts 17:31 declares that God has appointed a day in which He will judge the world in righteousness. On that day no lawyer with beguiling speech will be able to manipulate a jury into an unjust decision. Both believer and unbeliever will have to give an account directly before Christ Himself (John 5:22). Matthew 12:36 tells us that every idle word ever spoken will be carefully scrutinized. While the believer's actions in this life may allow him to either gain or lose unspecified rewards, his ultimate hope lies in knowing he will, with certainty, obtain eternal life (1 John 5:13). Jesus promised in John 5:24 that those who hear His word, and believe on Him, have (right now) eternal life. Those who place their total confidence and trust in the work of Christ will not be condemned, but they have already "passed from death unto life." They need not fear that the coming judgment will render them guilty and deserving of eternal damnation.

On the other hand, those who believe that personal merit will vindicate them will be horribly disappointed. Exposed as insufficient will be sin-tainted deeds performed with the anticipation of individual exaltation. A life dedicated to self-glorification will not be enough to assuage God's demand for perfection. A horrible end also lies in store for those who pride themselves in their false religion. Many souls will reside in hell who placed more importance on their membership in a certain religious organization or belief system than in the truth of God's Word, the Bible. How terrible it will be to see that Christ does not grant eternal happiness to those who trusted in false prophets and false messiahs but only to those who trusted in a personal Christ— the One who declared in John 14:6 that He alone was "the way, the truth, and the life." As stated before, not just any Christ will do. Since neither the Jesus of Mormonism nor the Jesus of any other false religion has any power to save, those who trust in such imagined "saviors" will be sorely disappointed. Jesus Himself declared in Matthew 7:22–23:

> Many will say to me in that day, Lord, Lord, have we not prophesied in thy name? and in thy name have cast out devils? and in thy name done many wonderful works? And then will I profess unto them, I never knew you: depart from me, ye that work iniquity.

CONCLUSION

Heaven and hell, according to Mormonism:

- There are technically six levels awaiting people after death
- Those who obtain the highest level of the celestial kingdom become gods and dwell with their families
- Damnation is not attaining godhood
- Hell, or outer darkness, is a place where very few people will go

Heaven and hell, according to Christianity:

- Heaven and hell are the only two destinations that await humanity
- In heaven the family of God spend eternity praising Him and dwelling in His glory
- Damnation awaits those who reject God's gift of salvation through His Son Jesus Christ
- The Bible says, "Broad is the way, that leadeth to destruction, and many there be which go in thereat" (Matt. 7:13)

Are You Keeping Celestial Law?

Most Latter-day Saints hope that their good works will be enough when they die to provide them entrance into the celestial kingdom. According to President Spencer Kimball in the book *The Miracle of Forgiveness,* the celestial kingdom involves obeying the whole law. Yet is the Latter-day Saint doing this?

Christian: According to *Doctrine and Covenants* 88:22, a person who "is not able to abide the law of a celestial kingdom cannot abide a celestial glory." Are you abiding a celestial law?

Mormon: What do you mean?

C: Celestial law has been defined by your leaders as keeping all of the laws of God.

M: Well, nobody can do that.

C: If that is the case, then how do you hope to reach exaltation?

M: I believe that God will allow me to make up for my imperfections after I die.

C: Your own prophet, Joseph Fielding Smith, said that if you refuse to comply with the provided laws and ordinances during this lifetime, you will be "assigned, after the resurrection, to some inferior sphere."

M: Perhaps that was his opinion.

C: Maybe, but Alma 34:32–33 found in the *Book of Mormon* says, "For behold, this life is the time for men to prepare to meet God; yea, behold the day of this life is the day for men to perform their labors . . . for after this day of life, which is given us to prepare for eternity, behold, if we do not improve our time while in this life, then cometh the night of darkness wherein there can be no labor performed." If there is no labor performed in the next life, how can you make up for any imperfections?

M: But this is what repentance is for. If we repent, then our transgressions are erased.

C: Every time you repent, you do nothing more than admit your disobedience and how short you have fallen of the requirement for exaltation. You've already admitted that you are not living all of the commandments. Are you aware that President Kimball said that it was only by living all the commandments that you can have the assurance of forgiveness? If you are not living all of the commandments, how do you know you are truly forgiven?

M: I guess I can't.

C: President Kimball also said that the only repentance that "merits forgiveness" is the kind that includes clearing the very desire or urge to sin out of your life." Is the urge to sin cleared out of your life?

M: No, but I'm trying my best!

C: This may seem commendable, but President Kimball said trying was not good enough. He said to try was weak. When you were baptized a member in the LDS Church, you promised to keep all of the laws and commandments of God. You fail, so each week at sacrament service, you again commit to keep the commandments. Each week you fail. President Kimball said that a person like you is a covenant breaker, likening you to the wicked man of *D&C* 3:12, 13. If Mormonism is true, you are doomed to failure and, accordingly, destined for damnation.

Romans 3:19 says that those who try to appease God by following the law are guilty before God. Therefore, we're incapable of saving ourselves. Jesus did not die just to make our resurrection possible; rather, Colossians 2:13 says He came to take away all sins! Since sin separates us from God, this barrier is removed by faith. Only the righteousness of Christ will satisfy the demands of an all-holy God. Nothing less will do. It is only when we rely on this biblical fact that we can have the assurance of God's forgiveness! As long as people insist on good works for exaltation, they will continue to be frustrated and bear the heavy burden of guilt.

Examining the LDS Concept of Ordinances

Communion and Baptism

All other churches are entirely destitute of all authority from God; and any person who receives Baptism or the Lord's supper from their hands will highly offend God, for he looks upon them as the most corrupt of all people.

Apostle Orson Pratt, The Seer, 255

Although they are not requirements for entrance into heaven, the Lord's Supper and water baptism play important roles in the life of the Christian. The Latter-day Saints also consider these to be integral to their faith. It is in their purpose and importance, however, that the two faiths differ.

REMEMBERING THE LAST SUPPER

Mormons call the ordinance of the Lord's Supper the Sacrament. According to the *Encyclopedia of Mormonism:*

Partaking of the Sacrament is the central act of worship and covenant renewal and resembles the simple commemorative meal described in the New Testament. . . . All members of the Church, including unbaptized children, are encouraged to partake of the bread and water as emblems in remembrance of the body and blood of Jesus Christ.[1]

Apostle Bruce McConkie explained further:

By partaking of the sacrament, worthy saints renew the covenant previously made by them in the waters of baptism (Mosiah 18:7–10). . . . Worthy partakers of the sacrament put themselves in perfect harmony with the Lord. (3 Ne. 18.) As indicated by our Lord's statement they gain "the remission of their sins."[2]

The earliest Mormons used bread and wine for the Sacrament. *D&C* 20:75 says, "It is expedient that the church meet together often to partake of bread and wine in the remembrance of the Lord Jesus." A few months later Smith had a "revelation," recorded in *D&C* 27, setting forth a new requirement. Verse 3 says that God's people should not "purchase wine neither strong drink of your enemies." Water became the substance used in the LDS sacrament service. Apostle James Talmage explained why:

In instituting the sacrament among both the Jews and the Nephites, Christ used bread and wine as the emblems of His body and blood; and in this, the dispensation of the fulness of times, He has revealed His will that the saints meet together often to partake of bread and wine in this commemorative ordinance. But He has also shown that other forms of food and drink may be used in place of bread and wine. Soon after the Church had been organized in the present dispensation, the Prophet Joseph Smith was about to purchase wine for sacramental purposes, when a messenger from God met him and delivered the following instructions: "For, behold, I say unto you, that it mattereth not what ye shall eat or what ye shall drink when ye partake of the sacrament, if it so be that ye do it with an eye single to my glory— remembering unto the Father my body which was laid down for you, and my blood which was shed for the remission of your sins. Wherefore, a commandment I give unto you, that you shall not purchase wine neither strong drink of your enemies; Wherefore, you shall partake of none except it is made new among you; yea, in this my Father's kingdom which shall be built up on the earth." Upon this authority, the Latter-day Saints administer water in their sacramental service, in preference to wine.[3]

Strangely, almost three years later, Joseph Smith received another revelation where God once again specifically said wine should be used "in assembling yourselves together to offer up your sacraments before him."[4] *D&C* 89:6 adds that it should be "pure wine of the grape of the vine, of your own make."

In the Christian tradition, the Lord's Supper, which is also known as communion or Eucharist (meaning "give thanks"), was administered to the disciples on the night before Jesus' death (Luke 22:7–23). Jesus took bread and wine, gave it to His disciples, and instructed them to eat it with Him. It was meant to encourage these men. Whenever they sat down to participate in the Lord's Supper, they were to do so in remembrance of Him.

This event was an obvious reference to the Old Testament sacrificial system, whereby the death of the animal sacrifice and the draining of its blood foreshadowed Christ's sacrifice for the forgiveness of sins; it was the Lamb of God who made all of this possible. First Corinthians 11:26 says Christians should continue to observe the Supper to remember the price paid on behalf of all Christian believers. It is not to be taken lightly.

Matthew 26:29 refers to the "fruit of the vine," so Christians have used wine or grape juice to remember the supreme price paid on Calvary. Since water is not a historical element within the universal Christian church, it is curious why this element has been chosen in the LDS tradition to symbolize the blood of Jesus.

BAPTISM AS PRACTICED BY THE LDS CHURCH

According to Mormonism, people must be baptized in the LDS Church if they hope to attain true salvation (exaltation). Mormon leaders have maintained that only priesthood members of its church have authority to administer baptism; all others are invalid. Baptismal regeneration—the doctrine that teaches one must be baptized in order to be saved—is not unique to Mormonism. This doctrine was strongly espoused by the Campbellites of Joseph Smith's time.[5] Consider the following quotes from LDS prophets:

Many talk of baptism not being essential to salvation; but this kind of teaching would lay the foundation of their damnation. I have the truth, and am at the defiance of the world to contradict me, if they can.[6]

It is present salvation and the present influence of the Holy Ghost that we need every day to keep us on saving ground. When an individual refuses to comply with the further requirements of Heaven, then the sins he had formerly committed return upon his head; his former righteousness departs from him, and is not accounted to him for righteousness; but if he had continued in righteousness and obedience to the requirements of Heaven, he is saved all the time, through baptism, the laying on of hands, and obeying the commandments of the Lord and all that is required of him by the heavens—the living oracles.[7]

Baptism for the remission of sins is an ordinance of the gospel. Says one, baptism is not essential to salvation. Jesus not only taught it, but rendered obedience himself to that requirement, not that he was baptized for the remission of sins—but, as he said, "to fulfil all righteousness," thus in this, as in all other respects giving the example for all who follow.[8]

No mortal man or woman will ever receive celestial glory unless he or she has been baptized, receiving this ordinance personally or by proxy. That is the order that God has established.[9]

Salvation will come only to those who repent and have their sins washed away by baptism, and who thereafter show by a godly life that their repentance is genuine.[10]

BAPTISM AS PRACTICED IN CHRISTIANITY

While true Christian baptism did not begin until John the Baptist, there have been important Jewish rites that have involved purification through water. For instance, the Jewish high priests made it an important part of their role as mediators between God and people. Jewish ritual immersion baths, called *miqva'ot* (singular, *miqveh*), have been discovered during the second half of the twentieth century. For example, archaeologist Yigael Yadin discovered two *miqva'ot* at Masada, the large fortress in Israel built by Herod but occupied by

960 Jews for three years during the Roman destruction of Israel ending in A.D. 70. Other *miqva'ot* have been found near the Temple Mount in Jerusalem. Purification by water was not necessarily a precursor to baptism, as brought out by Christian scholar G. R. Beasley-Murray:

> If proselyte baptism was a universally accepted institution in Judaism before the Christian era, how are we to explain the fact that there is not one clear testimony to it in pre-Christian writings and its complete absence of mention from the writings of Philo, Josephus and the Bible, particularly the New Testament?[11]

Whatever the influence of Jewish proselyte baptism, it must be admitted that the baptism of John the Baptist was more than a ceremonial cleansing. Different from Jewish ritual immersion, Christian baptism is a "one-time ritual that initiates" a person into the group.[12] According to Luke 3:8–14, the baptism of John the Baptist involved a baptism of repentance, a confession of sin, and the need to be morally cleansed. Both the cleansed Jew and the sinful Gentile were commanded to repent and be baptized because their sins stained them. This baptism "symbolized preparation to receive the salvation, the kingdom of God which John heralded, and did not imply entrance into that kingdom itself."[13]

Each of the four Gospel accounts records the narrative of Christ's baptism. Though it was Christ's disciples, not Jesus Himself, who baptized individuals, it is clear that Jesus never minimized the need for baptism in the lives of believers.[14] Even the Great Commission found in Matthew 28:19–20 refers to baptizing the new believers in the name of God the Father, Son, and Holy Spirit.

While some may see baptism as being the instrument of salvation, it should be pointed out that Jesus Himself said in Luke 24:46–47: "Thus it is written . . . that repentance and remission of sins should be preached in his name among all nations." No reference is made to water baptism, but consideration of all the Gospel accounts certainly shows that baptism summed up the Christian believer's new attitude as he or she identified with Christ.

During the next step of Christian history, as chronicled in the Book of Acts, water baptism continued to play an important role. There can be no argument that the normal procedure for those who had confessed Christ as their Savior was baptism with water. This was a willful act done by the new believer to identify with Jesus Christ and His death, burial, and resurrection.

Consider Acts 10:44–47 when the Gentiles first received the Holy Spirit. In verse 44 the Holy Spirit is said to have come upon these Gentiles. In verse 45 the Jews were "astonished" because the Spirit had been poured out even on the Gentiles, a people to whom the gospel was not initially directed. The verbs Luke used to declare that the Spirit had already been given are in the past tense. Then, in verse 46, the Gentile believers were speaking in tongues and praising God. After all of this, Peter declared in verse 47 that the Gentiles should be baptized with water because they had also received the Holy Spirit.

After the time of the apostles, this view was predominant in the historical Christian church. While different viewpoints arose about the formula needed to baptize, Christians considered baptism a most important doctrine. In fact, it was not even considered a possibility to be identified as a Christian without participating in this important rite. Referring to baptism in the early church, Beasley-Murray wrote:

> It would have sounded as strange to a first generation Christian as many other queries characteristic of our time such as, "Is it necessary for a Christian to join the Church? Is it necessary to pray? Is corporate worship necessary? Is preaching necessary? Is the Lord's Supper necessary? Is the Bible necessary?" Such matters are self-evident, for they belong to the very structure of the Christian life.[15]

Christian church historian Dr. Justo Gonzalez noted that the early church in the first few centuries was cautious as to whom they would allow into the fold, making some converts wait for up to three years before they were allowed to be baptized. He wrote:

> In Acts we are told that people were baptized as soon as they were converted. This was feasible in the early Christian community, where most converts came from Judaism or had been influenced by it, and thus had a basic understanding of the meaning of Christian life and proclamation. But, as the Church became increasingly Gentile, it was necessary to require a period of preparation, trial, and instruction prior to baptism. This was the "catechumenate," which, by the beginning of the third century, lasted three years.[16]

Many individual churches believed that baptism was so significant as the identifier of a person with the Christian community that the major doctrines and catechism were taught and memorized by the convert before this initiation ceremony. If baptism equaled salvation, it seems strange that this waiting period would have been enforced.

BIBLE PASSAGES USED BY THE LDS

Certain Bible passages have been misused in an attempt to show that baptism is required for salvation. The following passages are used to support this erroneous doctrine.

- *Mark 16:16:* "He that believeth and is baptized shall be saved; but he that believeth not shall be damned." Assuming that water baptism is meant, then the Mormon needs to explain the second half of the verse. If belief plus baptism truly equals salvation, then why wasn't this formula used when it says that a person who "believeth not" would be condemned? To support the LDS position, this passage should read: "he that believeth not and is baptized not shall be damned." Taken at face value, this says that a lack of *belief,* not a lack of water baptism, is what damns a person. This certainly would be supported by the rest of Scripture (see Acts 4:12; 16:31; Rom. 10:9–10).
- *Luke 3:3:* "And he came into all the country about Jordan, preaching the baptism of repentance for the remission of sins." The word *for* (Greek: *eis*) in "for the remission of sins" can mean *with a view to* or *because of.* Those who responded to John's invitation of baptism had already heard his message of coming judgment and of the "Lamb of God, which taketh away the sin of the world" (John 1:29). They responded to baptism based on the convicting message they had already heard. The word *eis* is also translated *at* in Matthew 12:41, where it says the men of Nineveh "repented *at* the preaching of Jonas." Did the men of Nineveh repent in order *to get* the preaching of Jonas? Or did they repent *because of* the preaching of Jonas? The latter, of course, is the proper answer.
- *John 3:5–6:* "Jesus answered, Verily, verily, I say unto thee, Except a man be born of water and of the Spirit, he cannot enter

into the kingdom of God. That which is born of the flesh is flesh; and that which is born of the Spirit is spirit." We must ask what being "born of water" would have meant to Nicodemus. In his commentary on John, Leon Morris writes:

> Nicodemus could not possibly have perceived an allusion to an as yet non-existent sacrament. It is difficult to think that Jesus would have spoken in such a way that His meaning could not possibly be grasped. His purpose was not to mystify but to enlighten. In any case the whole thrust of the passage is to put the emphasis on the activity of the Spirit, not on any rite of the church.[17]

The emphasis throughout the passage is on the Spirit, with no other reference to water. Verse 6 shows that, as each of us has had a physical birth, so we must have a spiritual birth to enter the kingdom of God.

- *Acts 2:38:* "Repent, and be baptized every one of you in the name of Jesus Christ for the remission of sins." Just as in Luke 3:3, so Peter was encouraging his hearers to be baptized in view of the remission of sins they had received when they were cut to the heart by his message regarding the Christ. It is interesting to note that Peter made no reference to baptism in his next recorded sermon (see Acts 3:19).

- *Acts 22:16:* "And now why tarriest thou? arise, and be baptized, and wash away thy sins, calling on the name of the Lord." Is Ananias stressing the act of water baptism in order to wash away a person's sins? Or is he emphasizing calling on the name of the Lord? In light of the many passages that stress calling on the name of the Lord (see Joel 2:32; Acts 2:21; Rom. 10:13), we must choose the latter interpretation.

- *Romans 6:3–4:* "Know ye not, that so many of us as were baptized into Jesus Christ were baptized into his death? Therefore we are buried with him by baptism into death: that like as Christ was raised up from the dead by the glory of the Father, even so we also should walk in newness of life." There is a strong connection between baptism and the believer's relationship to Christ through His death and resurrection. The use of the aorist (past) tense suggests that, at some specific moment, the believer actually becomes linked to Christ's death and resurrection.

Again, in New Testament times, faith and baptism were so closely identified because they normally took place so closely together. Paul's main message in this passage was that Christians should consider themselves dead to sin but alive in Christ. If the old nature has been washed away through the death and resurrection of Christ, why should the believer allow sin to reign? Baptism symbolizes a person's new identity with Christ.

- *Colossians 2:12–13:* "Buried with him in baptism, wherein also ye are risen with him through the faith of the operation of God, who hath raised him from the dead. And you, being dead in your sins and the uncircumcision of your flesh, hath he quickened together with him, having forgiven you all trespasses." The context of this passage deals with the physical act of circumcision that took place during the Old Testament times. It is significant that the New Testament tends to depreciate the external act of circumcision. It argues that circumcision is to be replaced, not by another external act (e.g., baptism) but by an internal act of the heart. Paul points out that Old Testament circumcision was an outward formality denoting the Judaic faith, but Romans 2:29 says the true Jew "is one inwardly; and circumcision is that of the heart, in the spirit, and not in the letter; whose praise is not of men, but of God." The New Covenant fulfilled the framework of circumcision and the Law.

- *1 Peter 3:18–20:* "For Christ also hath once suffered for sins, the just for the unjust, that he might bring us to God, being put to death in the flesh, but quickened by the Spirit: by which also he went and preached unto the spirits in prison; which sometime were disobedient, when once the longsuffering of God waited in the days of Noah, while the ark was a preparing, wherein few, that is, eight souls were saved by water." Baptism "saves" only in that it is "an appeal to God," an act of faith acknowledging dependence on Him. Verse 21 says that it comes not by washing of water but by an appeal to God. Christian author Bob L. Ross states that there is a four-step process of how both the ark and the ordinance of baptism symbolize the Christian's salvation in Christ:

1. The ark's occupants were inside *before* the waters came; the believer is likewise "in Christ" *before* water baptism.
2. The ark containing the occupants was surrounded by the waters of the flood, with water beneath and rain above; likewise, those in Christ go into the water.
3. Those in the ark had a resurrection from the waters; similarly, the believer is resurrected out of the water.
4. Those in the ark left behind their former world and started afresh; so also the believer, having risen from the waters of baptism, now goes forth to walk in newness of life.[18]

It needs to be remembered that baptism, like partaking of the Lord's Supper, is a work. It is something that an individual must personally perform. As such, it is not a requirement for receiving salvation under the guidelines of Ephesians 2:8–9. "For by grace are ye saved through faith; and that not of yourselves: it is the gift of God: not of works, lest any man should boast."

CONCLUSION

The Sacrament and baptism, according to Mormonism:

- The Sacrament is made up of bread and water
- Water baptism is a requirement for salvation
- Water baptism must be performed by a person with authority in the LDS Church

The Lord's Supper/Eucharist and baptism, according to Christianity:

- Bread and wine or grape juice are used in the ordinance of Holy Communion
- Water baptism is a vital part of the Christian practice, but a person receives salvation through faith alone
- The validity of water baptism depends on the person receiving it, not on the church or person performing the ordinance

The Word of Wisdom

SALVATION AND A CUP OF TEA. You cannot neglect little things. "Oh, a cup of tea is such a little thing. It is so little; surely it doesn't amount to much; surely the Lord will forgive me if I drink a cup of tea." If you drink coffee or tea, or take tobacco, are you letting a cup of tea, or a little tobacco stand in the road and bar you from the celestial kingdom of God, where you might otherwise have received a fullness of glory?

President Joseph Fielding Smith,
Doctrines of Salvation 2:16

The introduction to section 89 of the *Doctrine and Covenants* states:

Revelation given through Joseph Smith the Prophet, at Kirtland, Ohio, February 27, 1833. HC 1:327–329. As a consequence of the early brethren using tobacco in their meetings, the Prophet was led to ponder upon the matter; consequently he inquired of the Lord concerning it. This revelation, known as the Word of Wisdom, was the result.

So important is the Word of Wisdom to the faithful Latter-day Saint that, unless it is followed, no Mormon is allowed to enter the sacred LDS temple. This health code encompasses much more than the use of tobacco, however. It also covers use of such substances as alcohol, hot drinks, and meat. A close look at the Word of Wisdom doctrine reveals that few (if any) Mormons truly keep the Word of Wisdom as it was said to be given to Smith in 1833. Furthermore, documentation from LDS sources show that important Mormon leaders who emphasized the adherence to this doctrine broke it themselves.

THE WORD OF WISDOM DEFINED

According to *D&C* 89:3, the Word of Wisdom is "a principle with [a] promise, adapted to the capacity of the weak." This did not become a "command" for eighteen years, until it was proposed in 1851 by President Brigham Young.[1] If this was such an important teaching, it seems strange that it was not a command from God when this revelation was first given. Verse 5 reads: "That inasmuch as any man drinketh wine or strong drink among you, behold it is not good, neither meet in the sight of your Father, only in assembling yourselves together *to offer up your sacraments* before him."[2]

As previously mentioned, wine was to be used "to offer up your sacraments" when the church members gathered together, but the LDS Church advocates the use of water, not wine, in its celebration of the Lord's Supper. Verses 7–9 of the Word of Wisdom say:

> And again, strong drinks are not for the belly, but for the washing of your bodies. And again, tobacco is not for the body, neither for the belly, and is not good for man, but is an herb for bruises and all sick cattle, to be used with judgment and skill. And again, hot drinks are not for the body or belly.

It is not known how many Latter-day Saints wash their bodies with strong drinks, but the passage referring to "hot drinks" has been used as a prohibition against coffee and tea. George Q. Cannon, a member of the First Presidency under Brigham Young, took this admonition even further when he included chocolate, cocoa, and even soup on this list:

> We are told, and very plainly too, that hot drinks—tea, coffee, chocolate, cocoa and all drinks of this kind are not good for man. . . . We must not permit [our children] to drink liquor, or hot drinks, or hot soups or to use tobacco or other articles that are injurious.[3]

While most Mormons say caffeine is their reason not to drink coffee and tea, an article in the *Salt Lake Tribune* states that 90 percent of adults in North America consume caffeine on a regular basis through other products. While not covered in the Word of Wisdom, a cola soft drink may contain as much as forty milligrams of caffeine![4]

Continuing, *D&C* 89:12–13 says:

> Yea, flesh also of beasts and of the fowls of the air, I, the Lord, have ordained for the use of man with thanksgiving; nevertheless they are to be used sparingly; And it is pleasing unto me that they should not be used, only in times of winter, or of cold, or famine.

If meat is only to be eaten in times of winter or cold, are we to believe that those members who live in tropical or moderate climates never partake of meat? Does a season of the year really define when meat should be eaten? While a person might be able to make a case against the regular ingestion of fatty meats, the mention of "fowls of the air" raises another question. If regular consumption of these animals is so wrong, why did God Himself provide the children of Israel with quail on a daily basis during their wilderness journey to Canaan (Num. 11:31)? Consider also that once they arrived in the land of promise, God encouraged the Israelites to eat as much meat as their hearts desired (Deut. 12:15, 20). Mormon writer John J. Stewart admits, "The admonition to eat little meat is largely ignored, as are some other points of the revelation."[5]

While Christians cannot accept the Word of Wisdom as playing a role in a person's salvation, the importance of good health should not be minimized. Paul taught in 1 Corinthians 6:19 that our bodies are "temple(s) of the Holy Ghost." This is why many Christians abstain from tobacco, alcohol, and other destructive substances.[6] Exercise, a proper diet, and getting proper rest are just some of the important things Christians should consider in order to be fully fit and available to do the work of God.

Doctrine and Covenants section 89 ends with a pledge that states, "And I, the Lord, give unto them a promise, that the destroying angel shall pass by them, as the children of Israel, and not slay them. Amen." Clearly this passage is a reference to the original Passover as recorded in Exodus 12. Whether the destroying angel is something that should seriously concern a Latter-day Saint could be debated since angels sent specifically for the purpose of destruction are extremely rare in the Bible (e.g., Num. 22:21–35; 1 Chron. 21:15–30; Isa. 37:36–37). Some Mormon leaders have stated that verse 21 in section 89 of the *D&C* is not implying that Latter-day Saints shall never die. They insist that while many faithful LDS people have passed away, it should not be assumed that a "destroying angel" was responsible, since destroying angels only strike the disobedient and unrighteous.

HYPOCRISY IN THE LDS LEADERSHIP

If the principle known as the Word of Wisdom is a principle delivered by God, then why have Mormonism's leaders not always been faithful to it? For instance, Joseph Smith often used tobacco and liquor. He even stated:

> We then partook of some refreshments, and our *hearts were made glad* by the fruit of the vine. . . . Elders Orson Hyde, Luke S. Johnson, and Warren Parrish, then presented the Presidency with three servers of glasses filled with wine, to bless. . . . It was then passed round in order, the cake in the same order; and suffice it to say, our *hearts were made glad* while partaking of the bounty of earth which was presented, until we had taken our fill.[7]

According to the 22 January 1935 *Saint's Herald,* a newspaper owned by the Independence, Missouri–based Reorganized Church of Jesus Christ of Latter-day Saints, Smith ran a tavern from his home. His wife, Emma, disapproved and ordered him to get rid of it, which he did. Early Mormon Oliver B. Huntington told of one story concerning Smith and a man named Robert Thompson. Smith told Thompson that he should "get drunk and have a good spree. If you don't you will die." Robert did not do it. He was a very pious exemplary man and never guilty of such an impropriety as he thought that to be. In less than two weeks he was dead and buried.[8]

Mormon Church leaders and historians have sanitized some things in LDS publications to protect the reputation of their founding prophet. For instance, Joseph Smith is quoted as saying: "It was reported to me that some of the brethren had been drinking whisky that day in violation of the Word of Wisdom. I called the brethren in and investigated the case, and was satisfied that no evil had been done."⁹ The original account found in the *Millennial Star* adds these words: "and gave them a couple of dollars, with directions to replenish the bottle to stimulate them in the fatigues of their sleepless journey."¹⁰

Apparently, keeping the Word of Wisdom was difficult for many early Latter-day Saints. In 1873 Brigham Young reported that the cooperative store in Utah "was doing a great business in tea, coffee and tobacco."¹¹ On 10 March 1860 Young rebuked the LDS men for chewing tobacco in the semiannual conference and spitting it on the floor but came short of calling their habit "sin." He said:

> Many of the brethren chew tobacco, and I have advised them to be modest about it. . . . If you must use tobacco, put a small portion in your mouth when no person sees you, and be careful that no one sees you chew it. I do not charge you with sin. You have the "Word of Wisdom." Read it.¹²

Young's hesitancy to call this act a sin is noteworthy. Even though Smith revealed the Word of Wisdom in 1833, its observance did not become a requirement for entrance into a temple until almost a century later. According to the *Encyclopedia of Mormonism:*

> There is evidence that Church Presidents John Taylor, Joseph F. Smith, and Heber J. Grant wanted to promote adherence to the Word of Wisdom as a precondition for entering LDS temples or holding office in any Church organization; and indeed, by 1930 abstinence from the use of alcohol, tobacco, coffee, and tea had become an official requirement for those seeking temple recommends. While abstinence from these substances is now required for temple attendance and for holding priesthood offices or other Church callings, no other ecclesiastical sanctions are imposed on those who do not comply with the Word of Wisdom.¹³

While he did discourage the use of tobacco, Young seemed to be more concerned about the amount of money being spent on these substances. On 9 October 1865 he said:

> What I am now about to say is on the subject of the use of tobacco. Let us raise our own tobacco, or quit using it. In the years [18]'49, '50, '51, '52, and '53, and so long as I kept myself posted respecting the amount expended yearly by this people at the stores for articles of merchandise,

we spend upwards of 100,000 dollars a year for tobacco alone! We now spend considerably more than we did then.[14]

Many Mormons maintain that the supposed revelation from God as found in *D&C* 89 affirms Smith's position as a true prophet who recognized the dangers of tobacco, alcohol, and caffeine many years before the medical profession understood their effects. Dr. James Mason, a Mormon who was the director of the Centers for Disease Control in Atlanta, Georgia, said, "Few revelations have come under more scrutiny than this 'word of wisdom,' and few have served as well to vindicate Joseph Smith's calling as a prophet."[15]

While this may sound reasonable, it is far from the truth. What is not mentioned by these Mormons who boast about Smith's "revelation" is that the Word of Wisdom ideas were being advocated by others during the time of Joseph Smith. According to Dean D. McBrien, one group called the American Temperance Society was successful in "eliminating a distillery in Kirtland [OH] on February 1, 1833, just twenty-seven days before the Latter-day Saint revelation counseling abstinence was announced, and that the distillery at Mentor, near Kirtland, was also closed at the same time."[16]

Three years before the Word of Wisdom revelation, the 6 November 1829 edition of the *Wayne Sentinel,* which was published in the neighborhood where Smith grew up, talked about tobacco as being "an absolute poison." Regarding alcoholic drinks, warnings had been given years before by the temperance movement. It is extremely possible that Smith picked up his ideas from these other sources.

CONCLUSION

The Word of Wisdom, according to Mormonism:

- Is a health code practiced by the faithful Latter-day Saint
- Is a definite requirement for temple entrance
- Among other things, disallows the use of alcohol, drugs, smoking or chewing tobacco, or drinking certain drinks, including coffee and tea
- Was not followed by certain early LDS leaders

The Temple

Every foundation stone that is laid for a temple, and every temple completed according to the order the Lord has revealed for His holy priesthood, lessens the power of Satan on the earth, and increases the power of God and godliness, moves the heavens in mighty power in our behalf, invokes and calls down upon us the blessings of eternal gods, and those who reside in their presence.

Member of the First Presidency George Q. Cannon,
Logan Temple Dedication, 1877

Unlike the chapels where Mormons regularly meet to conduct worship services, LDS temples are places where worthy Mormons—known as patrons—attend to perform "sacred" works for both themselves and those who have already died, including deceased relatives. Mormons believe that God presides over the ceremonies in each of these temples scattered throughout the world. Among the rites are the endowment ceremony, baptisms for the dead, eternal marriages, and sealings of families for time and eternity.

The importance of the LDS temple and its ceremonies cannot be overstressed, for it is only by participating in the temple ritual that a faithful Latter-day Saint hopes to achieve exaltation and godhood.

ONLY THE WORTHY

When they are first built, Mormon temples are opened to the general public in an "open house" format for a short time. After this, the temple is then dedicated by LDS general authorities and reopened only to worthy members. A member is considered worthy if he or she holds a "temple recommend." The recommend is an identification card, which is renewed annually by the individual's bishop. Qualifying criteria include full payment of tithes, regular attendance to ward meetings, wearing temple garments under regular clothing, and an agreement to obey the Word of Wisdom.[1]

The temple has been called the faithful Mormon's "home." President Joseph Fielding Smith wrote:

> *If you would become a son or a daughter of God and an heir of the kingdom, then you must go to the house of the Lord and receive blessings which there can be obtained and which cannot be obtained elsewhere; and you must keep those commandments and those covenants to the end.* . . . The sons and daughters are not outside in some other kingdom. The sons and daughters go into the house, belong to the household, have access to the home. . . . Sons and daughters have access to the home where he dwells, and you cannot receive that access until you go to the temple.[2]

THE INSIDE WORKS OF THE LDS TEMPLE

There are a number of rites performed within the Mormon temple. Mormons are encouraged to perform these ceremonies for themselves, and once they have been completed, Mormons begin work on behalf of dead relatives and friends. By performing these ceremonies on behalf of those who have already died, they hope that these people will be able to improve their eternal standing as they await the judgment in "spirit prison." There are six major parts to these works: washing and anointing, new names, temple garments and the pre-endowment instructions, the endowment ceremony, baptism for the dead, and marriage for time and eternity.

WASHING AND ANOINTING

The first time patrons (temple participants) go through the temple, they go through an ordinance called "washing and anointing." After showing a temple recommend and gaining entrance into the temple, the temple participant first enters the men's or women's locker room, where street clothes are replaced with a poncholike "shield" that is open on both sides. Wearing nothing but the shield, the patron enters an area of the temple that contains the washing and anointing rooms. Here a temple worker ceremonially touches or "washes" and blesses the patron, making reference to various parts of his or her body. Men are separated from the women during this ceremony. Two temple workers lay hands on the member's head, and one of the workers prayerfully "confirms" the washing. The member is ceremonially anointed with olive oil, and then the anointing is confirmed.

TEMPLE GARMENTS AND NEW NAMES

After the washing and anointing, the patron is taken into a small curtained room. At this point, a temple worker actually puts the temple garment on the patron. Sewn into this "garment of the holy priesthood" are markings similar to those used in Freemasonry. Over the right breast is a mark that resembles a backward *L,* and over the left breast is a mark that resembles a capital *V.* Sewn over the abdomen and over the knee area is another marking that looks like an ordinary buttonhole.

After placing the "garment" on the patron and removing the "shield," the patron is given a new name as part of the ceremony. This name is considered sacred and never to be revealed, except at a certain time later in the ceremony. All men entering the temple on the same day are given the same name; the same is true for women.[3] These names are usually taken from either the Bible or the *Book of Mormon.* Historically, Mormon leaders have taught that the husband has the ability to call his wife from the grave by her new name on resurrection day. Every Mormon husband who has been through the temple is told his wife's "new name," though she is not permitted to know his. According to Charles W. Penrose, who later became a First Counselor to Heber J. Grant:

In the resurrection, they stand side by side and hold dominion together. Every man who overcomes all things and is thereby entitled to inherit all things, receives power to bring up his wife to join him in the possession and enjoyment thereof.[4]

In 1857 Apostle Erastus Snow proclaimed:

Do you uphold your husband before God as your lord? "What!—my husband to be my lord?" I ask, Can you get into the celestial kingdom without him? Have any of you been there? You will remember that you never got into the celestial kingdom without the aid of your husband. If you did, it was because your husband was away, and some one had to act proxy for him. No woman will get into the celestial kingdom, except her husband receives her, if she is worthy to have a husband; and if not, somebody will receive her as a servant.[5]

PRE-ENDOWMENT INSTRUCTIONS

After returning to the locker room and putting on white temple clothing over their garments, patrons are then welcomed to the temple and reminded to be "alert, attentive, and reverent during the presentation of the endowment." Patrons are told that if they are "true and faithful," the day will come when they will be called up and will be anointed "kings and queens, priests and priestesses."

During this time, further explanations of their temple garments are given. Patrons are told that their obedience to the covenants they are to make, along with their wearing the temple garments, will protect them. These garments are said to "be a shield, and a protection to you against the power of the destroyer until you have finished your work here on earth." By wearing these garments at all times, it is taught that the individual Mormon, depending on his or her faithfulness, is protected both physically and spiritually. For instance, President Spencer W. Kimball said on 31 May 1948:

Temple garments afford protection. I am sure one could go to extreme in worshiping the cloth of which the garment is made, but one could also go to the other extreme. Though generally I think our protection is a mental, spiritual, moral one, yet I am convinced that there could be and undoubtedly have been many cases where there has been, through faith, an actual physical protection, so we must not minimize that possibility.[6]

Wearing the garments is an indication of a person's righteousness. Seventy Carlos E. Asay thinks "of the garment as the Lord's way of letting us take part of the temple with us when we leave."[7] He wrote:

A few years ago, in a seminar for new temple presidents and matrons, Elder James E. Faust, then of the Quorum of the Twelve Apostles, told about his being called to serve as a General Authority. He was asked only one question by President Harold B. Lee: "Do you wear the garments properly?" to which he answered in the affirmative. He then asked if President Lee wasn't going to ask him about his worthiness. President Lee replied that he didn't need to, for he had learned from experience that how one wears the garment is the expression of how the individual feels about the Church and everything that relates to it. It is a measure of one's worthiness and devotion to the gospel.[8]

After quoting from Ephesians 6, Asay said the garment symbolized a part of the armor of God:

There is, however, another piece of armor worthy of our consideration. It is the special underclothing known as the temple garment, or garment of the holy priesthood. . . . This garment, worn day and night, serves three important purposes: it is a reminder of the sacred covenants made with the Lord in His holy house, a protective covering for the body, and a symbol of the modesty of dress and living that should characterize the lives of all the humble followers of Christ. . . . The piece of armor called the temple garment not only provides the comfort and warmth of a cloth covering, it also strengthens the wearer to resist temptation, fend off evil influences, and stand firmly for the right.[9]

In a letter to priesthood leaders on 19 October 1988, Mormons were told:

Church members who have been clothed with the garment in the temple have made a covenant to wear it throughout their lives. This has been interpreted to mean that it is worn as underclothing both day and night. . . . The fundamental principle ought to be to wear the garment and not to find occasions to remove it. Thus, members should not remove either all or part of the garment to work in the yard or to lounge around the home in swimwear or immodest clothing. Nor should they remove it to participate in recreational activities that can reasonably be done with the garment worn properly beneath regular clothing. When the garment must be removed, such as for swimming, it should be restored as soon as possible.[10]

Mormons who remain true to the faith and wear the garments believe they will be protected. There are numerous testimonies to how these garments have allegedly saved Mormons' lives. For instance, Bill Marriott of the Marriott hotel chain told CBS *60 Minutes* interviewer Mike Wallace in 1996 that his garment had protected him in a boat fire. Despite the testimonies of Mormons who believe their garment has protected them from physical harm, it should be pointed out that there are seemingly faithful Mormons who wear their garment and yet are killed or injured every day.

There is also no biblical support for this unusual practice. In the Old Testament, only priests from the line of Levi and not the common Jew wore the linen undergarments. Still, we find no biblical support for the notion that the priestly garments offered any special protection as described by various LDS authorities. In the New Testament, the Christian is told to have his "loins girt about with truth" and to put on the "breastplate of righteousness." However, such metaphorical language never implies that we should trust in actual physical objects. It appears that the idea of protective undergarments falls into the same category as the proverbial rabbit's foot or talisman.

THE ENDOWMENT CEREMONY

This ceremony is performed for both the living and the dead where "certain special, spiritual blessings [are] given [to] worthy and faithful saints in the temples . . . because in and through them the recipients are endowed with power from on high."[11] The ceremony includes a type of melodrama to explain the LDS view of the creation and fall of humanity. These dramas were originally performed by Mormon temple workers playing such parts as that of Elohim (God the Father), Jehovah (Jesus), and Lucifer. Video is utilized today in most temples.

The ordinance ceremony is made up of different sections. These include the following: the creation and fall, where the Mormon God sends "Jehovah" and "Michael" to organize unorganized matter into a world "like unto the other worlds" that have previously been formed; the law of obedience, when patrons vow to live up to the full law of God; the law of the gospel and the law of chastity, when additional vows are made; the law of consecration, when patrons consecrate themselves, their time, talents, and "everything with which the Lord has blessed them." As the vows are made, the patrons learn special handshakes, called "tokens," along with secret "signs" and "words" that they are told will be needed in the afterlife for admittance into heaven.

The temple ceremony was supposed to have been given to Joseph Smith and was to never change. Apostle John Widtsoe stated, "Joseph Smith received the temple endowment and its ritual, as all else he promulgated, by revelation from God."[12] Seventy Royden Derrick wrote:

> Temple ordinances instituted in the heavens before the foundation of the world are for the salvation and exaltation of God's children. It is important that the saving ordinances not be altered or changed, because all of those who will be exalted, from the first man, Adam, to the last, must be saved on the same principles.[13]

Despite the fact that Joseph Smith himself said that God "set the ordinances to be the same forever and ever,"[14] the LDS Church has continuously changed the ceremony over the years. It quietly made many drastic changes in April 1990. One such change concerned the portion where Lucifer hired a Christian minister to preach false doctrine. The false doctrine this character was preaching was ironically called "the orthodox religion." In the pre-1990 ceremony, Lucifer himself interviewed the pastor to see if he had "been to college and received training for the ministry."

If this pastor would covenant to convert people to his "orthodox religion," Lucifer promised, "I will pay you well." Adam and Eve were introduced to the pastor as those who "desire religion." The preacher then attempted to convince Adam to believe in a God surrounded by a myriad of beings who had been "saved by grace," in a God who filled the universe but was still so small that He could dwell in a person's heart.

Adam, the "good guy" in the scenario, rejects the pastor's teachings on God, salvation by grace alone, and the reality of hell. The entire scene was offensive because it was intended to make the Christian pastors look like they were in the employ of Satan. All mention of this scene was entirely dropped, and Mormons who did not enter the temple before 1990 may know nothing about it.[15]

BAPTISM FOR THE DEAD

The most often practiced ordinance in the Mormon temple is vicarious baptism for the dead. So important is this ritual that to neglect it can actually result in the Mormon losing his or her salvation. President Joseph Fielding Smith wrote:

> But greater than all this, so far as our individual responsibilities are concerned, the greatest is to become saviors, in our lesser degree which is assigned us, for the dead who have died without a knowledge of the Gospel. Joseph Smith said: "The greatest responsibility in this world that God has laid upon us, is to seek after our dead." . . . It will suffice here to say that the Lord has placed upon us this responsibility of seeing that our dead receive the blessings of the Gospel. Said Joseph Smith: "Those saints who neglect it, in behalf of their deceased relatives, do it at the peril of their own salvation."[16]

Since Christianity was said to be dead in apostasy from the time after the apostles until the nineteenth century, faithful living Mormons are baptized on behalf of all non-Mormons who have passed away. This takes place in a font resembling the description of King Solomon's "brazen sea."[17] Normally located in the lower part of the temple, the font is situated on top of twelve life-size oxen, which are said to symbolize the twelve tribes of Israel.

Mormons participating in the temple ceremony on behalf of the dead view their work as a means of binding the family unit together. President John Taylor said "we are the only people that know how to save our progenitors, how to save ourselves, and how to save our posterity in the celestial kingdom of God."[18] Today the doctrine continues to be most important for families:

> The glad message of the restored gospel of Jesus Christ is that ordinances performed in the temples of the Lord conditionally guarantee that these

family relationships can continue for eternity. . . . The events surrounding the Lord's death and resurrection clearly demonstrate that there is a place to which we go after we die where we await our resurrection and subsequent entry into "heaven." . . . Just as Jesus performed a labor for us that we could not perform for ourselves, so can we perform the ordinance of baptism for those who have died, allowing them the opportunity to become heirs of salvation.[19]

Since their work can help "save" those who have passed away, this doctrine should motivate living Mormons. Theodore M. Burton, a member of the Seventy, taught:

Thus, those living today must perform the physical ordinance work on the earth that will qualify persons in the spirit world to receive that proxy work done for them, even as we living today receive the proxy work done for us by Jesus Christ. In other words, we work in partnership here on the earth with those missionaries in the spirit world who preach the gospel of Jesus Christ to those persons living in the spirit world, that they might be judged according to men in the flesh. This combination effort can free them from their spiritual prison and heal their bruised souls through Jesus Christ. This is why the members of the Church who can qualify through righteous living must go to the temple in ever-increasing numbers and why they must attend the temple more frequently than they have ever done in the past.[20]

By 1997 there were an estimated 140 million proxy temple endowments for the dead, so only "about .13 percent (just over one-tenth of 1 percent) of the earth's estimated historic population of 105 billion" have had this ordinance done on their behalf.[21] Part of the problem is that numerous genealogical records from many generations have been destroyed or lost. Another reason is that there are so many people who have lived in this world, yet there are comparatively so few Mormons and temples. Mormonism's leaders have taught that this work will continue throughout the millennial reign of Christ.[22]

Despite the huge emphasis on this doctrine, Christianity teaches that salvation is offered to the living. The Bible is very clear in Hebrews 9:27 that judgment follows this life. Further hope of attaining favor with God is lost at death. In fact, Paul wrote in 2 Corinthians 6:2 that "now is the accepted time; behold, now is the day of salvation."

Although Mormons like to reference 1 Corinthians 15:29 to support this doctrine, there is no evidence that Christians actually participated in a rite that is similar to that practiced by Mormons. While biblical scholars have noted that heretical groups such as the Cerinthians and Marcionites practiced a form of baptism for the dead, Paul separated himself from such as these when he said, "Else what shall *they* do which are baptized for the dead, if the dead rise not at all? why are *they* then baptized for the dead?" (emphasis added). If baptism for the dead was, as *D&C* 128:17 puts it, the "most glorious of all subjects belonging to the everlasting gospel," it seems odd that Paul would not include himself as a participant.[23]

Another interesting point comes from D. A. Carson, a research professor of New Testament at Trinity Evangelical Divinity School in Deerfield, Illinois. He wrote:

> When something is mentioned only once, it cannot be given the same weight of importance as the central themes of Scripture. . . . When something is mentioned only once, there is more likelihood of misinterpreting it, whereas matters repeatedly discussed are clarified by their repetition in various contexts.[24]

MARRIAGE FOR TIME AND ETERNITY

Traditionally, "celestial marriages" of LDS couples for "time and eternity" take place in the temples.[25] This is an important teaching, since "only in the temple can we be sealed together forever as families."[26] Marriages performed outside of the temple are considered binding only "until death."

Eternal increase, or the ability to procreate throughout eternity, is a much sought-after goal of the faithful Mormon. According to the *History of the Church,* Joseph Smith said the following on 16 May 1843:

> Except a man and his wife enter into an everlasting covenant and be married for eternity, while in this probation, by the power and authority of the Holy Priesthood, they will cease to increase when they die; that is, they will not have any children after the resurrection. But those who are mar-

ried by the power and authority of the priesthood in this life, and continue without committing the sin against the Holy Ghost, will continue to increase and have children in the celestial glory.[27]

On 6 April 1845 Brigham Young declared:

And I would say, as no man can be perfect without the woman, so no woman can be perfect without a man to lead her, I tell you the truth as it is in the bosom of eternity; and I say so to every man upon the face of the earth; if he wishes to be saved he cannot be saved without a woman by his side.[28]

In an article titled "Temples and Eternal Marriage," President Spencer W. Kimball taught that the apostasy was the reason why Christians have not practiced this teaching. He wrote:

The way is well defined and clear. Eternal marriage was known to Adam and others of the prophets, but the knowledge was lost from the earth for many centuries. God has restored the truths and has provided the way. . . . It is inconceivable that otherwise intelligent, astute, and highly educated people should ignore or willfully disregard this great privilege. The doors can be unlocked. The gap can be bridged. And men can walk safely, securely, to never-ending happiness, making their marriages timeless and eternal.[29]

Indeed, "the full measure of progression in eternity is unattainable without the perpetuity of the family organization."[30] Combined with keeping "the covenant made in connection with this holy and perfect order of matrimony," celestial marriage is essential in this life.[31] According to *D&C* 131:2–4:

And in order to obtain the highest, a man must enter into this order of the priesthood [meaning the new and everlasting covenant of marriage]; And if he does not, he cannot obtain it. He may enter into the other, but that is the end of his kingdom; he cannot have an increase.[32]

D&C 132:20 says this allows them to become

gods, because they have no end; therefore shall they be from everlasting to everlasting, because they continue; then shall they be above all, because all things are subject unto them. Then shall they be gods, because they have all power and the angels are subject unto them.

Children born to a couple married in the temple are automatically "sealed" for eternity to their parents. Those couples not married in the temple will not only lose the right to be together after death, but they have no "claim upon their children, for they have not been born under the covenant of eternal marriage."[33] Quoting from *D&C* 132:17, which says that those who do not obey will "not (be) gods, but are angels of God forever and ever," President Kimball declared that such a fate was to be mourned:

> How conclusive! How bounded! How limiting! And we come to realize again as it bears heavily upon us that this time, this life, this mortality is the time to prepare to meet God. How lonely and barren will be the so-called single blessedness throughout eternity! How sad to be separate and single and apart through countless ages when one could, by meeting requirements, have happy marriage for eternity by marrying in the temple by proper authority and continue on in ever-increasing joy and happiness, growth, and development.[34]

Those not born "under the covenant" of celestial marriage must have their families "sealed" in a separate temple ceremony. President Howard W. Hunter wrote: "If children are born before the wife is sealed to her husband, there is a temple sealing ordinance that can seal these children to their parents for eternity, and so it is that children can be sealed vicariously to parents who have passed away."[35]

By itself, though, temple marriage does not guarantee exaltation. Joseph Fielding Smith also said: *"Blessings pronounced upon couples in connection with celestial marriage are conditioned upon the subsequent faithfulness of the participating parties."*[36] President Kimball added, "An eternal marriage plus a worthy continuing consecrated life will bring limitless happiness and exaltation."[37]

Although continued good works are essential, Mormonism teaches that a person must be married in the temple to have a chance at exaltation. But what happens if a person does not get married, for whatever reason, and dies single? Apparently this person is destined not to become a god. Smith was very clear about "celestial marriage (being) essential to exaltation" when he said:

> Another thing that we must not forget in this great plan of redemption and exaltation, is that *a man must have a wife, and a woman a husband, to receive the fulness of exaltation.* They must be sealed for time and for all eternity in a temple; then their union will last forever, and they cannot be separated because God has joined them together, as he taught the Pharisees. . . . The Lord has commanded us, as it is recorded in the revelations, that marriage among members of the Church should be performed in his holy house, and not for time only, but for time and all eternity. Therefore, those who are satisfied to receive a ceremony for time only, uniting them for this life, and are content with that, are *ignorant* of this fundamental principle of the gospel and its consequences, or they are in *rebellion* against the commandments of the Lord.[38]

Talking to the youth, President Ezra Taft Benson said:

> If youth are going to inherit the highest degree of glory in the celestial kingdom, this means marriage for time and all eternity in the temples of God. That is the only plan that has been provided by our Heavenly Father. We want them to keep their covenants after they have been in those sacred places. We want them to marry in the Church and to marry in the temple of God.[39]

In the LDS Church–produced student manual *Achieving a Celestial Marriage,* a story is told to show how essential this teaching is. When an unmarried Mormon man asked what the "law of exaltation" was, he was told:

> Well, it involves the whole of the gospel law. Everything required of us by God is associated with this law, but the major crowning point of the law which man must obey is eternal marriage. Therein lies the keys of eternal life or, as the Doctrine and Covenants puts it, "eternal lives."[40]

When the man was asked if he realized "the implications of this doctrine," he stated, "I think so. If God became God by obedience to all of the gospel law with the crowning point being the celestial law of marriage, then that's the only way I can become a god." "Right," was the response. Later, when asked what would happen to someone who obeyed the entire gospel law except for eternal marriage, the young man realized the answer: "They still could not be gods. Now I understand. Celestial marriage is the crowning ordinance of the gospel." Again, he was told, "Right."[41]

According to Apostle Bruce McConkie, singleness and divorce are possible ways a person could lose exaltation status.

> By definition and in its nature, exaltation consists in the continuation of the family unit through all ages yet to be. If the family unit continues, if husband and wife go into the spirit world as a married couple and come up in the resurrection continuing as husband and wife, then exaltation is assured. If they go there separately and singly—either not having entered into this celestial order or, having entered into it, having not kept the terms and conditions and laws that appertain to it—they will have immortality only and not eternal life.[42]

Apostle John A. Widtsoe wrote that the union of two people need not be limited to just the living:

> Several approaches to eternal marriage may be made: Two living person [sic] may be sealed to each other for time and eternity. A living man may be sealed for eternity to a dead woman; or a living woman to a dead man. Two dead persons may be sealed to each other. It is also possible, though the Church does not now permit it, to seal two living people for eternity only, with no association on earth.[43]

JESUS AND THE SADDUCEES

In an account given in the Synoptic Gospels, Jesus was approached by members of the Sadducees, the Jewish religious party that did not believe in a bodily resurrection from the dead (Matt. 22:23–33; Mark 12:18–27; Luke 20:27–28). Trying to trick Him, these leaders presented what appears to be a hypothetical situation involving seven brothers. When the oldest brother died, he left a wife and no children. As was the custom in those days, the next oldest unmarried brother took the woman for his wife. However, the second brother died, as did the third through seventh brothers. Before they died, each of them had married the old-est brother's wife, making her a widow seven times over.

In Mark 12:23 they asked, "In the resurrection therefore, when they shall rise, whose wife shall she be of them? for the seven had her to wife." Jesus chastised His inquisitors in verse 24, saying they did not know the Scriptures. "For when they shall rise from the dead, they neither marry, nor are given in marriage; but are as the angels which are in heaven" (v. 25).[44]

At face value and as it has been historically interpreted, Jesus appears to be saying that heaven will be much different from life as it is known on earth. While the gifts of sex and procreation are impor-tant parts of the earthly life, these will not be a part of the afterlife. The joys in store for the believer are incredibly more magnificent than the temporary pleasure of sexual fulfillment.

In addition, there will be no need to procreate in heaven. Thus, while it appears we will be able to recognize fellow believers in heaven, there is no indication from the Bible that we will be eternally paired with a particular mate. Historically, Christians view all believ-ers as part of God's great family rather than millions of smaller groups. However, Mormon leaders have interpreted this passage quite differ-ently than the historic Christian view. McConkie wrote:

> What then is the Master Teacher affirming by saying, "in the resurrection they neither marry, nor are given in marriage, but are as the angels of God in heaven"? He is not denying but limiting the prevailing concept that there will be marrying and giving in marriage in heaven. He is saying that as far as "they" (the Sadducees) are concerned, that as far as "they" ("the chil-dren of this world") are concerned, the family unit does not and will not continue in the resurrection. Because he does not choose to cast his pearls before swine, and because the point at issue is not marriage but resurrec-tion anyway, Jesus does not here amplify his teaching to explain that there is marrying and giving of marriage in heaven only for those who live the fulness of gospel law—a requirement which excludes worldly people.[45]

Saying that this was not "the Lord's final word on the subject," David H. Yarn Jr., a BYU professor emeritus of philosophy and reli-gion, said, "The Lord did not say there would be no people in the mar-ried state in the resurrection but that there would be no marriages made

in the resurrection."[46] Some Mormon leaders have read their own inter-
pretations into this passage, explaining that the fictional wife in the
parable had been eternally sealed to the first husband. For instance,
Apostle James E. Talmage wrote:

> The Lord's meaning was clear, that in the resurrected state there can be
> no question among the seven brothers as to whose wife for eternity the
> woman shall be, since all except the first had married her for the duration
> of mortal life only, and primarily for the purpose of perpetuating in mor-
> tality the name and family of the brother who first died.[47]

While these explanations may sound good to a Mormon audience
that cherishes the institution of marriage, the ability to read between
the lines of Jesus' teaching does not make a doctrine true. Mormon
leaders are unable to provide any additional support from the Bible
as to the importance of an "everlasting principle" and "eternal covenant" known as celestial marriage. How many people would, on reading this Synoptic Gospel account alone in conjunction with the teachings of the Bible, exclaim, "This proves the biblical principle of eternal
marriage"? Rather than supporting the view of eternal marriage, Jesus
explained that the institution of marriage was for this life only and not
the life to come. To assume anything more is biblically and exegeti-
cally unsound.

THE MASONIC AND OCCULTIC BACKGROUND OF THE CEREMONY

Because those who have participated in the LDS temple endowment ceremony make a covenant to not talk about what goes on inside
LDS temples, it is often asserted that this is a "secret ceremony." However, many Mormons become offended by this description, claiming
that the ceremony is not "secret" but rather "sacred." Apostle Boyd K.
Packer wrote:

> A careful reading of the scriptures reveals that the Lord did not tell all
> things to all people. There were some qualifications set that were prereq-
> uisite to receiving sacred information. Temple ceremonies fall within this

category. We do not discuss the temple ordinances outside the temples. . . . The ordinances and ceremonies of the temple are simple. They are beautiful. They are sacred. They are kept confidential lest they be given to those who are unprepared.[48]

It seems odd that categorizing the ceremony in such a manner would make this subject off-limits. Latter-day Saints deem many areas sacred, yet Mormons seem to have no problem discussing them. For instance, the *Book of Mormon* is a sacred book, yet few Mormons or missionaries would hesitate to tell their testimony about this book and the gospel contained within its pages.

If what goes on inside the temple is supposed to be kept from public knowledge, this would certainly fit the definition of secret. Although Mormons are told that the endowment is representative of the ancient ceremony mentioned in the Bible, there is no evidence to suggest that Jewish worshipers in Bible times were threatened for revealing what went on inside the Jerusalem temple. Nor is there any biblical evidence to suggest that the ancient temple rites were similar to those enjoined by Mormons in their temples today.

Although *D&C* 124:41 says that the LDS temple ordinances were "kept hid from before the foundation of the earth," they are suspiciously close to those used in Freemasonry. A person need only look closely at the outside structure of the Salt Lake City temple to see many designs peculiar to Freemasonry. These include the All-Seeing Eye, the inverted five-pointed star (known as the eastern star), and the clasped hands or grip. All of these were a part of Freemasonry long before Smith incorporated them. Markings in the priesthood garments also bear resemblance to the compass, square, and level of Freemasonry. Signs, grips, oaths, and tokens used in the ceremony are so similar that one can't escape the suspicion that Smith "borrowed" these Masonic practices, especially since he became a Mason on 15 March 1842.[49]

Apostle Heber C. Kimball, who was a Mason (as were the first three presidents of the LDS Church), saw a parallel between the endowment and Masonry. In 1842 he wrote: "thare is a similarity of preast Hood in masonary. Br Joseph ses masonry was taken from preasthood but has become degenerated. but menny things are perfect."[50]

Mormon historian Reed C. Durham Jr., insists Joseph Smith did, in fact, use the Masonic ritual as a springboard for the Mormon ceremony. He wrote:

> There is absolutely no question in my mind that the Mormon ceremony which came to be known as the Endowment, introduced by Joseph Smith to Mormon Masons initially, just a little over one month after he became a Mason, had an immediate inspiration from Masonry.[51]

There are other practices in Mormonism that are occultic in nature, such as contact with the dead. President Wilford Woodruff reported the following:

> The dead will be after you, they will seek after you as they have after us in St. George. . . . I will here say, before closing, that two weeks before I left St. George, the spirits of the dead gathered around me, wanting to know why we did not redeem them. . . . These were the signers of the Declaration of Independence, and they waited on me for two days and two nights.[52]

In the 1974 book *Temple Manifestations* (distributed at LDS-owned Deseret Bookstores), Joseph Heinerman reports matter-of-factly about numerous spirit sightings by Mormons at and around LDS temples. For instance, at the same St. George temple where the signers of the Declaration of Independence allegedly appeared to President Woodruff,[53] temple worker M. F. Farnsworth said "persons have told me of seeing their dead friends for whom they have officiated, manifesting themselves to them."[54] Horatio Pickett, another St. George temple worker, had the following vision on 19 March 1914:

> Do those people for whom this work is being done, know that it is being done for them, and, if they do, do they appreciate it? While this thought was running through my mind I happened to turn my eyes toward the southeast corner of the font room and there I saw a large group of women. The whole southeast part of the room was filled; they seemed to be standing a foot or more above the floor and were all intently watching the baptizing that was being done.[55]

Still another temple worker, John Mickleson Lang, said that in 1928 he "distinctly heard a voice at the east end of the font, very close to the ceiling, calling the names of the dead to witness their own baptism, allowing a moment for each spirit to present itself."[56] Meanwhile, at the Manti temple, spirits of early LDS Church leaders appeared at the 1888 dedication ceremony, including Joseph Smith and Brigham Young. The apostles were said to look like they had halos of light on top of their heads.[57] Apostle Anthon H. Lund told a chilling story:

> I remember one day in the Temple at Manti, a brother from Mount Pleasant rode down to the Temple to take part in the work, and as he passed the cemetery in Ephraim, he looked ahead (it was early in the morning), and there was a large multitude all dressed in white, and he wondered how that could be. Why should there be so many up here; it was too early for a funeral, he thought; but he drove up and several of them stepped out in front of him and they talked to him.
>
> They said, "Are you going to the Temple?" "Yes." "Well, these that you see here are your relatives and they want you to do work for them." "Yes," he said, "but I am going down today to finish my work. I have no more names and I do not know the names of those who you say are related to me." "But when you go down to the Temple today you will find there are records to give our names." He was surprised. He looked until they all disappeared, and drove on. As he came into the Temple, Recorder Farnsworth came up to him and said, "I have just received records from England and they all belong to you." And there were hundreds of names that had just arrived, and what was told him by these persons that he saw was fulfilled. You can imagine what joy came to his heart, and what a testimony it was to him, that the Lord wants this work done.[58]

Numerous other manifestations are said to have taken place in other temples such as Kirtland, Nauvoo, Salt Lake, and Hawaii.[59] It seems curious that Mormons would desire to have contact with the dead when the Old Testament clearly warns against necromancy and conjuring up "familiar spirits."[60] Playing around with spirits is dangerous, something that certainly would not be recommended for Christians. If God was not the creator of the ceremony, then could it be possible that Smith—using his imaginative creativity and pagan practices—created an atmosphere that would be a conduit for evil spirits? It certainly appears that this has taken place, and for this reason Christians should have nothing to do with such a practice.

TEMPLES: THE CHRISTIAN PERSPECTIVE

The Old Testament temple was a place where sacrifices were made on behalf of the sins of pious Jews. The blood of the slain animal symbolized propitiation (appeasement for God's anger) and expiation (cancellation of sin). Blood sacrifices included burnt, sin, trespass and fellowship offerings of several kinds of animals; bloodless sacrifices involved grain offerings and libations. The bloodless sacrifices were made, however, only if they followed blood sacrifices.[61] Forgiveness was received through the faith of those who offered these sacrifices.

Unfortunately, Mormons fail to acknowledge that the temple and its priesthood foreshadowed the coming Great High Priest, Jesus Christ, to whom Hebrews 4:16 says Christians can now go to obtain mercy. Because Jesus is alive forevermore, there is no need for a human high priest. This office has been filled. The blood shed in the temple ceremonies foreshadowed the work that would be performed by Christ Himself. Hebrews 9:26 and 10:14 vividly depict how Christ "put away sin by the sacrifice of himself . . . for by one offering he hath perfected for ever them that are sanctified."

CONCLUSION

The Temple, according to Mormonism:

- Once dedicated, LDS temples are open only to Mormons who hold special passes called temple recommends
- In the endowment ceremony participants learn necessary handshakes (tokens) and passwords (key words) necessary to gain entrance into God' presence
- Marriages in the temple bind the couple as husband and wife beyond the grave
- Work for the dead makes it possible for those who did not hear the "restored gospel" during their earthly lives to be joined with family members in eternity

Is the Temple Really Necessary?

While Mormonism teaches that the work done in the LDS temple is necessary for a person who hopes to attain true salvation, the Bible and the *Book of Mormon* do not support such a teaching. It is true that a temple-worthy Mormon is not supposed to talk about specific ceremonies performed in the temple, but the topic of whether or not temples are needed today can be discussed without stepping on the Mormon's toes.

Christian: I notice that the Mormon Church builds its temples all over the world.

Mormon: Yes, we believe that God's people need to attend the Lord's house like the Christians did in the days of the apostles.

   C: Are you temple worthy?

   M: I am.[62]

   C: It seems strange that neither the Bible nor the *Book of Mormon* talks about Christians going to temples to do good works for both the living and the dead.

   M: But don't you believe that the temples existed during the time of Jesus?

   C: There was one recognized temple. However, the Bible never implies that regular temple participation was to be a part of Christians' worship. If this were such an important part of the Christian walk, you would think Paul, for instance, would have stressed regular temple attendance. We do know that the Jews used the temple in Jerusalem until it was finally destroyed for good in A.D. 70. According to the Old Testament, one of the most important reasons for the temple was the Old Covenant ritual of blood sacrifices. Because Jesus shed His blood on our behalf in full payment of our sins, we are under a New Covenant and no longer need the blood of these animals. So why do we need a temple?

M: To perform important works for the living and dead.

C: But there is no support for these works in either the Bible or the *Book of Mormon.*

M: Certainly there is. First Corinthians 15:29 talks specifically about baptism for the dead.

C: Notice that Paul did not identify himself with those who did practice this rite as he switched from first person pronouns used in the text surrounding this verse to third person. It was as if he distanced himself from such a ritual. His main purpose was to support resurrection from the dead. Besides, both the Bible and the *Book of Mormon* teach that salvation cannot occur after death.[63]

M: I'm sure there is other support for the temple. It just seems so right, and I feel such peace when I go there. Besides, look at how beautiful these structures are!

C: Certainly your temples are unique and magnificent, but if what goes on in there is not of God, does it really matter? Besides, there was only one Jewish temple at a time in Jerusalem, yet the LDS Church has dozens of temples around the world.

M: But God's people will be a temple-building people!

C: Not back in the biblical times. As long as their temple was standing and did not need to be rebuilt, the Jews made no effort to build more.[64]

While this conversation can go a number of different ways, the Mormon should realize that the Christian church has never participated in temple ceremonies that even remotely resemble those of the LDS Church. Without this justification and with no biblical or historical support regarding the rites of the Mormon temples, it doesn't matter how special the temple or its ceremonies make a person feel. Participating in such activities is not part of the road to salvation!

PART SIX

Examining the LDS Concept of Revelation

Lamanites, the Seed of Cain, and Polygamy

I would not want you to believe that we bear any animosity toward the Negro. "Darkies" are wonderful people, and they have their place in our church.

President Joseph Fielding Smith,
Look magazine, 22 October 1963, 79

Since LDS leaders claim that their church has a "latter-day" authority once possessed by the Christian church of the New Testament apostles, Mormons often like to refer to the authenticity of their scriptures and leadership. These leaders are said to have been picked by God to guide His people in these days. Are these men receiving true revelations from God?

THE LAMANITES

The *Book of Mormon* opens with the story of a Jewish man by the name of Lehi who is warned by God to leave Jerusalem just prior to its capture by the Babylonians in 587 B.C. Lehi had a wife, Sariah, and four sons named Laman, Lemuel, Nephi, and Sam. They, along with some others, traveled across the ocean to the Western Hemisphere. A great portion of the *Book of Mormon* narrative revolves around the story of Laman and Nephi and their respective followers and descendants, the Lamanites and Nephites. Apparently Laman was always a problem child, and once they arrived in America, both Laman and Lemuel proved to be quite wicked. At one point they even plotted to kill their father and brother Nephi. God punished them for their wickedness, and in order to identify them and their followers, they were given a "skin of blackness." Second Nephi 5:21–23 says:

> And he [God] had caused the cursing to come upon them, yea, even a sore cursing, because of their iniquity. For behold, they had hardened their hearts against him, that they had become like unto a flint; wherefore, as they were white, and exceedingly fair and delightsome, that they might not be enticing unto my people the Lord God did cause a skin of blackness to come upon them. And thus saith the Lord God: I will cause that they shall be loathsome unto thy people, save they shall repent of their iniquities. And cursed shall be the seed of him that mixeth with their seed; for they shall be cursed even with the same cursing. And the Lord spake it, and it was done.

Throughout much of the *Book of Mormon,* the dark-skinned Lamanites are found plaguing the light-skinned Nephites. Eventually the Lamanites succeeded in annihilating their light-skinned counterparts at the battle of Hill Cumorah. According to Mormon belief, American Indians are descendants of these Lamanite people and are therefore Semitic in heritage. Despite the curse placed on them, the *Book of Mormon* did predict that the curse could, and would, be lifted. Prior to 1981, 2 Nephi 30:6 reads, ". . . their scales of darkness shall begin to fall from their eyes; and many generations shall not pass away among them, save they shall be a white and a delightsome people." In 1981 the LDS Church made several revisions to the *Book of Mormon* and in doing so changed the word *white* in 2 Nephi 30:6 (page 117 in the original 1830 edition of the *Book of Mormon*) to the word *pure*.

Some have insisted that the word *pure* is the correct rendering, since this word is found in the 1840 edition of the *Book of Mormon.* Those who argue this point insist that skin color was not the issue at all.

Rather, the passage was speaking more of a spiritual purity. While it is true that the 1840 edition did use the word *pure,* for some reason later editions of the *Book of Mormon* went back to using the word *white.* Insisting that the word *pure* is the correct rendering does not explain why so many LDS leaders ignored the 1840 correction.[1]

Perhaps this is explained by the fact that 3 Nephi 2:15 in the *Book of Mormon* also states that the Lamanites' skin color would change after conversion, saying, "And their [the Lamanites] curse was taken from them, and their skin became white like unto the Nephites." A number of Latter-day Saints have verified that the context refers to skin color. For instance, Joseph Smith was given a revelation foretelling of a day when intermarriage with the Lamanites would produce a white and delightsome posterity. To say Smith corrected the word *white* in 1840 is odd, since he himself used the expressions "white" and "delightsome" in 1831. Mormon writer George Smith wrote:

> This unpublished 17 July 1831 revelation was described three decades later in an 1861 letter from W. W. Phelps to Brigham Young quoting Joseph Smith: "It is my will, that in time, ye should take unto you wives of the Lamanites and Nephites, that their posterity, may become white, delightsome and just." In the 8 December 1831 Ohio Star, Ezra Booth wrote of a revelation directing Mormon elders to marry with the natives.[2]

Brigham Young certainly believed skin color had something to do with spirituality when he said in 1859:

> You may inquire of the intelligent of the world whether they can tell why the aborigines of this country are dark, loathsome, ignorant, and sunken into the depths of degradation. . . . When the Lord has a people, he makes covenants with them and gives unto them promises: then, if they transgress his law, change his ordinances, and break the covenants he has made with them, he will put a mark upon them, as in the case of the Lamanites and other portions of the house of Israel; but by-and-by they will become a white and delightsome people.[3]

At the October 1960 LDS general conference, President Spencer Kimball utilized the language of 2 Nephi 30:6 when he stated how the Indians "are fast becoming a white and delightsome people." He said:

The day of the Lamanites is nigh. For years they have been growing delight-some, and they are now becoming white and delightsome, as they were promised. In this picture of the twenty Lamanite missionaries, fifteen of the twenty were as light as Anglos; five were darker but equally delight-some. The children in the home placement program in Utah are often lighter than their brothers and sisters in the hogans on the reservation.

At one meeting a father and mother and their sixteen-year-old daugh-ter were present, the little member girl—sixteen—sitting between the dark father and mother, and it was evident she was several shades lighter than her parents—on the same reservation, in the same hogan, subject to the same sun and wind and weather. There was the doctor in a Utah city who for two years had had an Indian boy in his home who stated that he was some shades lighter than the younger brother just coming into the pro-gram from the reservation. These young members of the Church are chang-ing to whiteness and to delightsomeness. One white elder jokingly said that he and his companion were donating blood regularly to the hospital in the hope that the process might be accelerated.[4]

Mormon writer George Edward Clark gives a similar account in his book *Why I Believe:*

The writer has been privileged to sit at table with several members of the Catawba tribe of Indians, whose reservation is near the north border of South Carolina. That tribe, or most of its people, are members of the Church of Jesus Christ of Latter-day Saints (Mormon). Those Indians, at least as many as I have observed, were *white and delightsome;* as white and fair as any group of citizens of our country. I know of no prophecy, ancient or modern, that has had a more literal fulfillment.[5]

It appears that not every Mormon, including some LDS prophets, believed the word *pure* was a correct translation of 2 Nephi 30:6. To argue for *pure* only serves to undermine the credibility of Brigham Young, Spencer Kimball, and other Mormons who honestly felt that converted Indians were indeed becoming white. Not only did Brigham Young feel that righteousness produced white skin, but he also taught that unrighteousness could result in black skin. In 1857, he declared:

I feel to bless this people, and they are a God-blessed people. . . . You can see men and women who are sixty or seventy years of age looking young and handsome; but let them apostatize, and they will become gray-haired, wrinkled, and black, just like the Devil.[6]

THE 1978 "REVELATION" AND THE SEED OF CAIN

According to LDS teaching, a person's behavior in the preexistence determines "why some persons are born in one race or caste and some in another."[7] Joseph Fielding Smith taught:

There is a reason why one man is born black and with other disadvantages, while *another is born white* with great advantages. The reason is that we once had an estate before we came here, and were obedient, more or less, to the laws that were given us there. *Those who were faithful in all things there received greater blessings here, and those who were not faithful received less.*[8]

Before the foundation of the world, a "council of the Gods" was called to decide who was to become the savior of humanity. Joseph Smith taught, "In the beginning, the head of the Gods called a council of the Gods; and they came together and concocted a plan to create the world and people it."[9] When Lucifer's plan was rejected, he rebelled and convinced one-third of God's spirit children to join him. Joseph Fielding Smith explained:

When the plan of redemption was presented and Jesus was chosen to be the Redeemer of the world, some rebelled. They were not willing to accept him as "the Lamb slain from the foundation of the world." . . . In this great rebellion in heaven, Lucifer, or Satan, a son of the morning, and one-third of the hosts thereof were cast out into the earth because Lucifer sought to destroy the free agency of man and the one-third of the spirits sided with him. . . . There were no neutrals in the war in heaven. *All took sides either with Christ or with Satan.* Every man had his agency there, and men receive rewards here based upon their actions there, just as they will receive rewards hereafter for deeds done in the body. The Negro, evidently, is receiving the reward he merits.[10]

The spirit children of God who did not fight valiantly for the cause of Christ were allowed to progress to mortality and gain physical bodies, but they were not allowed to hold the priesthood authority necessary to enter the temple and progress to godhood. Without access to the ordinances of the temple, those who were less valiant were invariably given a sentence of damnation.[11] The less valiant spirits who did not perform adequately in the preexistence would be known by their black skin. In a 1939 general conference speech, Elder George F. Richards taught:

> The Negro is an unfortunate man. He has been given a black skin. But that is as nothing compared with that greater handicap that he is not permitted to receive the Priesthood and the ordinances of the temple, necessary to prepare men and women to enter into and enjoy a fulness of glory in the celestial kingdom.[12]

Many Mormons felt that black people had nobody but themselves to blame for their dark skin and the "disadvantages" that accompanied it. Mormon leaders have been very strong in their words regarding their opinion of this race of people. Joseph Smith said, "Had I anything to do with the negro, I would confine them by strict law to their own species, and put them on a national equalization."[13] Brigham Young, who preached that Cain's mark was "the flat nose and black skin," taught: "You see some classes of the human family that are black, uncouth, uncomely, disagreeable and low in their habits, wild, and seemingly deprived of nearly all the blessings of the intelligence that is generally bestowed upon mankind."[14] President John Taylor felt the existence of the black race served to be the devil's representative:

> And after the flood we are told that the curse that had been pronounced upon Cain was continued through Ham's wife, as he had married a wife of that seed. And why did it pass through the flood? Because it was necessary that the devil should have a representative upon the earth as well as God.[15]

He later added:

> Why is it, in fact, that we should have a devil? Why did the Lord not kill him long ago? Because he could not do without him. He needed the devil and a great many of those who do his bidding to keep men straight, that we may learn to place our dependence upon God, and trust in Him, and

to observe his laws and keep his commandments. When he destroyed the inhabitants of the ante*diluvian* world, he suffered a descendant of Cain to come through the flood in order that he might be properly represented upon the earth.[16]

On 17 August 1951 the LDS First Presidency issued a statement regarding the "Negro Question," saying "the conduct of spirits in the premortal existence has some determining effect upon the conditions and circumstances under which these spirits take on mortality." Because they apparently were not as valiant, those preexistent spirits were "willing to come to earth and take on bodies no matter what the handicap may be as to the kind of bodies they are to secure." The handicap was "failure of the right to enjoy in mortality the blessings of the priesthood." John Lund, who at the time was the assistant LDS Church historian, claimed this was a result of a lack of preparation in the preexistence:

> It is vitally important to re-emphasize at this point that Cain's descendants are not being denied the Priesthood because of the sins of Cain. The fact that they are required to wait this great length of time in order to receive the Priesthood is not because of Cain's slaying of Abel, but because of their own individual preparation and worthiness in the pre-existence.[17]

Since it is taught that a loss of memory about the preexistence accompanies mortality, those with black skin are being punished for something they could not remember doing. Saying that his God knew what he was doing when he sent some preexistent spirits to black homes and others to white homes, John J. Stewart admitted that he believed the white race is born with important spiritual advantages:

> The circumstances of our birth in this world are dependent upon our performance in the spirit world, just as the circumstances of our existence in the next world will depend upon what use we make of the blessings and opportunities we enjoy in this world. According to LDS doctrine, Dr. George Washington Carver—who, incidentally, was a mulatto rather than a Negro—will be far ahead of many of us born under more favorable circumstances in this life, for he made the most of his opportunities, while many of us are forfeiting our birthright. We were ahead of him in the first lap of the race, but he has gone far ahead of many of us in the second. . . .

There were those in the spirit world whose performance caused them to forfeit the right to bear the Priesthood of God and enjoy its attendant blessings in this world.[18]

Because of these priesthood restrictions, many outside of the LDS Church have assumed blacks were not welcomed as members. This is not true. However, their spiritual status was looked on as second-rate:

Negroes in this life are denied the priesthood; under no circumstances can they hold this delegation of authority from the Almighty. The gospel message of salvation is not carried affirmatively to them. . . . Negroes are not equal with other races where the receipt of certain spiritual blessings are concerned.[19]

If exaltation in the celestial kingdom was not a reachable goal, then what would be the final destination for the black man or woman? In a speech given at BYU in 1954, Apostle Mark E. Petersen taught that they could become "servants" in the celestial kingdom: "If that Negro is faithful all his days, he can and will enter the celestial kingdom. He will go there as a servant, but he will get a celestial resurrection."[20]

Petersen believed in complete segregation, although he claimed to have no animosity toward blacks:

Now we are generous with the Negro. We are willing that the Negro have the highest kind of education. I would be willing to let every Negro drive a Cadillac if they could afford it. I would be willing that they have all the advantages they can get out of life in the world. But let them enjoy these things among themselves. I think the Lord segregated the Negro and who is man to change that segregation?[21]

What would prevent someone from achieving the priesthood and thus godhood? According to Petersen, even one drop of proverbial "Negro blood" would disqualify a person.

If I were to marry a Negro woman and have children by her, my children would all be cursed as to the priesthood. Do I want my children cursed as to the priesthood? If there is one drop of Negro blood in my children, as I have read to you, they receive the curse. There isn't any argument, therefore, as to inter-marriage with the Negro, is there? There are 50 million

Negroes in the United States. If they were to achieve complete absorption with the white race, think what that would do. With 50 million Negroes inter-married with us, where would the priesthood be? Who could hold it, in all America? Think what that would do to the work of the church![22]

John Lund affirmed that "the mark of a black skin deals specifically with the problems of intermarriage. The Lord did not want the seed of Cain to intermingle with the rest of Adam's children."[23] To even have relations with a black woman would warrant death, according to Brigham Young: "Shall I tell you the law of God in regard to the African race? If the white man who belongs to the chosen seed mixes his blood with the seed of Cain, the penalty, under the law of God, is death on the spot. This will always be so."[24]

A DOCTRINE THAT WAS TO ALWAYS BE

On 3 December 1854 Brigham Young insisted that blacks would not be able to gain the priesthood until after the resurrection:

When all the other children of Adam have had the privilege of receiving the Priesthood, and of coming into the kingdom of God, and of being redeemed from the four quarters of the earth, and have received their resurrection from the dead, then it will be time enough to remove the curse from Cain and his posterity.[25]

While some might blame Young as the originator of this teaching, Seventy Milton R. Hunter said the doctrine really should be traced back to Joseph Smith:

Brigham Young did not originate the doctrine that Negroes could not hold the Priesthood in this life but some day some of them may be granted that privilege, but he was taught it by the Prophet Joseph. The minutes of a meeting of the general authorities of the Church which was held on August 22, 1895, read as follows: "President George Q. Cannon remarked that the Prophet taught this doctrine: That the seed of Cain could not receive the Priesthood nor act in any of the offices of the Priesthood until the seed of Abel should come forward and take precedence over Cain's offspring."[26]

Mormon leaders tenaciously held to this position, even during the Civil Rights movement of the 1960s, claiming that this doctrine was to continue "while time endures."[27] When a reporter asked in 1964 if blacks would receive the priesthood, LDS Prophet David O. McKay replied, "Not in my lifetime, young man, nor yours."[28] In 1967 John Lund explained that this was a doctrine that would always remain

> because Negroes must first pass through mortality before they may possess the Priesthood. . . . Those who believe that the Church "gave in" on the polygamy issue and subsequently should give in on the Negro question are not only misinformed about Church History, but are apparently unaware of Church doctrine. . . . Therefore, those who hope that pressure will bring about a revelation need to take a closer look at Mormon history and the order of heaven.[29]

In light of the previous teachings, no doubt many Mormons were surprised to learn that President Kimball supposedly received a revelation that would officially take away the restrictions barring those of black heritage from priesthood blessings. On 8 June 1978 a statement was read that included the following words:

> Aware of the promises made by the prophets and presidents of the Church who have preceded us that at some time, in God's eternal plan, all of our brethren who are worthy may receive the priesthood. . . . He has heard our prayers, and by revelation has confirmed that the long-promised day has come when every faithful, worthy man in the Church may receive the holy priesthood.[30]

One question is, "To which 'promises' is Kimball referring?" Prior to 1978 it was generally understood that the promise of priesthood for the "seed of Cain" would only come to pass *after* the resurrection and not before. One can only speculate as to why the LDS leadership made the change at this time. Many feel that the October 1978 opening of a temple in São Paulo, Brazil, may have been a contributing factor. Brazil has been a hotbed for Mormon growth but it is also a country comprised of people of mixed descent. Because many Brazilians are descendants of former slaves, it would be impossible to tell who was "unqualified" to participate in the priesthood under the old standard.

Mormons often make an issue that their four scriptures are to be the measuring rod for truth and that revelation cannot contradict what they contain. Harold B. Lee stated, "If it is not in the standard works, we may well assume that it is speculation, man's own personal opinion; and if it contradicts what is in the scriptures, it is not true."[31] Given the fact that Abraham 1:26 in the *Pearl of Great Price* was used as a proof text to ban blacks from the priesthood, the 1978 reversal appears to violate Lee's admonition.[32]

All of this information raises other questions. If the Mormon God has removed the curse that was once on the black race, why has he not also removed the mark? If the sole purpose of the black skin was merely to identify those who should not receive priesthood blessings, and that no longer applies, why are people still being born with this mark?

The restrictions once imposed on black members are a fading memory. We have personally spoken with many black members of the LDS Church who had no idea that this discrimination was once a tenet of their faith. Today the official position of the Mormon Church allows all worthy male members, regardless of race, to hold the position of priest.

POLYGAMY: ONE MAN, MANY WIVES

Another controversial issue of Mormonism was the teaching of polygamy. Its practice was, and still is, looked on by many Bible-believing Christians as a detestable arrangement. Its proliferation among Joseph Smith's followers was more than enough evidence to convince them that Smith was not a true prophet and his church was not Christian.

Mormon historians and apologists have given numerous reasons as to why Joseph Smith established the covenant of plural marriage. One of the main arguments used to support this practice was the example of Old Testament patriarchs and kings. It would be foolish to argue otherwise since this was a lifestyle for both the ungodly (such as Lemech, the son of Cain, and Belshazzar, the king of Babylon) as well as men whose lives reflected the blessings of God.

Biblically, polygamy was merely tolerated by God. It was never a requirement for one's salvation. The mere fact that in the beginning

God created Eve alone for the companionship of Adam points to the monogamous relationship between a man and a woman as the ideal. This is confirmed by 1 Corinthians 7:2, in which the apostle Paul stated that "every man have his own *wife*," not *wives*. According to Titus 1:6 and 1 Timothy 3:2, monogamy was a qualification for church office, and in Matthew 19:5 even Jesus affirmed monogamy when He stated "and they twain [two] shall be one flesh."

A person would be hard-pressed to support polygamy by using the *Book of Mormon*. In fact, Jacob 2:27 reads, "Wherefore, my brethren, hear me, and hearken to the word of the Lord: For there shall not any man among you have save it be one wife; and concubines he shall have none." Some Mormons have countered with Jacob 2:30. This *Book of Mormon* passage reads, "For if I will, saith the Lord of Hosts, raise up seed unto me, I will command my people; otherwise they shall hearken unto these things."

The usual argument insists that polygamy was allowed in the early years of Mormonism in order to "raise up seed." Proponents of this view say that God allowed polygamy because there was an over-abundance of women in the LDS Church, making it necessary for the men to each marry more than one wife. This argument is not supported by the facts and is actually refuted by Apostle John Widtsoe:

> The United States census records from 1850 to 1940, and all available Church records, uniformly show a preponderance of males in Utah, and in the Church. Indeed, the excess in Utah has usually been larger than for the whole United States, as would be expected in a pioneer state. The births within the Church obey the usual population law—a slight excess of males. Orson Pratt, writing in 1853 from direct knowledge of Utah conditions, when the excess of females was supposedly the highest, declares against the opinion that females outnumbered the males in Utah. (*The Seer*, p. 110) The theory that plural marriage was a consequence of a surplus of female Church members fails from lack of evidence.[33]

According to the introduction to volume 5 of the *History of the Church,* the revelation on plural marriage was written down in order to convince Smith's wife Emma of its authenticity. When exactly this "revelation" came to Joseph Smith is somewhat confusing. According to page 501 of the same volume, Joseph Smith was *given* this revelation on 12 July 1843.

However, the heading of section 132 states it was only recorded on that date and that "this revelation had been known by the Prophet since 1831." It would seem that the latter would be more correct, since *D&C* 132:52 records a warning to Emma to "receive all those *that have been given* unto my servant Joseph." Emma never liked the idea of polygamy. Despite a warning in verse 54 saying that Emma would be destroyed if she did "not abide this commandment," she lived a full life. Her husband, on the other hand, would be dead within a year. Mormon historian Richard S. Van Wagoner writes:

> As God's earthly agent, he [Smith] believed he had been given powers that transcended civil law. Claiming sole responsibility for binding and unbinding marriages on earth and in heaven, he did not consider it necessary to obtain civil marriage licenses or divorce decrees. Whenever he deemed it appropriate he could release a woman from her earthly marriage and seal her to himself or to another with no stigma of adultery.[34]

Although many members of the LDS Church knew polygamy was being practiced,[35] the doctrine was not officially announced until 1852.[36] For years Mormon leaders taught that the practice of polygamy was necessary for a man to receive exaltation, yet the majority of the membership remained monogamous.[37] According to *The Encyclopedia of Mormonism:*

> Although polygamy had been practiced privately prior to the exodus, Church leaders delayed public acknowledgment of its practice until 1852. In August of that year, at a special conference of the Church at Salt Lake City, Elder Orson Pratt, an apostle, officially announced plural marriage as a doctrine and practice of the Church. A lengthy revelation on marriage for eternity and on the plurality of wives, dictated by Joseph Smith on July 12, 1843, was published following this announcement (*D&C* 132).[38]

No doubt this practice came as a surprise to many of the converts who came to Utah from Europe. As far as they knew, polygamy was merely a vicious rumor propounded by enemies of the church. Why should they think otherwise? After all, the idea that Mormons were practicing polygamy was denied outright in the European edition of the *Doctrine and Covenants*. For example, *D&C* section CIX:4, printed in Liverpool, England, in 1866, reads:

> Inasmuch as this Church of Christ has been reproached with the crime of fornication and polygamy: we declare that we believe that one man should have one wife: and one woman but one husband, except in case of death, when either is at liberty to marry again.[39]

In Utah the message was quite different. The same year that the above-mentioned Liverpool edition came out in 1866, Brigham Young proclaimed, "The only men who become Gods, even the Sons of God, are those who enter into polygamy."[40] When this practice came under severe criticism, it was evident church leaders would not easily abandon this teaching. The defense of this doctrine by Mormon leaders can be easily documented, including the following examples:

> You might as well deny "Mormonism," and turn away from it, as to oppose the plurality of wives.[41]

> We are told that if we would give up polygamy—which we know to be a doctrine revealed from heaven, and it is God and the world for it—but suppose this Church should give up this holy order of marriage, then would the devil, and all who are in league with him against the cause of God, rejoice that they had prevailed upon the Saints to refuse to obey one of the revelations and commandments of God to them. . . . Will the Latter-day Saints do this? No; they will not to please anybody.[42]

> Where did this commandment come from in relation to polygamy? It also came from God. . . . When this commandment was given, it was so far religious, and so far binding upon the Elders of this Church, that it was told them if they were not prepared to enter into it, and to stem the torrent of opposition that would come in consequence of it, the keys of the kingdom would be taken from them. When I see any of our people, men or women, opposing a principle of this kind, I have years ago set them down as on the high road to apostasy, and I do to-day; I consider them apostates, and not interested in this Church and kingdom.[43]

> If we were to do away with polygamy, it would only be one feather in the bird, one ordinance in the Church and kingdom. Do away with that, then we must do away with prophets and Apostles, with revelation and the gifts

and graces of the Gospel, and finally give up our religion altogether and turn sectarians and do as the world does, then all would be right. We just can't do that, for God has commanded us to build up His kingdom and to bear our testimony to the nations of the earth, and we are going to do it, come life or come death. He has told us to do thus, and we shall obey Him in days to come as we have in days past.[44]

This doctrine of eternal union of husband and wife, and of plural marriage, is one of the most important doctrines ever revealed to man in any age of the world. Without it man would come to a full stop; without it we never could be exalted to associate with and become gods . . .[45]

If plurality of marriage is not true or in other words, if a man has no divine right to marry two wives or more in this world, then marriage for eternity is not true, and your faith is all vain, and all the sealing ordinances and powers, pertaining to marriages for eternity are vain, worthless, good for nothing; for as sure as one is true the other also must be true.[46]

Despite the rhetoric, the federal government began its efforts to force the abandonment of polygamy on 1 July 1862. The Anti-bigamy Act defined the illegality of polygamy but it was not really enforced for another twenty years. In 1882 the government enacted what was known as the Edmunds Law. This provision

made the "cohabiting" with more than one woman a crime, punishable by a fine not to exceed three hundred dollars, and by imprisonment not to exceed six months. This law also rendered persons who were living in polygamy, or who believed in its rightfulness, incompetent to act as grand or petit jurors; and also disqualified all polygamists for voting or holding office.[47]

Five years later the Edmunds-Tucker Act became law. Its effects on the LDS Church proved to be most devastating. In 1890 President Wilford Woodruff signed what has come to be known as the Manifesto, or Declaration 1.[48] This document was basically a promise to the United States stating that the Mormon Church would submit to the laws of the land and desist from solemnizing plural marriages. The document denied any accusations that the church was encouraging or performing any such marriages.

The signing of the Manifesto was certainly a major blow to the "prophetic insight" of Mormonism's leaders. Perhaps Woodruff forgot that it was he himself who said his church would continue to practice polygamy "come life or come death." In light of the numerous statements supporting polygamy made by several Mormon leaders, it is surprising that Woodruff claimed he acted according to the will of God. In saying this, he would have to admit that either God has a very short memory or that the previous declarations from LDS leaders were outside of God's will.

It would also appear that the signing of the Manifesto was merely a ploy to get the federal government to relax its sanctions against the LDS Church and to allow Utah to become a state in 1896. History shows that the promise to abolish plural marriage was really disingenuous. Except for Lorenzo Snow, who lived with his youngest wife, "not a single apostle or member of the First Presidency discontinued connubial relationships with plural wives."[49]

For instance, Heber J. Grant, who would later become the LDS Church's seventh president, was arrested, tried, and convicted for unlawful cohabitation in 1899 and fined $100. He fathered 76 children by 27 plural wives during the years 1890–1905. On 25 November 1906 the *Salt Lake Tribune* reported that sixth LDS President Joseph F. Smith "pleaded guilty before Judge M. L. Ritchie in the District Court Friday to the charge of cohabitating with four women in addition to his lawful wife." He was fined $300.[50]

In today's world of Mormonism, Joseph Smith, Brigham Young, Orson Pratt, John Taylor, and many other well-known heroes of the LDS faith would be promptly excommunicated for their participation in practicing their view of celestial marriage. Apostle Bruce McConkie declared, "All who pretend or assume to engage in plural marriage in this day, when the one holding the keys has withdrawn the power by which they are performed, are guilty of gross wickedness."[51]

It would be incorrect to think polygamy is a dead issue within the LDS Church. Section 132 of the *Doctrine and Covenants,* the portion of LDS scripture that established its validity, is still included in the LDS canon.

While McConkie denounced the practice of polygamy in this life, he did say, "Obviously the holy practice will commence again after the Second Coming of the Son of Man and the ushering in of the millennium."[52] Many Mormons insist that the reason plural marriage is no longer practiced is because it violates the law. Such an argument begs the following questions, Does God really care what American law says? If it were truly God's will, wouldn't He expect plural marriages among His people, despite the law?

A Mormon may argue that present circumstances reflect God's will regarding this subject, but a Mormon who chooses such a defense will find no support for this from leaders prior to 1890. Almost without exception, pressure from the United States to eliminate polygamy was looked on as a direct refusal to recognize God's will.

POLYGAMY TODAY

In the late nineteenth century many Latter-day Saints viewed the abandonment of polygamy as religious treason. Almost immediately splinter groups were formed to carry on the "everlasting covenant" of celestial marriage. Today plural marriage is still defiantly practiced in the United States, and it is doubtful that the government, with its liberal view of sexuality, will ever be able to effectively enforce existing laws against polygamy.

Many of today's polygamists skirt the letter of the law by legally marrying one wife, then perform private marriage ceremonies for additional wives in what they feel is in accord with "God's law." According to the 11 December 1997 issue of the *New York Times,* it is estimated that between 30,000 and 35,000 people practice polygamy in the United States today—the majority residing in Utah and Arizona—although some estimates have been as high as 100,000. Since so much secrecy surrounds this practice, it is impossible to obtain accurate figures.

President Spencer Kimball warned his people to stay away from those who belong to polygamous "cults." In a 1974 general conference address he said:

> We warn you against the so-called polygamy cults which would lead you astray. Remember the Lord brought an end to this program many decades ago through a prophet who proclaimed the revelation to the world. People are abroad who will deceive you and bring you much sorrow and re-

morse. Have nothing to do with those who would lead you astray. It is wrong and sinful to ignore the Lord when he speaks. He has spoken—strongly and conclusively.[53]

Fundamental Mormon groups feel that the LDS leadership has sinfully ignored the Lord's leading by denying the efficacy of plural marriage. Within the whole scope of Mormonism, those who practice polygamy today are probably much more consistent with the teachings of Joseph Smith and Brigham Young than the Church of Jesus Christ of Latter-day Saints that condemns them.

CONCLUSION

Mormonism teaches:

- Indians were Jews by nationality whose forefathers came to the Western Hemisphere from Jerusalem
- Those with black skin were cursed because they were less valiant in the previous life, known as preexistence
- Until 1978 blacks were unable to hold the priesthood
- Although the doctrine of polygamy ended in 1890, the doctrine was an important part of the Mormon lifestyle, and its practice will be reinstituted in the next life

Christianity teaches:

- Galatians 3:28 says that all people were created equal, whatever their sex, nationality, or social status
- 1 Peter 2:9 says that every believer is able to hold the priesthood (it does not exclude anyone)
- Monogamy was the New Testament norm despite the example of some who practiced polygamy in the Old Testament

Joseph Smith

Mormonism, as it is called, must stand or fall on the story of Joseph Smith. He was either a prophet of God, divinely called, properly appointed and commissioned, or he was one of the biggest frauds this world has ever seen. There is no middle ground.

President Joseph Fielding Smith,
Doctrines of Salvation 1:188

Joseph Smith Jr. was born on 23 December 1805 in Sharon, Vermont. He was the fifth of eleven children born to Joseph and Lucy Mack Smith. According to the quote above and as demonstrated throughout history, the Latter-day Saint religion centers around this individual who claimed to have restored the Christian faith to the world after an apostate hiatus of many centuries.

Having made regular visits to Temple Square in Salt Lake City, Utah, we have noticed a more subdued reference to Mormonism's founder by tour guides and various displays. In the public arena, emphasis on Smith seems to be diminishing; however, he still plays a prominent and highly visible role in lectures and publications geared toward the LDS membership. For instance, in the July 1999 *Ensign* magazine (p. 32), Richard Neitzel Holzapfel wrote:

> Yet Joseph Smith was more than an uncommon man with a common name. Few individuals' lives and labors have been foreknown and foretold like those of this great and long-hoped-for seer. The Prophet Joseph Smith's life and ministry were seen by ancient prophets "since the world began" as part of the "restitution of all things." . . . From the days of Adam, prophets like Enoch, Joseph of Egypt, Moses, Isaiah, Ezekiel, Daniel, Malachi, and the Apostle Peter looked forward to his ministry and the establishment of the kingdom of God through his labors.

Telling the story of the origins of the LDS Church and of Joseph Smith has been in itself controversial. According to former Mormon historian D. Michael Quinn:

> Few Mormons today can grasp the polarizing charisma of their founding prophet. Some may feel uncomfortable when confronted with the full scope of Joseph Smith's activities as youthful mystic, treasure-seeker, visionary, a loving husband who deceived his wife regarding about forty of his polygamous marriages, a man for whom friendship and loyalty meant everything but who provoked disaffection by "testing" the loyalty of his devoted associates, an anti-Mason who became a Master Mason, church president who physically assaulted both Mormons and non-Mormons for insulting him, a devoted father who loved to care for his own children and those of others, temperance leader and social drinker, Bible revisionist and esoteric philosopher, city planner, pacifist and commander-in-chief, student of Hebrew and Egyptology, bank president, jail escapee, healer, land speculator, mayor, judge and fugitive from justice, guarantor of religious freedom but limiter of freedom of speech and press, preacher and street-wrestler, polygamist and advocate of women's rights, husband of other men's wives, a declared bankrupt who was the trustee-in-trust of church finances, political horse-trader, U.S. presidential candidate, abolitionist, theocratic king, inciter to riot, and unwilling martyr.[1]

Such a description would seem unfathomable by many faithful Latter-day Saints. At times we almost feel sympathetic toward the Mormon apologist who has to defend Smith's bad social behavior before he can even attempt to justify LDS theological positions. Some may argue that Smith was merely a man, complete with his failures. While that certainly is true, should people accept Smith as a prophet of God when his behavior was sometimes less than what we would expect from political leaders? Should character be ignored when it comes to men who claim to be prophets of God? (See 1 Timothy 3.)

POLYANDRY AND THE PROPHET

In his book *Sidney Rigdon, A Portrait of Religious Excess,* LDS historian Richard Van Wagoner devotes a whole chapter describing the temperament and behavior of Mormonism's founder. He wrote:

> His backwoods savoir-faire sometimes impressed visitors whom he lav-ished with food, wine, and tall tales, but his frequent misuse of Latin, Hebrew, and German were plainly pedantic. His relish for competition in sports, matched by his ambition in commerce and politics, was not what people expected from a divine. Nor could Smith resist the flourishes of military dress and parade, or dramatic staging of ritual and ceremony of all kinds. Embracing friends and lashing out verbally and physically at enemies, he was no Buddah [sic]. But perhaps the most scandalous man-ifestation of Smith's lust for manly achievement was his inclination toward extra-marital romantic liaisons, which he believed were licensed by the Old Testament and countenanced by God's modern revelation.[2]

Van Wagoner documents several instances of Smith's amorous advances toward women while the Saints were settled in Nauvoo, Illi-nois. Some of the women were still teenagers. He notes that "Emma spent the last three years of her husband's life jealously battling his errant yearnings, more than once threatening to return to her family in New York."[3]

Smith did not limit his secret marriages to single women. LDS his-torian Todd Compton notes that many of Smith's plural wives were already married:

> One misconception concerning Joseph's polyandry is that it was a prac-tice represented in only one or two unusual marriages; however, fully one-third of Joseph's plural wives, eleven of them, were polyandrous. If we superimpose a chronological perspective, we see that of Joseph's first twelve wives, nine were polyandrous.[4]

Some might argue that these relationships were strictly platonic. Compton disagrees, "Though it is possible that Joseph had some marriages in which there were no sexual relations, there is no explicit or convincing evidence for such a marriage (except, perhaps, in the cases of the older wives). And in a significant number of Joseph's marriages, there is evidence for sexual relations."[5]

It is difficult to justify this behavior in light of the strict biblical prohibition against it. Leviticus 20:10 declares that an adulterous act such as this was punishable by death: "And the man that committeth adultery with another man's wife, even he that committeth adultery with his neighbour's wife, the adulterer and the adulteress shall surely be put to death."

Smith also targeted the young daughters of two of his closest associates. For instance, Joseph Smith attempted to make nineteen-year-old Nancy Rigdon one of his secret plural wives but was soundly rebuffed. When her father, Sidney, heard of the incident, he confronted Smith. Van Wagoner notes that Smith at first denied the story but recanted when Nancy failed to back off from her accusation. Shortly thereafter Smith had a letter sent to Nancy in which he said, "That which is wrong under one circumstance, may be, and often is, right under another."[6]

In May 1843 the thirty-seven-year-old prophet of Mormonism convinced fifteen-year-old Helen Mar Kimball to be sealed as his plural wife. The daughter of Heber C. Kimball stated how Smith promised that if she would "take this step," it would insure the eternal salvation and exaltation of her father's household and kindred. Helen was led to believe that the relationship was more of a spiritual nature and claimed she would have never gone through with it had she known otherwise.[7]

Speaking at the October 1999 general conference, Apostle M. Russell Ballard stated that one of the characteristics of a false prophet was someone who attempted "to change the God-given and spiritually based doctrines that protect the sanctity of marriage, the divine nature of the family, and the essential doctrine of personal morality." Ballard said such false prophets tend to redefine morality to justify, among other things, adultery and fornication.[8] It's odd that many Latter-day Saints fail to hold Joseph Smith accountable to such standards.

Could a modern Mormon in good conscience sustain a leader who lied to his wife about his affairs with other women and who secretly married women already married to other men? It is generally agreed among Mormon historians that Emma Smith was adamantly against the plural wife system. The fact that she married a nonmember after the death of Joseph tends to prove that she did not believe plural marriage (or marriage at all) had anything to do with true salvation, as was taught in the LDS Church.[9]

Despite this less than flattering description, some Mormon apologists have argued that if Smith could somehow be transported into modernity, the general membership would not find anything out of order with his behavior or teaching. For instance, in Dr. Hugh Nibley's rebuttal to Fawn McKay Brodie's biography *No Man Knows My History*, Nibley stated that should Smith speak in a modern LDS congregation, no one would find anything strange or out of place.[10] Not every Latter-day Saint agrees with Nibley's conclusion. Former University of Utah professor Dr. Richard J. Cummings wrote:

> Hugh Nibley declared some years ago that "if Joseph Smith were to walk into a conference of the Mormon church today he would find himself completely at home; and if he were to address the congregation, they would never for a moment detect anything the least bit strange, unfamiliar or old-fashioned in his teaching." However, anyone willing to face the Mormon identity crisis realistically must ask if Joseph Smith's imagined return to the church might not bear a closer resemblance to Christ's less-than-cordial reception in fifteenth-century Seville as conceived by Dostoevsky in the Grand Inquisitor episode of The Brothers Karamazov than to the cheery scenario depicted by Nibley.[11]

Some Mormon writers have admitted that Smith would not at all fit into a modern LDS world. For instance, would Mormons living in today's society follow as their prophet a man who was known to be a money digger and advocate of folk magic? According to Quinn, Smith and his family were well versed in such things:

> Joseph Smith, the founding prophet and president of the new church organized on 6 April 1830, had unquestionably participated in treasure seeking and seer stone divination and had apparently also used divining rods, talismans, and implements of ritual magic. His father, one of the Eight

Witnesses to the divinity of the Book of Mormon and later the church patriarch, had also participated in divining and the quest for treasure. His older brother Hyrum, another of the Eight Witnesses, a member of the First Presidency, and church patriarch following the death of his father, was custodian of the family's implements of ritual magic at his death, and his younger brother William, one of the original twelve apostles, accepted his brother's seer stone divination and presumably found nothing objectionable with the other folk magic practices of his father and brothers. His brother Samuel, another of the Eight Witnesses, may have also shared the folk perspectives of his parents and brothers.[12]

The fact that Smith owned a Jupiter talisman shows that his fascination with the occult was not just a childish fad. At the time of his death, Smith had on his person this talisman that contained the astrological symbol of Jupiter as well as the words "Confirmo O Deus potentissimus." Mormon historians disagree as to the exact translation of the words, but generally they have to do with asking God (Jupiter) for power or strength.[13]

THE PROUD PROPHET

According to *D&C* 135:3, "Joseph Smith, the Prophet and Seer of the Lord, has done more, save Jesus only, for the salvation of men in this world, than any other man that ever lived in it." There is no question that many Mormon historians have painted Smith as a man of high morals and impeccable integrity. Any reports to the contrary are often assumed to have been made by enemies of the church or disgruntled ex-Mormons. Despite what may have been written about him, it is evident that Smith had an ego and expected to be followed without question.

Smith's role was said to be so important that God allowed him to be visited by a number of heavenly messengers.[14] Brigham Young said Smith's character was on the same level as that of Jesus and others of both the Old and New Testament. He stated in 1871:

Well, now, examine the character of the Savior, and examine the characters of those who have written the Old and New Testaments; and then

compare them with the character of Joseph Smith, the founder of this work
. . . and you will find that his character stands as fair as that of any man's
mentioned in the Bible. We can find no person who presents a better character to the world when the facts are known.[15]

Listen to several boasts made by Smith in the sixth volume of the
History of the Church:

I combat the errors of ages; I meet the violence of mobs; I cope with ille-
gal proceedings from executive authority; I cut the gordian knot of powers, and I solve mathematical problems of universities, with truth—dia-
mond truth; and God is my "right hand man."[16]

God made Aaron to be the mouthpiece for the children of Israel, and He
will make me to be god to you in His stead, and the Elders to be mouth
for me; and if you don't like it, you must lump it.[17]

Come on! ye prosecutors! ye false swearers! All hell, boil over! Ye burning mountains, roll down your lava! for I will come out on the top at last.
I have more to boast of than ever any man had. I am the only man that has
ever been able to keep a whole church together since the days of Adam.
A large majority of the whole have stood by me. Neither Paul, John, Peter,
nor Jesus ever did it. I boast that no man ever did such a work as I. The
followers of Jesus ran away from Him; but the Latter-day Saints never ran
away from me yet.[18]

Despite the bravado displayed by Mormonism's founder, Alma
5:27–28 in the *Book of Mormon* warns:

Have ye walked, keeping yourselves blameless before God? Could ye say,
if ye were called to die at this time, within yourselves, that ye have been
sufficiently humble? That your garments have been cleansed and made white
through the blood of Christ, who will come to redeem his people from their
sins? Behold, are ye stripped of pride? I say unto you, if ye are not ye are
not prepared to meet God. Behold ye must prepare quickly; for the kingdom of heaven is soon at hand, and such an one hath not eternal life.

If the *Book of Mormon* is actual scripture, as many Mormons believe, would it not appear that Smith was not prepared to meet God
and therefore did not have eternal life?

NO SALVATION WITHOUT JOSEPH SMITH

Despite the fact that Christians throughout the centuries have pointed to Jesus Christ as the only way to eternal life, Mormon leaders have taught that Joseph Smith will apparently be a deciding factor as well. Brigham Young said:

> If I can pass brother Joseph, I shall stand a good chance for passing Peter, Jesus, the Prophets, Moses, Abraham, and all back to Father Adam, and be pretty sure of receiving his approbation. . . . If we can pass the sentinel Joseph the Prophet, we shall go into the celestial kingdom, and not a man can injure us. If he says, "God bless you, come along here"; if we will live so that Joseph will justify us, and say, "Here am I, brethren," we shall pass every sentinel.[19]

Concerning judgment day, Young stated that entrance into the celestial kingdom was conditional on Smith's consent.

> No man or woman in this dispensation will ever enter into the celestial kingdom of God without the consent of Joseph Smith. From the day that the Priesthood was taken from the earth to the winding-up scene of all things, every man and woman must have the certificate of Joseph Smith, junior, as a passport to their entrance into the mansion where God and Christ are—I with you and you with me. I cannot go there without his consent. He holds the keys of that kingdom for the last dispensation—the keys to rule in the spirit world.[20]

George Q. Cannon agreed that Smith holds the keys to everyone's salvation when he wrote:

> He stands, therefore, at the head of this dispensation and will throughout all eternity, and no man can take that power away from him. If any man holds these keys, he holds them subordinate to Joseph Smith. . . . If we get our salvation, we shall have to pass by him; if we enter into our glory, it will be through the authority that he has received. We cannot get around him.[21]

President Joseph Fielding Smith affirmed this, saying that nobody could reject this "testimony without incurring the most dreadful consequences, for he cannot enter the kingdom of God."[22]

Either Smith was called of God or he wasn't. Mormon Church historian Andrew Jenson wrote:

> If Joseph Smith is what he professed to be: A true Prophet of God, no one can reject his testimony without being condemned, while on the other hand, if he was an impostor, or a false prophet, we can reject him without fear of Divine punishment, and the condemnation will rest upon the man who assumes to speak in the name of the Lord presumptuously.[23]

This veneration for Smith even extends to the point of modifying Scripture to accommodate the Mormon prophet. For instance, on 9 September 1860 Brigham Young proclaimed:

> For unbelievers we will quote from the Scriptures—"Whosoever believeth that Jesus is the Christ is born of God." Again—"Hereby know ye the Spirit of God: Every spirit that confesseth that Jesus Christ is come in the flesh, is of God." I will now give my scripture—"Whosoever confesseth that Joseph Smith was sent of God to reveal the holy Gospel to the children of men, and lay the foundation for gathering Israel, and building up the kingdom of God on the earth, that spirit of God; and every spirit that does not confess that God has sent Joseph Smith, and revealed the everlasting Gospel to and through him, is of Antichrist, no matter whether it is found in a pulpit or on a throne, nor how much divinity it may profess, nor what it professes with regard to revealed religion and the account that is given of the Saviour and his Father in the Bible."[24]

The Bible clearly states that every person—both believer and nonbeliever—will be judged by Jesus, not Joseph! There is no hint that somebody like Smith would assist in the judgment. Jesus said in John 5:22–23a, "For the Father judgeth no man, but hath committed all judgment unto the Son: That all men should honour the Son, even as they honour the Father." Both believer and nonbeliever alike will someday acknowledge that Jesus is Lord (Phil. 2:9–11). Unfortunately, those who refuse to submit themselves to the lordship of Christ in this life will only have Him to be their judge in the next. They will not have the opportunity to make Jesus their much-needed Savior.

JOSEPH SMITH AS PROPHET

Looking back into history, one can't help but be amazed at the trust Smith's followers had in him. Early LDS history is replete with accounts of faithful Mormons who left friends and loved ones to respond to the prophet's latest revelation. A classic example of this type of obedience can be traced to the early 1830s when hundreds of Latter-day Saints left for Missouri on the hope that God was going to establish Zion. Smith proclaimed that cities would be established in the area and prophesied that three temples would be built in the following areas: Independence, Far West, and Adam-ondi-Ahman. None of the predicted temples were ever built, and by 1838, the Mormons had been driven out of Missouri.

To this day the Mormons cite cases of persecution in Missouri as a fulfillment of Bible verses such as 2 Timothy 3:12. The problem with this assumption is that persecution is only one of many signs following true faith. If persecution was the only determinate of truth, the Mormons would have to recognize that the very groups they claim are apostate must also be true, since Christians are persecuted on a daily basis throughout the world, many of them to death.

Those Latter-day Saints who rely on reading only faith-promoting history fail to see that there are two sides to the persecution story. Many have been led to believe that the trouble early Mormons faced in Missouri was based solely on their religious convictions. Knowledgeable historians deny this conclusion:

> Fear of being overwhelmed politically, socially, culturally, economically by Mormon immigration was what fueled anti-Mormonism wherever the Latter-day Saints settled during Joseph Smith's lifetime. Religious belief, as non-Mormons understood it, had little to do with anti-Mormonism. On the other hand, by the mid–1830s Mormons embraced a religion that shaped their politics, economics, and society. Conflict was inevitable.[25]

> Impressed by the Mormon image of group solidarity, some old settlers expressed fears that as a group the Mormons were determined to take over all of their lands and business.[26]

In his excellent work *The 1838 Mormon War in Missouri,* LDS historian Stephen C. LeSueur noted on page 3, "Non-Mormon land speculators could not hope to compete with the Mormons, who were purchasing large tracts of land with Church funds," and that the huge immigration of Mormons to the area also "threatened to displace older towns as the political and commercial centers for their counties. The Missouri settlers saw their status and security threatened by the burgeoning Mormon population."

Many Mormons believe that the early Saints were merely innocent victims of religious bigotry. However, LDS historians James B. Allen and Glen M. Leonard write:

> The Saints themselves may not have been totally without blame in the matter. The feelings of the Missourians, even though misplaced, were undoubtedly intensified by the rhetoric of the gathering itself. They were quick to listen to the boasting of a few overzealous Saints who too-loudly declared a divine right to the land. As enthusiastic millennialists, they proclaimed that the time of the gentiles was short, and they were perhaps too quick to quote the revelation that said that "the Lord willeth that the disciples and the children of men should open their hearts, even to purchase this whole region of country, as soon as time will permit." Even though the Saints were specifically and repeatedly commanded to be peaceful and never to shed blood, some seemed to unwisely threaten warfare if they could not fulfill the commandment peacefully.[27]

Continued disagreements and violence resulted in Smith's arrest in 1838. Shortly thereafter, his followers were forced to leave Missouri. They eventually settled in a swampland in western Illinois and founded the city of Nauvoo.[28] It should come as no surprise that among the many excuses Mormons have raised for the failure of Smith's Missouri predictions, few admit it was due to his lack of prophetical insight. When the state of Missouri failed to "redress the wrongs" against the Saints, Smith declared:

> I prophesy in the name of the Lord God of Israel, unless the United States redress the wrongs committed upon the Saints in the state of Missouri and punish the crimes committed by her officers that in a few years the government will be utterly overthrown and wasted, and there will not be so much as a potsherd left. [29]

The United States never met Smith's demands and continued as a nation, despite Smith's threat.[30]

THE "MARTYRDOM" OF THE PROPHET

As could be expected, Smith's controversial nature earned him not only devoted followers but also many enemies. His pronouncements upset many of those who were outside the LDS Church, and he also angered many that were once considered his closest advisors.

Some within the church felt that Smith had abused his power as mayor of Nauvoo because he was introducing doctrines and practices contrary to the will of the Lord. On 7 June 1844, seven men, some of whom were prominent in Nauvoo, published a newspaper to call Joseph Smith into account.[31] The severe criticism of the *Nauvoo Expositor* led Smith to declare it a nuisance, and on June 10 he ordered the printing press destroyed. Thomas Ford, then governor of Illinois, was called into the matter and subsequently charged the Nauvoo city council with abuse of power. He also called for the arrest of Smith and others guilty of the destruction.

Knowing full well that he would be in great danger by placing himself in the hands of his enemies, Smith attempted to flee into Iowa and ultimately to the Rockies. While waiting for horses, his wife Emma sent him a message stating that the Latter-day Saints were accusing Smith of cowardice and urged him to return. Smith did so.

On his way to the jail in Carthage, Smith and his party were approached by sixty mounted militia known as the Carthage Greys. It was at that moment that Smith is recorded as saying, "I am going like a lamb to the slaughter."[32] He was jailed in a minimum-security cell at the Carthage Jail.[33] Smith was visited by Cyrus H. Wheelock who, as he was about to leave, "drew a small pistol, a six-shooter from his pocket, remarking at the same time, 'Would any of you like to have this?'" The narrative states that Smith "immediately replied, 'Yes, give it to me.'" He then proceeded to take the pistol and put it into his pants pocket.[34]

After dinner, Smith and several church officials ordered some wine to be brought to the jail. John Taylor, who was present with Smith at the time, wrote:

> Sometime after dinner we sent for some wine. It has been reported by some that this was taken as a sacrament. It was no such thing; our spirits were generally dull and heavy, and it was sent for to revive us. I think it was Captain

Jones who went after it, but they would not suffer him to return. I believe we all drank of the wine, and gave some to one or two of the prison guards.[35]

Soon after the dinner, about a hundred armed men with their faces painted black stormed the jail, taking justice into their own hands.[36] The men in the cell tried to defend themselves. Joseph "Smith sprang to his coat for his six-shooter, Hyrum for his single barrel, Taylor for Markham's large hickory cane, and Dr. Richards for Taylor's cane."[37] Hyrum Smith fell with a mortal wound to the face. Several bullets hit Taylor while Richards received a slight wound to one of his ears. John Taylor stated that before Smith was shot, he used his smuggled gun to shoot three of his attackers, killing two of them.[38] Historian Reed C. Durham describes Smith's final moments:

> Joseph Smith, Master Mason and widow's son, went to the window and with upraised hands, commenced giving the Masonic distress call to fraternal Masons who were present in the mob: "Oh Lord, My God." He was unable to complete his plea and fell out of the window to his death.[39]

The differences between Jesus and Joseph Smith are obvious. On the one hand, Jesus quietly and humbly went like a lamb to the slaughter. He went peacefully and without resistance. When Peter attempted to defend his Lord from the mob by drawing his sword, he was told to put it away (John 18:11). Although one might sympathize with Smith's attempt to defend himself against an unruly mob, it is wrong for Mormons to draw a similarity between Smith's final actions and those of the Savior. There can be no comparison between the sacrificial death of Christ and the way Smith died!

C O N C L U S I O N

Mormonism teaches that Joseph Smith is the prophet who:

- restored true Christianity to this world
- was inspired by God to bring forth true scriptures from God
- was martyred as a "lamb led to slaughter"

The Church and Its Leadership

Your safety and ours depends upon whether or not we follow the ones whom the Lord has placed to preside over his church. He knows whom he wants to preside over this church, and he will make no mistake. The Lord chooses whom he wants to preside over his church, and he will make no mistake. The Lord doesn't do things by accident. . . . Let's keep our eye on the President of the Church.

> President Harold B. Lee,
> *Living Prophets for a Living Church,* 32

For the Mormon, it is essential that a living "prophet" guide the true church. Mormon leaders teach that this is "not a reformist church but a restored church."[1] Therefore, it is taught that the LDS Church is a true picture of Christianity, and all other religious groups lack the proper guidance from God.[2] Without this structure, the Mormon Church's claim to "latter-day" authority is nonexistent.

A CHURCH WITH AUTHORITATIVE LEADERS

From the very beginning, Mormonism's leaders have been the figureheads of the LDS Church. What they say goes. Apostle Heber C. Kimball declared on 8 November 1857, "If you are told by your leader to do a thing, do it. None of your business if it is right or wrong."[3] This message has not changed. After quoting *D&C* 1:30, which claims that the LDS Church is "the only true and living church upon the face of the whole earth," President Gordon Hinckley said:

> Here lies the truth. Here lies the priesthood. Hold to the Church. Do not ever lose sight of the fact that the Church must ever remain preeminent in your lives if you are going to be happy as the years pass. Never let yourselves be found in the position of fighting The Church of Jesus Christ of Latter-day Saints. You cling to it and be faithful to it. You uphold and sustain it. You teach its doctrines and live by it. And I do not hesitate to say that your lives will be the richer and happier because of that. You cannot find happiness fighting the work of God. Those who have done so have gone down to a dismal end.[4]

While acknowledging that his listeners had been "taught to think critically," Hinckley made it clear that this must be done without "looking for flaws in the church or in its leaders."[5] There is no doubt that the general authorities, or "the Brethren" as they are commonly known, are very important to Mormons. In explaining who these were, James Faust, a second counselor in the First Presidency, said:

> When I was first named as a General Authority many years ago, I went to see President Hugh B. Brown, then in the First Presidency, and asked him, "President Brown, what advice have you got for a new, young, inexperienced General Authority?" This wise and venerable man responded simply and directly, "Stick with the Brethren." Who are the Brethren? The Brethren are those who hold the keys of the kingdom of God on earth. They are the First Presidency and the Quorum of the Twelve Apostles, each of whom is an apostle and prophet; the Seventy; and, in temporal matters, the Presiding Bishopric. The rise of the Church from Palmyra to Kirtland, from Kirtland to Nauvoo, from Nauvoo to the West, and in over 150 countries all over the world has come about because the body of the Church, wherever it was, has been loyal to the Brethren.[6]

It is taught that listening to the counsel of these men will lead the faithful Mormon to the celestial kingdom and godhood. Seventy

L. Aldin Porter gave an October 1994 general conference speech warning those Mormons who would consider trusting in their own rationale rather than the counsel of general authorities:

> One's intentions may be of the purest kind. The sincerity may be total and complete. Nevertheless, pure intentions and heartfelt sincerity do not give members of the Church authority to declare doctrine which is not sustained by the living prophets. While we are members of the Church, we are not authorized to *publicly declare* our speculations as doctrine nor to extend doctrinal positions to other conclusions based upon the reasoning of men and women, even by the brightest and most well-read among us. . . . When you see any document, any address, any letter, any instruction that is issued by the Council of the First Presidency and the Quorum of the Twelve, it should be recognized for what it surely is—the mind and the will of the Lord to his people in this day.[7]

In a message directed to teachers in the LDS Church, President Ezra Taft Benson reminded them that doctrinal interpretation was only for church leaders: "Doctrinal interpretation is the province of the First Presidency. The Lord has given that stewardship to them by revelation. No teacher has the right to interpret doctrine for the members of the Church."[8]

Do most Mormons accept this role of such authority, even to trust these men to lead them to eternal life? Apparently so. What if they are wrong? Some seem to think that they will be forgiven and the issue will be forgotten. Speaking at an LDS Sunstone Symposium on 8 August 1997, Clay Chandler said, "Our leaders can be forgiven for occasionally deceiving us if they don't violate our trust."

Some Christians may not completely understand such rationale, but it must be remembered that for Mormons, rejecting the prophet and other church leaders is akin to rejecting God Himself. To speak out against them is to risk excommunication from the one true church. James Faust explained that there are "four absolutes" of the Mormon faith:

> The first is that Jesus is the Christ, the Savior, the Mediator and Redeemer of the world. The second is that Joseph Smith was a prophet of God and reestablished the Church of Christ upon the earth with its keys and authority. The third is that all of the Presidents of the Church since Joseph Smith

have been successors in that power and authority. The fourth is that President Gordon B. Hinckley is the only prophet of God upon the earth, holding all of the keys, powers, and authorities of the Church in the earth today.[9]

Notice that three of the four "absolutes" pertain to the LDS prophet. Mormonism definitely holds to the idea that the prophet holds the preeminent role when it comes to guidance. Consider the words of these Mormons from the 1990s:

> When we sustain the President of the Church by our uplifted hand, it not only signifies that we acknowledge before God that he is the rightful possessor of all the priesthood keys; it means that we covenant with God that we will abide by the direction and the counsel that comes through His prophet. It is a solemn covenant.[10]

> We declare with soberness, and yet with the authority of God in us vested, we have a prophet today. The President of the Church, as a prophet, is God's representative on earth and is appointed to lead his church. This has been true in the past as recorded in the Old Testament, the New Testament, the Book of Mormon, and in this, the last dispensation of the fulness of times with the restoration of The Church of Jesus Christ of Latter-day Saints. He who holds all the priesthood keys authorizing those saving blessings is the living prophet.[11]

At the conclusion of the October 1994 general conference, President Howard W. Hunter proclaimed: "Let us study their words [the prophets and other general authorities], spoken under the Spirit of inspiration, and refer to them often. The Lord has revealed his will to the Saints in this conference."[12]

While the Mormon leaders may say that they and their organization are above reproach, such a position of ultimate authoritarianism is not a New Testament trait. If the leaders of the early church had claimed ultimate authority, then we could rightly conclude that Paul would never have become an apostle. After his conversion, Acts 9:26 says Paul tried to join the disciples but he was rebuffed due to a lack of trust. The apostles were reluctant to believe that Paul had actually converted. Although it is unclear as to the role Barnabas played in leading the early church, he did stand up for Paul and defended him before the apostles.

Paul took a position opposite to that held by the leaders of Mormonism. He invited his followers in Galatians 1:8–9 to closely scrutinize his teachings: "But though we, or an angel from heaven, preach any other gospel . . . let him be accursed." He made it clear that even he was not above criticism. When he saw an inconsistency in Peter's behavior among the Gentiles, Paul saw no problem in confronting Peter "to the face" about the matter (Gal. 2:11). This is especially significant, since Peter's seniority far surpassed that of Paul.

THE PROPHET AND LDS DOCTRINE

When it comes to doctrine, Mormons are not limited merely to the written word as found in the standard works. Latter-day Saints can find authoritative teachings "through conferences, Church publications, and instructions to local priesthood leaders."[13] These teachings are placed on par with their scripture. Apostle James Talmage affirmed, "We rely therefore on the teachings of the living oracles of God as of equal validity with the doctrines of the written word."[14]

Apostle J. Reuben Clark affirmed, "We have the Scriptures which other Christian sects use, namely the Bible, including the Old and New Testaments, but we also have the Book of Mormon, the Doctrine and Covenants, the Pearl of Great Price, and the Living Oracles of the Church."[15] Another apostle, Henry D. Moyle, said, "That which the Presidency of this Church have said, and say now, is as much the law and the gospel as anything that has ever been said or written before for our guidance."[16] Moyle made it sound as if he believed living prophets were more authoritative than the standard works when he said:

> The older I get and the closer the contact I have with the President of the Church, the more I realize that the greatest of all scriptures which we have in the world today is current scripture. What the mouthpiece of God says to His children is scripture. It is intended for all the children of God upon the earth. It is His word and His will and His law made manifest through scripture, and I love it more than all other. It applies to me today specifically, and to you all.[17]

Many Latter-day Saints feel confident that their prophet could never mislead them. On 31 August 1873 Brigham Young challenged his audience to give proof that he had ever given incorrect counsel.

> I am here to give this people, called Latter-day Saints, counsel to direct them in the path of life. . . . If there is an Elder here, or any member of this Church, called the Church of Jesus Christ of Latter-day Saints, who can bring up the first idea, the first sentence that I have delivered to the people as counsel that is wrong, I really wish they would do it; but they cannot do it, for the simple reason that I have never given counsel that is wrong; this is the reason.[18]

That counsel, however, can fluctuate when a prophet dies. Harold B. Lee said:

> We have some today willing to believe someone who is dead and gone and to accept his words as having more authority than the words of a living authority today. . . . We are not dependent only upon the revelations given in the past as contained in our standard works—as wonderful as they are—but we have a mouthpiece to whom God does reveal and is revealing His mind and will. God will never permit him to lead us astray. As has been said, God would remove him out of his place if he should attempt to do it.[19]

Ezra Taft Benson concurred with this thought when he wrote, "Keep your eye on the prophet—for the Lord will never permit His prophet to lead this Church astray."[20] Claiming church members needed to be fully obeying their leadership, Apostle Neal Maxwell said, "In the future, a discernable distinction of the true followers of Christ will be the heed and attention they give to the living prophets and Apostles."[21]

Some modern LDS scholars have discounted past statements from Mormon leaders by arguing that they should not be held accountable for positions that go beyond the realm of theology. President Wilford Woodruff would have disagreed with this view, stating that the word of the prophet reigns supreme despite any contradicting evidence.

> Now, whatever I might have obtained in the shape of learning, by searching and study respecting the arts and sciences of men,—whatever principles I may have imbibed during my scientific researches, yet, if the Prophet

of God should tell me that a certain principle or theory which I might have
learned was not true, I do not care what my ideas might have been, I should
consider it my duty, at the suggestion of my file leader, to abandon that
principle or theory.[22]

Ezra Taft Benson echoed the same sentiments:

Sometimes there are those who feel their earthly knowledge on a certain
subject is superior to the heavenly knowledge which God gives to His
prophet on the same subject. They feel the prophet must have the same
earthly credentials or training which they have had before they will accept
anything the prophet has to say that might contradict their earthly school-
ing. . . . We encourage earthly knowledge in many areas, but remember
if there is ever a conflict between earthly knowledge and the words of the
prophet, you stand with the prophet and you'll be blessed and time will
vindicate you.[23]

According to page 21 of the church manual *Teachings of the Living Prophets:* "Not every word they speak should be thought of as an
official interpretation or pronouncement. However, their discourses
to the Saints and their official writings should be considered products
of their prophetic calling and should be heeded."

What about when a former prophet's teachings disagree with the
current prophet? In a speech given on 26 February 1980 called "14
Fundamentals in Following the Prophets," Ezra Taft Benson, then an
apostle, made a number of points about the prophet, including the idea
that he would never mislead the church, that he does not need to say
"Thus saith the Lord" for something to be authoritative, and that he
speaks for the Lord in everything. He also made it a point to say that
the living prophet is more important than a dead prophet. Perhaps this
point was given to offset a number of bizarre teachings given by past
leaders.

One would think that if Mormon leaders were all getting their information from the same source (Elohim), such a loophole would not be
necessary. Mormon history shows that many of its leaders have taught
principles that were diametrically opposed to current LDS thought.
For instance, Brigham Young declared how Adam was God and "the
only God with whom we have to do."[24] Despite the fact that Young
defended this position into the latter years of his life, some Latter-day

Saints have relegated this teaching to a mere "theory."[25] Some Mormons even outright deny that he ever taught such a doctrine.

Both Wilford Woodruff and Brigham Young taught that God was progressing in knowledge. In 1857 Woodruff stated, "God himself is increasing and progressing in knowledge, power, and dominion, and will do so, worlds without end. It is just so with us."[26] Orson Pratt was reluctant to believe such a notion. In a sermon given on 13 January 1867 Young rebuked Pratt:

> Brother Orson Pratt, has in theory, bounded the capacity of God. According to his theory, God can progress no further in knowledge and power; but the God that I serve is progressing eternally, and so are his children: they will increase to all eternity, if they are faithful.[27]

Despite the fact that Young felt he was never wrong in his counsel, modern LDS leaders have sided with Pratt. For instance, Joseph Fielding Smith questioned Young's position:

> It seems very strange to me that members of the Church will hold to the doctrine, "God increases in knowledge as time goes on." . . . I think this kind of doctrine is very dangerous. I don't know where the Lord has ever declared such a thing. . . . I believe that *God knows all things and that his understanding is perfect, not "relative."* I have never seen or heard of any revealed fact to the contrary.[28]

In his "Seven Deadly Heresies" speech, Bruce McConkie declared:

> There are those who say that God is progressing in knowledge and is learning new truth. This is false, utterly, totally and completely. There is not one sliver of truth in it. . . . I have been sorely tempted to say at this point that any who so suppose have the intellect of an ant and the understanding of a clod of miry clay in a primordial swamp. But of course I would never say a thing like that.[29]

While this late apostle's comments were met with chuckles from the audience, it should make one wonder if his past leaders such as Brigham Young or Wilford Woodruff had the "intellect of an ant and the understanding of a clod of miry clay," since what McConkie condemned as heresy was taught by such leaders as divine truth. Such contradictions must surely weigh heavy on Latter-day Saints who strive for some consistency in their doctrinal life. To say that the LDS leaders are incapable of leading their followers astray is certainly not supported by history.

CONCLUSION

Mormonism teaches that the LDS Church is true because:

- It alone has living prophets to guide the church
- Its prophets' words are equal to and even surpass the authority of written scripture
- Its prophets cannot lead the church astray

Applying Pascal's Wager to Mormonism

With Latter-day Saints risking so much to trust in their leadership, the question we end this book on is: Are you willing to gamble with your eternal life that you are right? Although many Mormons may joke about the differences between Christianity and Mormonism and say, "We'll all find out who's right at the end," how one believes is not a light matter. We have used a tactic called Pascal's Wager (developed by sixteenth-century mathematician and philosopher Blaise Pascal) to get many Mormons to consider the importance of faith and facts. The strategy involves two parts:

A. Ask the Mormon: "Are you willing to bet with your life that you're right about truth?" Consider the following scenarios.

1. The Mormon and Christian are both wrong. Therefore, both Mormonism and Christianity are false religions.
2. The Mormon is right and the Christian is wrong. If this is true, then Mormonism as brought forth by Joseph Smith is God's restored gospel. Therefore, the Christian belongs to an apostate faith.

3. The Christian is right about truth and the Mormon is wrong. If this is correct, then the historic Christian faith is the only true gospel. Therefore, the Mormon belongs to an apostate faith.
4. There is no fourth possibility because both faiths cannot be right when they contradict each other.

B. Once these principles have been shown to be mutually exclusive—and we have never had trouble getting a Mormon to agree with the fourth statement—the "wager" should be explained. Tell the Mormon: "Now that we have established that there are three choices, let's discuss the implications of each possibility."

1. If the first possibility is correct, then both the Mormon and the Christian are wrong. Perhaps the Hindu, Muslim, or Jehovah's Witness is correct, or maybe the other side of death is nonexistence. If this were true, both parties should explore all avenues since they are in need of truth.
2. If the second possibility is correct, then the Mormon is right and the Christian is wrong. With individual salvation in mind as explained above, the Mormon would therefore have a chance to make it to the top level of the celestial kingdom if, as 2 Nephi 25:23 states, he or she is able to do all that he or she can do.

   Interestingly enough, if the Mormon is right, then the Christian's eternal destiny appears to be pretty secure. Bruce McConkie said "good" people who were not worthy of becoming gods would still benefit in the afterlife. He said, "Honorable men of the earth who are blinded by the craftiness of men and who therefore do not accept and live the gospel law" will achieve the second level of heaven known as the terrestrial kingdom.[30] While this level is not as desirable as the celestial kingdom, *D&C* 76:77 says the presence of the Son is evident there. Apostle Dallin H. Oaks said that everyone

   > will ultimately be resurrected and go to a kingdom of glory. The righteous—regardless of current religious denomination or belief—will ultimately go to a kingdom of glory more wonderful than any of us can comprehend. Even the wicked, or almost all of them, will ultimately go to a marvelous—though lesser—kingdom of glory.[31]

The Christian doesn't have much to lose in this scenario. True, he or she may not be eligible for exaltation, but then again, one must wonder how many of the millions who have been Mormon will be eligible to become gods after death. A great many LDS Church members do not even have temple recommends, a certain celestial requirement! But not all is lost for those destined to the terrestrial kingdom; indeed, this populace will be allowed to abide in the glory of Jesus and comfortably exist in an eternal state.

3. This brings us to the third choice. What if the Christian is right and the Mormon is wrong? It is the difference between heaven and hell. According to the Bible, heaven is the place where believers will abide with God for all eternity in His presence. Only true believers in Christ will be allowed entrance (John 3:16–21; Rev. 2:11; 20:6).

   It should be pointed out how real hell is for unbelievers (Matt. 8:12; 25:41–46). It is eternal separation from God in a painful and final state (2 Thess. 1:9; Rev. 14:10–11). It is, in actuality, a second death. Biblical Christianity leaves no room for obtaining salvation after rejecting it in this life (2 Cor. 6:2; Heb. 9:27). If Christianity is true and Mormonism is false, the Mormon has everything to lose. Hell is a real place, and every person who does not believe in the true God will go there.

As might be expected, the above presentation appears to shock most Mormons. In effect, too many Mormons risk losing an eternal existence with God simply because they have blindly based their eternal destinies on the reputation of Joseph Smith and his successors. Because many Mormons place such an inordinate amount of faith in their feelings (and testimony), too few have done adequate research into the possibility that they might be wrong. While this tactic cannot—or should not—coerce belief or be proof that Christianity is true, it can be an incentive for Mormons to take another look at the essentials of their faith and compare it to the historic Christian faith. To do any less would not make a safe bet.

PASCAL'S WAGER

I would like to compare our faiths.

3 Possibilities

A	B	C
Both are wrong	LDS = Right Christian = Wrong	Christian = Right LDS = Wrong

A

Christian and Mormon are both in deep trouble
because another faith is true or there is no God.

B

Mormon headed to celestial or terrestrial kingdoms,
depending on how life was lived on earth.
Christian headed to terrestrial or telestial kingdoms,
depending on how life was lived on earth.

C

Christian heading to heaven to live eternally with God.
Mormon who does not have a true faith is heading to hell.

Place Your Wager

Consider all avenues. . . . Don't just "accept" a religion.

Past and Present Important Leaders in the LDS Church

Since there are so many LDS Church leaders, we have provided this alphabetical listing of those general authorities who have been quoted throughout this book. Each man's current or final position is included. The president of the church, also known as the prophet, is the top position in the LDS Church. He and two counselors make up the First Presidency. Next in line after the twelve apostles is the First Quorum of the Seventy, followed by the Second Quorum of the Seventy.

Ballard, M. Russell (1928–) Apostle
Bangerter, William G. (1918–) Emeritus Seventy
Benson, Ezra Taft (1899–1994) Thirteenth President
Brockbank, Bernard P. (1909–) Emeritus Seventy
Brown, Hugh B. (1883–1975) First Counselor in the First Presidency
Cannon, George Q. (1827–1901) First Counselor in the First Presidency
Clark, J. Reuben, Jr. (1871–1961) First Counselor in the First Presidency
Cowdery, Oliver (1806–1850) Assistant President under Joseph Smith
Derrick, Royden G. (1915–) Emeritus Seventy
Dunn, Paul H. (1924–1997) Emeritus Seventy
Eyring, Henry B. (1933–) Apostle
Faust, James E. (1920–) Second Counselor in the First Presidency
Grant, Heber J. (1856–1945) Seventh President
Haight, David B. (1906–) Apostle
Hales, Robert D. (1932–) Apostle

Hinckley, Gordon B. (1910–) Fifteenth President
Holland, Jeffrey R. (1940–) Apostle
Hunter, Howard W. (1907–1995) Fourteenth President
Hunter, Milton R. (1902–1975) First Council of the Seventy
Hyde, Orson (1805–1878) Apostle
Kimball, Heber C. (1801–1868) First Counselor in the First Presidency
Kimball, Spencer W. (1895–1985) Twelfth President
Lee, Harold B. (1899–1973) Eleventh President
Lund, Anthon (1844–1921) First Counselor in the First Presidency
Lyman, Francis M. (1840–1916) Apostle
McConkie, Bruce R. (1915–1985) Apostle
McKay, David O. (1873–1970) Ninth President
Maxwell, Neal A. (1926–) Apostle
Monson, Thomas S. (1927–) First Counselor in the First Presidency
Moyle, Henry D. (1889–1963) First Counselor in the First Presidency
Nelson, Russell M. (1924–) Apostle
Oaks, Dallin H. (1932–) Apostle
Packer, Boyd K. (1924–) Apostle
Penrose, Charles W. (1832–1925) First Counselor in the First Presidency
Perry, L. Tom (1922–) Apostle
Petersen, Mark E. (1900–1984) Apostle
Pratt, Orson (1811–1881) Apostle
Pratt, Parley P. (1807–1857) Apostle
Richards, LeGrand (1886–1983) Apostle
Rigdon, Sidney (1793–1876) First Counselor in the First Presidency
Roberts, B. H. (1857–1933) Seventy
Scott, Richard G. (1928–) Apostle
Smith, George A. (1870–1951) Eighth President
Smith, Hyrum (1800–1844) Assistant President under Joseph Smith
Smith, Joseph, Jr. (1805–1844) First President and Mormon Church founder
Smith, Joseph F. (1838–1918) Sixth President
Smith, Joseph Fielding (1876–1972) Tenth President
Smoot, Reed (1862–1941) Apostle
Snow, Lorenzo (1814–1901) Fifth President
Talmage, James E. (1862–1933) Apostle
Taylor, John (1808–1887) Third President
Whitney, Orson F. (1855–1931) Apostle
Widtsoe, John A. (1872–1952) Apostle
Wirthlin, Joseph B. (1917–) Apostle
Woodruff, Wilford (1807–1898) Fourth President
Young, Brigham (1801–1877) Second President

The Top 101 Events in the History of Mormonism

1805—Joseph Smith Jr., the founder of the movement, is born the fourth child of Joseph and Lucy Mack Smith in Sharon, Windsor County, Vermont (December 23).

1820—Smith claims to be visited by God the Father and Jesus Christ and is told that all the churches are wrong.

1823—Smith claims to be visited by the angel Moroni who reveals the alleged existence of gold plates that tell the story of ancient peoples (Nephites and Lamanites) on the American continent.

1826—Smith goes on trial in Bainbridge, New York, and is fined for "glass looking."

1827—Smith marries Emma Hale in South Bainbridge, New York.

　—Smith claims to be shown the gold plates on the Hill Cumorah; he says that he is given the Old Testament stones known as the Urim and Thummim to help in the translation.

1828—The first part of the *Book of Mormon* (Book of Lehi) is stolen by Martin Harris's wife. Rather than risk trying to retranslate these 116 pages and having Harris's wife discredit him by reproducing them, Smith is told to repent and then not to retranslate them (*D&C* 3, 10).

1829—Smith and Oliver Cowdery are said to have received the Aaronic priesthood from John the Baptist along the banks of the Susquehanna River near Harmony, Pennsylvania. They then baptize each other. A month later the two men are said to have received the Melchizedek priesthood from the apostles Peter, James, and John.

1830—Five thousand copies of the translation of the gold plates (officially known as the *Book of Mormon*) are produced in March.

　—The church begins in April as the "Church of Christ" in Fayette, New York, with six members.

1831—Smith moves the church to Kirtland, Ohio, saying he received a revelation that is recorded in *D&C* 37.

—Smith says he receives another revelation that Independence, Missouri, is the New Jerusalem and the center place of the kingdom of God on the western hemisphere. A temple site is also dedicated.

1833—The moral code known as the "Word of Wisdom" (found in *D&C* 89) is finished.

—The Joseph Smith Translation of the Bible (JST) is finished on July 2.

1834—Mormon leaders vote to take Christ's name out of their church's name. It is known as *Church of the Latter-day Saints* until 1838, when it becomes the *Church of Jesus Christ of Latter-day Saints*.

1835—Twelve apostles and the First Quorum of the Seventy are chosen.

—The Mormons purchase four Egyptian mummies and some scrolls of papyrus, later to be "translated" by Smith as the Book of Abraham in the *Pearl of Great Price*.

—The LDS Church modifies some of the revelations in the *Book of Commandments* and republishes it as the *Doctrine and Covenants*.

1836—The Kirtland Temple, the first LDS temple, is dedicated after a three-year construction.

1837—One thousand baptisms are reported in England as Mormonism's message spreads abroad.

—Martin Harris, one of the three witnesses to the *Book of Mormon,* is excommunicated in December (*Doctrines of Salvation* 3:229).

1838—Spring Hill, a place twenty-five miles north of Far West, Missouri, is named Adam-ondi-Ahman, the place where Adam is said to have gone after being cast out of the Garden of Eden.

—Oliver Cowdery and David Whitmer, two of the three witnesses, join Martin Harris as excommunicated witnesses.

—In an attempt to prevent certain dissenters, including Oliver Cowdery, from damaging the reputation of the LDS Church, Sidney Rigdon, a counselor to Joseph Smith, demands in his June 19 "salt sermon" that these complainers leave the church or be punished.

—Soon after, in a vigorous July 4 address, Rigdon declares a "war of extermination" against those who would disturb the Mormons. These two sermons further incense the public against expanding LDS influence.

—Seventeen Mormons are killed in the "Haun's Mill Massacre." A group of Mormons are attacked by local Missourians in response to a previous attack made by the Mormons at Crooked River. The Missouri governor forces the Mormons to leave Missouri the following year. They then settle in Nauvoo, Illinois.

1840—The first Mormons arrive from England. By 1890, an estimated 85,000 LDS emigrants crossed the Atlantic.

1841—Baptism for the dead is introduced as a temple ordinance.

1842—The 14 Articles of Faith are written by Smith and published for the first time in the LDS publication *Times and Seasons* in Nauvoo, Illinois. They were later changed and revised to only thirteen articles, the number used today.

—The Female Relief Society of Nauvoo is established.

—Smith becomes a Mason and soon thereafter introduces the temple endowment ceremony.

—Smith changes the name of the angel who allegedly appeared to him in 1823, saying he called himself Moroni, not Nephi.

1843—The revelation on plural marriage is recorded in *D&C* 132.

1844—Smith is nominated for U.S. president in Nauvoo.

—Seven LDS dissenters print the *Nauvoo Expositor's* first and only edition on June 7. Smith orders the printing press to be destroyed and is later jailed.

—On June 27, Smith and his brother Hyrum are killed in a gun battle at the Carthage Jail. According to the *Documentary History of the Church* 7:101–3, Smith uses a smuggled pistol to kill two of his attackers.

—A power struggle ensues between Sidney Rigdon and Brigham Young. The Church votes Young as the new leader on August 8.

1845—Between December and February 1846, some five thousand endowments are performed in the Nauvoo Temple.

—Church leaders state their intent to move to the Rocky Mountains.

1846—The first of the volunteer companies of the Mormon Battalion depart to help in the war against Mexico. They arrive in San Diego six months later, but the war had already ended.

1847—A majority of Mormons leave Nauvoo and go with Brigham Young, arriving in the Great Salt Lake Valley in Utah on July 24. As soon as they arrive, they begin planting crops and digging irrigation ditches.

1848—Millions of crickets infest the crops of the pioneers, but the "miracle of the sea gulls" devoured the crickets, saving what was left of the crops.

1850—Apostle Orson Hyde, in Israel, dedicates the nation to the Jews.

1852—The doctrine of plural marriage is publicly announced, although many had already been practicing it since it was the doctrine taught by Smith.

—Young preaches the controversial Adam-God sermon, claiming that Adam is God the Father (*Journal of Discourses* 1:50–51).

1856—Many members rededicate themselves to God after being admonished forcefully from the pulpit. Polygamy and holy living are emphasized. This "reformation" continued through 1857.

1857—The Utah War begins as the U.S. government attempts to deal with what it perceives as the LDS Church's rebellion against the nation. Young declares Utah to be under martial law and orders missionaries to come home to help prevent entry of federal soldiers into Salt Lake City.

—A group of about 120 immigrants from Arkansas and Missouri are killed by Mormons and Indians north of St. George, Utah. It becomes known as the Mountain Meadows Massacre.

1858—After having been stopped for the winter by the delaying tactics of the Mormons, the government enters the Salt Lake Valley peacefully more than a year after being dispatched.

1860—The Reorganized Church of Jesus Christ of Latter-day Saints (RLDS) is founded in Missouri. Joseph Smith's son, Joseph Smith III, becomes the first prophet and president of this church.

1862—Despite a federal law that defined plural marriage as bigamy—making it a crime—the Mormons continue in their polygamous ways.

1873—Young preaches both in January and October that he has never given a sermon that cannot be called scripture.

1874—Young addresses his opponents of the Adam-God doctrine, claiming God has revealed the teaching to him.

1877—Young dies on August 29. The Church has no prophet for three years.

1880—After a reorganization of the First Presidency, John Taylor, the only non-American-born LDS president, becomes the third prophet. George Q. Cannon and Joseph F. Smith become counselors, remaining in this role for the terms of the next three prophets.

1887—Taylor dies. The church goes without a prophet for almost two years.

—David Whitmer, one of the three witnesses to the *Book of Mormon,* writes a pamphlet titled *An Address to All Believers in Christ.* Among other things, Whitmer testifies that God spoke to him and told him that the LDS Church was not true and that Joseph Smith was a fallen prophet.

1889—Wilford Woodruff becomes the church's fourth prophet.

1890—Pressured by the U.S. government, Woodruff signs the Manifesto, which *officially* abolishes polygamy among the Mormons. Unofficially, though, plural marriages continue.

1893—The Salt Lake temple is dedicated after forty years of construction at a total cost of $3.5 million.

1894—The law of adoption is officially denounced by Woodruff, who claimed he had a revelation from God. This doctrine taught that a person could be eternally sealed to prominent church leaders instead of direct ancestors. From this point on, genealogical research by LDS members increases.

1895—Utah becomes the forty-fifth state.

1898—Woodruff dies. Lorenzo Snow becomes the church's fifth prophet.

1899—Heber J. Grant, who would later become Mormonism's seventh prophet, pleads guilty to unlawful cohabitation and is fined $100.

1901—Snow dies. Joseph F. Smith becomes the church's sixth prophet.

1904—Smith issues an official statement upholding provisions of the 1890 Manifesto and invoking excommunication against persons violating the "law of the land" by contracting new plural marriages.

1906—Smith pleads guilty to unlawful cohabitation and is fined $300.

1907—Reed Smoot, a U.S. senator from Utah, is investigated by the Senate. During the three-year investigation, LDS leaders are questioned about polygamy continuing within the LDS Church and their involvement in politics, including the attempt to establish a political kingdom of God.

1915—Apostle James E. Talmage's influential book *Jesus the Christ* is published. It remains popular to this day.

1918—A month and a half before he dies, Smith says he received a vision of Jesus visiting the dead spirits while his body was still in the garden tomb. This is added to the *Doctrine and Covenants* as section 138.

—Joseph F. Smith dies. Heber J. Grant becomes the church's seventh prophet.

1920—The *Book of Mormon* is divided into chapters and verses.

1929—The Mormon Tabernacle begins a weekly network radio broadcast on NBC.

1930—The centennial of the LDS Church is celebrated in Salt Lake City.

1937—The Hill Cumorah pageant, "America's Witness for Christ," begins on an outdoor stage on the side of the Hill Cumorah in New York. To this day it remains an annual summer event.

1945—Grant dies. George Albert Smith becomes the church's eighth prophet.

1947—After being in existence for 117 years, the LDS Church reaches the one-million-member mark.

1951—George Albert Smith dies. David O. McKay becomes the church's ninth prophet.

1965—Family Home Evening program begins. The LDS Church publishes a manual that is to be placed in every LDS home. Five years later Monday evenings were designated for this day.

1966—A new visitors center is built on Temple Square in Salt Lake City, beginning a trend of constructing public relations buildings at LDS sites and temples.

1967—The Egyptian papyri used by Smith to translate the Book of Abraham found in the *Pearl of Great Price* are discovered at the New York Metropolitan Museum of Art. Since the field of Egyptology has grown considerably since the nineteenth century, the scrolls embarrass the LDS Church because they show that Smith did not know how to translate hieroglyphics.

1970 McKay dies. Joseph Fielding Smith becomes the church's tenth prophet.

1972—Joseph Fielding Smith dies. Harold B. Lee becomes the church's eleventh prophet.

1973—Lee dies. Spencer W. Kimball becomes the church's twelfth prophet. He is the third in a period of only three years.

1978—Kimball is said to have received a revelation that would allow all worthy male members, including blacks, to hold the Mormon priesthood.

1981—The *Book of Mormon* undergoes another two hundred changes, including 2 Nephi 30:6, which previously stated that converted Lamanites (Indians) would become "white" after embracing Mormonism. This is now changed to "pure." There have been close to four thousand changes since the 1830 edition, most of which are grammatical and spelling corrections.

1982—The LDS Church records its 5 millionth member.

1983—Six temples are dedicated throughout the year as the LDS Church leadership attempts to build their temples throughout the world. From 1983 to 1986, a total of twenty temples are dedicated, doubling the worldwide total to forty.

1985—Kimball dies. Ezra Taft Benson becomes the church's thirteenth prophet.

1987—Mark Hofmann is imprisoned for the 1985 bombing deaths of Steven Christensen and Kathleen Sheets. Hofmann confesses to selling forgeries of historical documents to the LDS Church.

1990—The LDS temple ceremony undergoes a drastic modification. Much of the revision deleted offensive portions, including a section mocking Christian pastors. These changes were made by church leadership without a vote or advance notification to its members.

1991—The church's membership rolls continue to expand. Only two years after membership hit the 7-million-member mark in 1989, it is now at 8 million.

1993—Nine outspoken LDS intellectuals are excommunicated, including historian D. Michael Quinn. Steve Benson, the grandson of President Benson, resigns his membership because the LDS Church has kept the incapacitated president as the leader despite his physical inability to lead.

1994—Benson dies. Howard W. Hunter becomes the church's fourteenth prophet.

1995—Hunter dies after only 270 days as prophet, the shortest reign of any LDS president. Gordon B. Hinckley becomes the church's fifteenth prophet, its third prophet in two years.

1996—For the first time in its history, more LDS members reside outside than within the United States.

1997—The St. Louis temple is dedicated in the spring by Hinckley, who has dedicated fully half of all fifty LDS temples located throughout the world. Thirty-four have been built in the last twenty years.

—The LDS Church reaches 10 million members. At this rate of growth, one projection estimates that there will be 160 million Mormons by the year 2057.

1998—Hinckley makes a historic visit to West Africa and promises that a temple will be built in Accra, Ghana. At the spring general conference, Hinckley says that his church will concentrate on building smaller temples to accommodate members living in areas where the church is smaller in number.

1999—Hinckley announces that a temple will be built in Palmyra, New York, where Joseph Smith is said to have found the *Book of Mormon* plates. In addition, the Nauvoo, Illinois, temple, originally dedicated in 1846 but later destroyed, will be rebuilt on the original site.

2000—BYU President Merrill Bateman predicts that there will be 125,000 LDS missionaries by the year 2025. He also predicts that there could be "a thousand or more temples" by that same year.

Notes

Preface

1. Brigham H. Roberts, who was a member of the LDS Quorum of the Seventy as well as a church historian, claimed, "Nothing less than a complete apostasy from the Christian religion would warrant the establishment of the Church of Jesus Christ of Latter-day Saints. Of sects there were already enough in existence. Division and subdivision had already created of confusion more than enough, and there was no possible excuse for the introduction of a new Christian sect. But if men through apostasy had corrupted the Christian religion and lost divine authority to administer the ordinances of the Gospel, it was of the utmost importance that a new dispensation of the true Christian religion should be given to the world" (*History of the Church of Jesus Christ of Latter-day Saints,* 7 vols. [Salt Lake City: Deseret Book Co., 1973], 1:XL).

Introduction

1. Not all the Latter-day Saints ventured west with Brigham Young. Emma Smith, Joseph's widow, had a strong dislike for Young. She remained behind with her three sons. The oldest, Joseph Smith III, later became president of the Reorganized Church of Jesus Christ of Latter-day Saints (RLDS), which is based today in Independence, Missouri.

2. Even though those found practicing polygamy are promptly excommunicated from the LDS Church, many who have a very limited understanding of the Mormons still think it is accepted among them.

3. Brigham Young, *Discourses of Brigham Young,* comp. John A. Widtsoe (Salt Lake City: Deseret Book Co., 1978), 433.

4. Ibid., 126.

Chapter 1 God the Father

1. Bruce R. McConkie, *Mormon Doctrine,* 2d ed. (Salt Lake City: Bookcraft, 1966), 270.

2. Bruce R. McConkie, *A New Witness for the Articles of Faith* (Salt Lake City: Deseret Book Co., 1985), 55.

3. Ibid.

4. "Our Relationship with the Lord" speech. BYU devotional, 2 March 1982, p. 3. In the same speech McConkie emphasized, "There is no salvation in believing any false doc-

trine, particularly a false or unwise view about the Godhead or any of its members" (p. 2). To this we heartily agree. Deuteronomy 8:19 tells us that those who walk after other gods "shall surely perish." The question is, which view is best supported from the Bible?

5. Dallin H. Oaks, general conference speech, *Ensign* (May 1995): 84–85, emphasis ours.

6. Joseph Fielding Smith, *Teachings of the Prophet Joseph Smith* (Salt Lake City: Deseret Book Co., 1938), 345.

7. Mormon theology makes a distinction between Elohim and Jehovah. Mormon leaders such as President Joseph F. Smith have claimed that these are the names of two separate Gods. He said: "Among the spirit children of Elohim, the first-born was and is Jehovah, or Jesus Christ, to whom all others are juniors" (Joseph F. Smith, *Gospel Doctrine,* comp. John A. Widtsoe [Salt Lake City: Deseret Book Co., 1919], 70). It should be noted that the English form "Jehovah" was developed from four consonants (YHWH) known as the Tetragrammaton. Since this was considered to be the personal name of God, the pious Jew felt it was too holy to pronounce and therefore did not include vowels. From these four letters, we get the word "Yahweh," translated "LORD" in many passages of the Bible. On literally hundreds of occasions, the words "Yahweh" and "Elohim" are used together to demonstrate that Jehovah is Elohim (see Gen. 2:4–22; Deut. 4:1; Judg. 5:3; 1 Sam. 2:30). These words are also used together as "LORD our God," "LORD my God," "LORD his God," "LORD your God," and "LORD thy God." Even Joseph Smith in his Inspired Version of the Bible (also known as the Joseph Smith Translation) "translated" 1 Kings 8:60 as "The Lord is God" or "Jehovah is Elohim." (See also Exodus 34:14 in the JST.)

8. Orson Pratt, *The Seer* (Salt Lake City: Eborn Books, 1990), 132. Being a polygamist, the LDS Elohim sexually created spirit children with his heavenly wives. All spirit beings in existence were produced this way. The Heavenly Mother doctrine finds no scriptural support within any of the four LDS scriptures. On page 516 of *Mormon Doctrine,* 2d ed. (Salt Lake City: Bookcraft, 1966), Bruce McConkie said the Heavenly Mother doctrine was an "unspoken truth." The *Encyclopedia of Mormonism* (vol. 2, "Mother in Heaven") admits that Latter-day Saints must "infer from authoritative sources of scripture and modern prophecy that there is a Heavenly Mother as well as a Heavenly Father. . . . Today the belief in a living Mother in Heaven is implicit in Latter-day Saint thought" (ed. Daniel H. Ludlow [New York: Macmillan, 1992], 961).

9. Orson Hyde, as quoted in *Journal of Discourses,* ed. George D. Watt, 26 vols. (Liverpool, England: F. D. Richards, 1854–86), 1:123.

10. James E. Talmage, *The Articles of Faith* (Salt Lake City: Deseret Book Co., 1987), 430.

11. Brigham Young in Watt, ed., *Journal of Discourses,* 3:93.

12. Spencer W. Kimball, *Teachings of Spencer W. Kimball,* comp. Edward L. Kimball (Salt Lake City: Bookcraft, 1982), 26.

13. Spencer W. Kimball, *The Miracle of Forgiveness* (Salt Lake City: Bookcraft, 1969), 2.

14. *Ensign* (June 1993): 10.

15. Milton R. Hunter, *The Gospel through the Ages* (Salt Lake City: Stevens and Wallis, 1945), 114.

16. John A. Widtsoe, *A Rational Theology As Taught by the Church of Jesus Christ of Latter-day Saints,* 7th ed. (Salt Lake City: Deseret Book Co., 1968), 24.

17. Herman Bavinck, *The Doctrine of God* (Great Britain: Banner of Truth Trust, 1991), 147.

18. Smith, *Teachings of the Prophet Joseph Smith,* 354.

19. Joseph Fielding Smith, *Doctrines of Salvation: Sermons and Writings of Joseph Fielding Smith,* 3 vols., ed. Bruce R. McConkie (Salt Lake City: Bookcraft, 1954–56), 2:47.

20. Joseph Fielding Smith, *Answers to Gospel Questions,* 4 vols. (Salt Lake City: Deseret Book Co., 1957–63), 2:144.

21. Young, *Discourses,* 22.

22. Brigham Young in Watt, ed., *Journal of Discourses,* 7:284. This quote is used in *Teachings of Presidents of the Church Brigham Young,* a 1997 manual used that year in Sunday school classes. Titled "Knowing and Honoring the Godhead," chapter 4 of this book states that the God of the Mormon Church is completely different from the God as historically taught in Christian history.

23. Joseph Fielding McConkie and Robert L. Millet, *Doctrinal Commentary on the Book of Mormon* (Salt Lake City: Bookcraft, 1987), 1:193.

24. Hunter, *The Gospel through the Ages,* 107.

25. Parley P. Pratt, *Key to the Science of Theology: A Voice of Warning* (Salt Lake City: Deseret Book Co., 1978), 21.

26. Orson Whitney, as quoted in *Collected Discourses,* ed. Brian H. Stuy, 5 vols. (Burbank, Calif., and Woodland Hills, Utah: B.H.S. Publishers, 1987–92), 4.

27. Bruce R. McConkie, *The Mortal Messiah* (Salt Lake City: Deseret Book Co., 1982), 35. No clearer description can be given than the one in the LDS manual *Achieving a Celestial Marriage* (Salt Lake City: The Church of Jesus Christ of Latter-day Saints, 1976), which reads, ". . . our Father in heaven was once a man as we are now, capable of physical death."

28. Don Lattin, "Musings with the Prophet," *San Francisco Chronicle,* 13 April 1997, sec. Z1, p. 3.

29. *Ensign* (July 1996): 53.

30. Smith, *Teachings of the Prophet Joseph Smith,* 345.

31. Ibid.

32. Numbers 23:19 follows the same line of thought: "God is not a man, that he should lie; neither the son of man, that he should repent."

33. Orson Hyde, "A Diagram of the Kingdom of God," *Millennial Star* 9 (15 January 1847): 23–24, as quoted in *The Words of Joseph Smith* (Orem, Utah: Grandlin Book Co., 1993), 299. According to Andrew F. Ehat and Lyndon W. Cook, the book's authors, there was "probably no clearer statement of Joseph's theology" than this editorial by Orson Hyde (297).

34. Cleon Skousen, *The First 2,000 Years* (Salt Lake City: Bookcraft, 1979), 355–56.

35. Widtsoe, *A Rational Theology,* 12.

36. This attribute should not be construed to mean that God, in His infinite perfection, could or would ever do anything contrary to His righteous nature. For instance, God cannot sin or in any way deny His holy character.

37. Brigham Young in Watt, ed., *Journal of Discourses,* 6:345.

38. Talmage, *The Articles of Faith,* 42–43.

39. McConkie, *Mormon Doctrine,* 359.

40. John A. Widtsoe, *Evidences and Reconciliations,* 3 vols. in 1, comp. G. Homer Durham (Salt Lake City: Bookcraft, 1960), 76–77.

41. Pratt, *Key to the Science of Theology,* 1855, 29. It should be noted that when this was reprinted after Pratt's death, this portion was changed to read: "Jesus Christ, a little babe like all the rest of us have been, grew to be a man, and received a fullness of the

glory of the Father; and he received all power, both in heaven and on earth; and the glory of the Father was with him, for he dwelt in him" (1978 ed., 19).

42. R. C. Sproul, *Essential Truths of the Christian Faith* (Wheaton: Tyndale House, 1992), 43.

43. This same thought is found in Isaiah 66:1: "Thus saith the LORD, The heaven is my throne, and the earth is my footstool: where is the house that ye build unto me?"

44. Literally the Greek reads "God is spirit."

45. Bruce McConkie wrote, "False creeds teach that God is a spirit essence that fills the immensity of space and is everywhere and nowhere in particular present. In a vain attempt to support this doctrine, formulated by councils in the early days of the great apostasy, it is common for apologists to point to the statement in the King James Bible which says, 'God is a Spirit.' (John 4:22–24.) The fact is that this passage is mistranslated; instead, the correct statement, quoted in context reads: 'The hour cometh, and now is, when the true worshippers shall worship the Father in spirit and in truth; for the Father seeketh such to worship him. For unto such hath God promised his Spirit. And they who worship him, must worship in spirit and in truth.' (Inspired Version, John 4:25–26.)" (*Mormon Doctrine,* 318). It should be noted that absolutely no ancient manuscript supports McConkie's position.

Chapter 2 *Jesus*

1. *Ensign* (May 1977): 26.

2. *Church News,* 7 February 1987, 13, emphasis ours.

3. *Church News,* 20 June 1998, 7. In the spring general conference held several months earlier, Hinckley said, "We acknowledge without hesitation that there are differences between us [and other faiths]. Were this not so there would have been no need for a restoration of the gospel," *Ensign* (May 1998): 4.

4. McConkie, *Mormon Doctrine,* 129, 323. Many Mormons have told us that they don't accept many of the teachings of this book, jokingly referring to it as "Brother Bruce's" opinion. Were his teachings "Mormon doctrine" as the title suggests? Since this work is often referenced in LDS publications, we see no reason why it should be disregarded.

5. Gnosticism should be considered an entirely different religion, not just a heresy. Gnosticism taught that a person could reach God through knowledge, not faith in Christ. The apostle John dealt with important Gnostic issues in his epistles.

6. Docetism was created by Gnosticism and taught that Jesus could not be human but was completely and totally God.

7. This taught that Jesus was man but not completely God (a supernaturally endowed human).

8. This taught that Jesus was not always God, but He evolved to godhood and lost His humanity. Origen was the main proponent of this heresy, and he also was the originator of the LDS doctrine known as "preexistence."

9. Also known as Sabellianism, which teaches that God has different forms. Its proponents teach that God is sometimes the Father, sometimes the Son, and sometimes the Holy Ghost.

10. This taught that Jesus was merely a god, a created being lower than the Father.

11. Harold O. J. Brown, *Heresies: The Image of Christ in the Mirror of Heresy and Orthodoxy from the Apostles to the Present* (Grand Rapids: Baker, 1984), 21.

12. Ezra Taft Benson, *Teachings of Ezra Taft Benson* (Salt Lake City: Bookcraft, 1988), 7. This was quoted in the *Ensign* (April 1997): 15.

13. *Gospel Principles* (Salt Lake City: The Church of Jesus Christ of Latter-day Saints, 1992), 64.

14. Brigham Young in Watt, ed., *Journal of Discourses,* 8:115.

15. Heber C. Kimball in Watt, ed., *Journal of Discourses,* 8:211.

16. Joseph F. Smith, *Family Home Evening Manual* (Salt Lake City: The Church of Jesus Christ of Latter-day Saints, 1972), 125–26.

17. McConkie, *Mormon Doctrine,* 547, 742.

18. McConkie, *The Promised Messiah,* 468.

19. Talmage, *The Articles of Faith,* 466–67.

20. James Talmage, *Jesus the Christ* (Salt Lake City: Deseret Book Co., 1981), 81.

21. *Messages for Exaltation: Eternal Insights from the Book of Mormon* (Salt Lake City: Deseret Sunday School Union, 1967), 378–79.

22. BYU professor Stephen E. Robinson in *The Mormon Puzzle* video produced in 1997 by the Southern Baptist Convention.

23. McConkie, *The Promised Messiah,* 466.

24. Hunter, *The Gospel through the Ages,* 51, 200.

25. *Ensign* (November 1995): 87, italics his. Unless a god can be imperfect, this would seem to contradict McConkie's notion that Jesus became God in the preexistence.

26. It should be noted that Joseph Smith radically changed verse 1 of this passage in his Inspired Version to read: "In the beginning was the gospel preached through the Son. And the gospel was the word, and the word was with the Son, and the Son was with God, and the Son was of God." No ancient biblical manuscript supports such a translation. The idea that Jesus was eternally God can be supported from many other passages, including John 5:17–18; 8:58 (in conjunction with Exod. 3:14); 10:30–33; 14:7–11; 17:5 (in conjunction with Isa. 42:8); 20:28–29; 2 Corinthians 8:9; Colossians 1:19; 2:3, 8–9; Titus 2:13; 2 Peter 1:1; 1 John 5:20.

27. This doctrine is known as the kenosis. Basically this position holds that Christ did not give up His divine attributes. Rather, He voluntarily gave up the exercise of those attributes while here on earth (see Phil. 2:5–11).

28. Although some Mormon leaders, including Joseph Fielding Smith in *Doctrines of Salvation,* 1:14, say prayers should only be offered to the Father, 3 Nephi 19:17ff in the *Book of Mormon* supports the biblical practice.

29. Kimball, *Teachings of Spencer W. Kimball,* 32–33.

30. Hunter, *The Gospel through the Ages,* 15.

31. Jess L. Christensen in *A Sure Foundation: Answers to Difficult Gospel Questions* (Salt Lake City: Deseret Book Co., 1988), 223–24. Other places where this doctrine is discussed include the LDS Church–produced *Gospel Principles,* 17; Kimball, *Teachings of Spencer W. Kimball,* 33–34; *Journal of Discourses,* 6:8.

32. Lest there be confusion over the term *firstborn,* it should be pointed out that the Greek word used is not *protoktistos* (meaning *first created*) but rather *prototokos* (meaning *firstborn*). Both Hebrews 1:3 and 2 Corinthians 4:4 point out that Christ is the exact representation of God. The title of *firstborn* is used to show preeminence as it does in Colossians 1:18. First Samuel 16:1–3 and Psalm 89:27 show that David was the last of Jesse's sons, yet the same Greek word in the Septuagint is used to declare the preeminence of David, not his order of birth. Also, if Jesus was first created, how could He create "all things"?

33. Brigham Young in Watt, ed., *Journal of Discourses,* 14:71–72.

34. Ibid., 7:333.

35. McConkie, *The Mortal Messiah,* 4:434. McConkie's use of Philippians 2:12 ("work out") also misses the meaning of the passage. Paul does not use this expression to mean "work for" as so many Mormons often insist. Still, we find it reprehensible to suggest that the perfect Christ was in need of any salvation at all.

36. Brigham Young in Watt, ed., *Journal of Discourses,* 13:309.

37. Pratt, *The Seer,* 172.

38. Orson Hyde in Watt, ed., *Journal of Discourses,* 4:259. See also 2:81–82, 210. The idea that Jesus was married at Cana is an argument from silence, since there is no proof of this whatsoever. It needs to be assumed that Jesus was actually the groom at the wedding. The context, however, shows that Jesus was merely a guest. Finally, at the cross, why was Jesus only concerned about the welfare of His mother? If He were married, it would have been logical for Him to have made instructions for the welfare of His wives and children as well.

39. Jedediah M. Grant in Watt, ed., *Journal of Discourses,* 1:346.

40. Smith, *Doctrines of Salvation,* 2:43–44; Smith, *Teachings of the Prophet Joseph Smith,* 301; Kimball, *Miracle of Forgiveness,* 245.

Chapter 3 *The Trinity*

1. Larry Dahl, "The Morning Breaks, the Shadows Flee," *Ensign* (April 1997): 14–15. He quoted from Talmage's *The Articles of Faith,* 12th ed. (1966), 47–48.

2. Smith, *Teachings of the Prophet Joseph Smith,* 370, 372.

3. Bruce R. McConkie, *The Promised Messiah,* The Messiah Series, vol. 1 (Salt Lake City: Deseret Book Co., 1978), 117–18. For other such quotes, see *History of the Church,* 6:476 and *The Articles of Faith* by Talmage, 47–48.

4. Gordon B. Hinckley, *Church News,* 4 July 1998, 2, from a member meeting in Leon, Mexico (11 March 1998).

5. Deuteronomy 6:4 says, "Hear, O Israel: The LORD our God is one LORD."

6. Rex E. Lee, *What Do Mormons Believe?* (Salt Lake City: Deseret Book Co., 1992), 21.

7. To assume that the Father, Son, and Holy Spirit are three separate Gods is, in the least, tritheism.

8. McConkie, *Mormon Doctrine,* 511.

9. *Defining the Mormon Doctrine of Deity,* a pamphlet printed in the Mormon Miscellaneous series, 1985, 5.

10. McConkie, *Mormon Doctrine,* 579.

11. Ronald Youngblood, as quoted in the *Evangelical Dictionary of Theology,* ed. Walter A. Elwell (Grand Rapids: Baker, 1984), 732. While Mormons may use Genesis 1:26 in an attempt to show that there is more than one God and that He has a body of flesh and bones, it should be pointed out that God is not a man, according to Numbers 23:19; 1 Samuel 15:29; and Hosea 11:9. The image and likeness talked about in Genesis refers not to God's physical nature but rather His spiritual nature. While metaphorical language is found throughout the Bible, references that point to God having a nose, hand, or eyes should not be taken any more literally than Psalm 91:4 (God is a bird?), John 10:7 (Jesus is a door?), or Hebrews 12:29 (God is hot?), among others.

12. J. N. D. Kelly, *Early Christian Doctrines* (New York: Harper San Francisco: 1978), 89.

13. Brown, *Heresies,* 20.

Chapter 4 *Preexistence and the Second Estate*

1. *Ensign* (January 1998): 15, as quoted from the *Ensign* (November 1983): 16–18.

2. Smith, *Doctrines of Salvation,* 1:74–75.

3. McConkie, *Mormon Doctrine,* 169.

4. *Ensign* (February 1996): 15.

5. *Gospel Principles,* 21. This is the idea that all people were given the freedom to choose between right and wrong in the preexistence as well as today on this earth.

6. Ibid., 18–19.

7. McConkie, *Mormon Doctrine,* 590.

8. *Gospel Principles,* 13–14.

9. *Ensign* (November 1993): 72.

10. George Q. Cannon, *Gospel Truth* (Salt Lake City: Deseret Book Co., 1987), 7.

11. Ludlow, ed., *Encyclopedia of Mormonism,* vol. 3, s.v. "Preesixtence (pre-earthly existence)," 1123.

12. Brigham Young, *Discourses of Brigham Young,* comp. John A. Widtsoe (Salt Lake City: Deseret Book Co., 1978), 197.

13. "LDS Handbook Says Family Size Up to Couple, God," *Salt Lake Tribune,* 5 December 1998, p. A1.

14. Smith, *Doctrines of Salvation,* 2:88–89.

15. David O. McKay, *Conference Report* (October 1947): 119; David O. McKay, *Gospel Ideals,* comp. G. Homer Durham (Salt Lake City: Improvement Era, 1953), 487.

16. Smith, *Doctrines of Salvation,* 2:87.

17. Ibid., 2:89.

18. Stephen E. Robinson, *BYU Studies* 17, no. 2 (winter 1977): 133.

19. Charles R. Harrell, *BYU Studies* 28, no. 2 (spring 1988): 77.

20. Ibid., 79. Charles Harrell writes: "The only other Book of Mormon passage that might have been construed as referring to preexistence is Ether 3:15." Any overtone of preexistence in this declaration tends to be overshadowed by the text immediately before and after it that discusses humanity's creation in the flesh. For Orson Pratt, in the light of his later understanding of the concept of preexistence, the clear implication was that all people were created spiritually in the beginning in the image and likeness of Christ's spirit. However, it is unlikely that the earliest converts who did not have the additional revelation would have connected this verse to such a doctrine. Orson Pratt himself reported that he saw a reference to preexistence in this verse only after reading "the new translation of the Scriptures, that throwing so much light and information of the subject, I searched the Book of Mormon to see if there were indications in it that related to the preexistence of man." It would seem, then, that neither the Bible nor the *Book of Mormon* was sufficient to establish the idea of preexistence in the minds of the Saints.

21. Ibid., 77.

22. Ibid., 88.

23. Job 15:7; Malachi 2:10; and John 9:2 are other passages sometimes referred to in support of this doctrine.

24. One passage that may be used by Mormons is Acts 17:28–29. Mormons assume Paul's reference to a Greek poet supports their notion that we are literally the offspring of God. This conclusion fails to take into account that the Greek poet mentioned by Paul referred to Zeus. Furthermore, the Greeks did not believe mankind was the literal offspring of Zeus. For further information see chapter 13 of our book *Questions to Ask Your Mormon Friend* (Minneapolis: Bethany, 1994), "Do You Really Believe You Can Become a God?"

25. Even the *Book of Mormon* tends to discount this idea that we have always been the children of God. Ether 3:14 says, "Behold, I am Jesus Christ. I am the Father and the Son. In me shall all mankind have life, and that eternally, even they who shall believe on my name; and they shall become my sons and my daughters." See also Mosiah 5:7; 3 Nephi 9:17; and Moroni 7:26, 48. A Mormon may argue that this only refers to a spiritual sonship. However, this objection has validity only if it can be demonstrated that the *Book of Mormon* teaches the LDS concept of the preexistence, which it does not.

Chapter 5 *The Fall*

1. Mormon leaders have taught that the Garden of Eden was located in what is today the state of Missouri. President Joseph Fielding Smith said in *Doctrines of Salvation,* 3:74: "In accord with the revelations given to the Prophet Joseph Smith, we teach that the Garden of Eden was on the American continent located where the City Zion, or the New Jerusalem, will be built. When Adam and Eve were driven out of the Garden, they eventually dwelt at a place called Adam-ondi-Ahman, situated in what is now Daviess County, Missouri."

2. Talmage, *Articles of Faith,* 70. He added, "With understanding of the nature of his act," Adam "also partook of the fruit that grew on the tree of knowledge" (65).

3. Joseph Fielding Smith, *Search These Commandments: Melchizedek Priesthood Personal Study Guide* (Salt Lake City: The Church of Jesus Christ of Latter-day Saints, 1984), 237.

4. McConkie, *The Promised Messiah,* 222.

5. Widtsoe, *Evidences and Reconciliations,* 195.

6. *Ensign* (January 1994): 10.

7. *Ensign* (November 1993): 73.

8. Also see Moses 5:10–11 in the *Pearl of Great Price.*

9. John 8:44 says, "Ye are of your father the devil, and the lusts of your father ye will do. He was a murderer from the beginning, and abode not in the truth, because there is no truth in him. When he speaketh a lie, he speaketh of his own: for he is a liar and the father of it." Even 2 Nephi 9:9 in the *Book of Mormon* agrees that Satan is the "father of lies."

10. Smith, *Doctrines of Salvation,* 1:115.

11. *Ensign* (November 1993): 73.

12. For instance, Exodus 34:7 lists iniquity, transgression, and sin as being synonymous. Psalm 32:1 and Micah 6:7 also follows this pattern.

13. Joseph Smith Jr., *Doctrine and Covenants of the Church of Jesus Christ of Latter-day Saints* (Salt Lake City: The Church of Jesus Christ of Latter-day Saints, 1981), 132:26.

Chapter 6 *Apostasy*

1. *Gospel Principles,* 105. If a Mormon chooses to argue that a lack of communication between leaders in the church caused them all to perish without successors, it suggests a concurrent genocide that history does not support.

2. Lee, *What Do Mormons Believe?* 4–5.

3. *Joseph Smith—History,* 1:19–20a in the *Pearl of Great Price.*

4. Mark E. Petersen, *Conference Reports of the Church of Jesus Christ of Latter-day Saints* (Salt Lake City: The Church of Jesus Christ of Latter-day Saints, April 1945), 43.

5. Benson, *Teachings of Ezra Taft Benson,* 86.

6. These would be results from "persecution" (Matt. 24:9–10), false teachers (Matt. 24:11), temptation (Luke 8:13), defective knowledge of Christ (1 John 2:19), moral lapse (Heb. 6:4–6), forsaking spiritual living (Heb. 10:25–31), and unbelief (Heb. 3:12).

7. Found in the section on "hell" (vol. 2, 586). In order to explain Matthew 16:18, Mormons are compelled to spiritualize the passage. For instance, LDS Apostle Orson Pratt stated "that the Church of Christ still exists in heaven and that the gates of hell have not prevailed against her" (*Divine Authenticity of the Book of Mormon—The Bible Alone an Insufficient Guide* [Liverpool, England, 1851], 44). Numerous passages in the *Doctrine and Covenants* give the impression that the church spoken of in Matthew 16:18 now refers to the LDS Church (see sections 10:69, 18:1–5).

8. Harold B. Lee, *Conference Report* (April 1953): 26.

9. Harold B. Lee, *Stand Ye in Holy Places: Selected Sermons and Writings of President Harold B. Lee* (Salt Lake City: Deseret Book Co., 1975), 127.

10. First Corinthians 12:3 says, "Wherefore I give you to understand, that no man speaking by the Spirit of God calleth Jesus accursed: and that no man can say that Jesus is the Lord, but by the Holy Ghost."

11. First Corinthians 3:10–11 says, "According to the grace of God which is given unto me, as a wise masterbuilder, I have laid the foundation, and another buildeth thereon. But let every man take heed how he buildeth thereupon. For other foundation can no man lay than that is laid, which is Jesus Christ."

12. Although the *Book of Mormon* does not call these men "apostles," Apostle Bruce McConkie does so in *Mormon Doctrine,* 793.

13. The *Encyclopedia of Mormonism,* vol. 1, s.v. "Book of Abraham," says, "Although it is not known whether Joseph Smith actually had this document, he provided a translation of it" (136).

14. Jesus did tell Peter in John 21:22, "If I will that he [John] tarry till I come, what is that to thee? follow thou me." John gave a personal note in the next verse to head off any faulty interpretation of Jesus' statement: "Then went this saying abroad among the brethren, that that disciple should not die; yet Jesus said not unto him, He shall not die; but, If I will that he tarry till I come, what is that to thee?" This contradicts Joseph Smith's interpretation.

15. Interview with David Whitmer, *Millennial Star* (9 December 1878): 40:773.

16. John Taylor in Watt, ed., *Journal of Discourses,* 18:308.

17. Wilford Woodruff, *The Discourses of Wilford Woodruff,* comp. G. Homer Durham (Salt Lake City: Bookcraft, 1946), 95.

18. Franklin Dewey Richards in Stuy, ed., *Collected Discourses,* vol. 3 (3 April 1892).

19. For example, see *About the Three Nephites* by Doug Beardall (Salt Lake City: LDS Book Publications, 1992).

20. Ludlow, ed., *Encyclopedia of Mormonism,* vol. 4, s.v. "Three Nephites," 1477.

21. Ibid.

22. This brings up the question, "Why were there twenty-four apostles on the earth at the same time?" Today the LDS Church only has twelve apostles.

23. This account shows the reorganization of the disciples after the Ascension of Christ. They apparently felt compelled to replace Judas.

24. Ludlow, ed., *Encyclopedia of Mormonism,* vol. 1, s.v. "Aaronic Priesthood," 3.

25. Ibid.

26. Ludlow, ed., *Encyclopedia of Mormonism,* vol. 2, s.v. "Melchizedek Priesthood," 886.

27. Robert J. Matthews, "The Role of the House of Israel in the Last Days," in *Watch and Be Ready: Preparing for the Second Coming of the Lord* (Salt Lake City: Deseret Book Co., 1994), 84ff. Matthews, who noted that he had held the position of a teacher in the Church Educational System for forty years, cited *D&C* 86:8–11, 96:7, 113:6–8, and 132:30–31 as well as Abraham 2:11 in the *Pearl of Great Price.*

28. Bruce R. McConkie, "The Patriarchal Order," address delivered to a religion class at BYU on 8 August 1967, as quoted in Matthews, "The Role of the House of Israel in the Last Days," 85. In what is known as a patriarchal blessing, a "patriarch" tells each Mormon the tribe from which he descends. Most Mormons are told they come from the tribe of Ephraim.

29. For more information see our book *Questions to Ask Your Mormon Friend,* chapter 9 ("Is the Mormon Priesthood Really of Ancient Origin?").

Chapter 7 *The Bible*

1. Bruce R. McConkie, *The Millennial Messiah* (Salt Lake City: Deseret Book Co., 1982), 160, 161, 164.

2. We see no need to debate the validity of the apocryphal books for the reason that Mormons, like Protestants, do not consider them authoritative. In *D&C* 91:3, Joseph Smith was supposedly told by God that "it is not needful that the Apocrypha should be translated" in his Inspired Version because, as the previous verse says, "there are many things contained therein that are not true, which are interpolations by the hands of men."

3. A. Berkeley Mickelsen, *Interpreting the Bible* (Grand Rapids: Eerdmans, 1963), 94–95.

4. *Ensign* (January 1995): 7.

5. See our book *Questions to Ask Your Mormon Friend* ("What If the Bible Is Translated Correctly After All?").

6. Not even LDS Church leaders can claim that their non-English *Book of Mormon* translations are taken from a first-generation source, since the original plates are no longer available. Since all of the dozens of foreign translations of the *Book of Mormon* have been derived from the admittedly second-generation English rendition (see *Ensign* [May 1995]: 10), all other translations into foreign languages are really third-generation texts. It would therefore appear that this argument (the Bible is a translation of a translation of a translation) would better apply to the *Book of Mormon!*

7. While many Mormons are fond of pointing out "contradictions" of biblical passages to question the accuracy of the Bible, we need to point out that this accusation of inconsistency is a very shallow argument. Unfortunately, room does not permit answering any specific objections here. However, numerous reference sources are available to Christians who are told that their Bible cannot be trusted. Four of the better resources are: *When Cultists Ask* by Norman Geisler and Ron Rhodes (Grand Rapids: Baker, 1997); *When Critics Ask* by Norman Geisler and Thomas Howe (Wheaton, Ill.: Victor, 1992); *Encyclopedia of Bible Difficulties* by Gleason Archer (Grand Rapids: Zondervan, 1982); and *Hard Sayings of the Bible* with Walter Kaiser Jr., Peter Davids, F. F. Bruce, and Manfred Brauch (Downers Grove, Ill.: InterVarsity Press, 1996).

8. See also Talmage, *Articles of Faith,* 210.

9. The LDS Church officially sanctions the King James Version Bible, although church manuals and publications have been increasingly giving more attention to Joseph Smith's Inspired Version, a "translation" of the Bible he claimed to have "finished" in 1833 (*History of the Church of Jesus Christ of Latter-day Saints* [Salt Lake City: Deseret Book Co., 1973], 1:368; *Deseret News 1999–2000 Church Almanac* [Salt Lake City: Deseret

News, 1998], 483). In the June 1999 edition of the LDS magazine *Ensign* (21), Andrew Skinner, department chair of ancient scripture at BYU, apparently agreed with its importance: "In the words of Elder Bruce R. McConkie (1915–85) of the Quorum of the Twelve Apostles, 'The Joseph Smith Translation, or Inspired Version, is a thousand times over the best Bible now existing on earth.'" Skinner went on to say, "The JST is a special gift given of the Lord. It is one of the great evidences of the Prophet Joseph Smith's divine calling." Despite such accolades, the LDS Church does not give away copies of the Joseph Smith Translation.

10. For instance, the name of King Benjamin was later changed to King Mosiah in Mosiah 21:28 and Ether 4:1; the phrase "son of" was added in passages such as 1 Nephi 11:18, 21, 32, and 13:40; the word "not" was inserted in 2 Nephi 12:9 to completely change the meaning.

Chapter 8 *The* Book of Mormon

1. For a discussion as to whether the Christian should pray about the *Book of Mormon*, see *Questions to Ask Your Mormon Friend* ("Why Should a Person Pray about the *Book of Mormon* When the Bible Says We Should Not Rely on Such a Subjective Test?").

2. "Our Best Books," *Parade* (29 December 1991), 20.

3. *History of the Church of Jesus Christ of Latter-day Saints* (Salt Lake City: Deseret Book Co., 1973), 4:537.

4. Ludlow, ed., *Encyclopedia of Mormonism,* vol. 1, s.v. "Book of Mormon plates and records," 200.

5. McConkie, *Mormon Doctrine,* 99, emphasis ours.

6. *Ensign* (November 1984): 7.

7. David Whitmer, *An Address to All Believers in Christ* (Richmond, Mo.: David Whitmer, 1887), 12. This story is quoted and confirmed by LDS Apostle Russell M. Nelson in the *Ensign* (July 1993): 62.

8. B. H. Roberts, comp., *Comprehensive History of the Church of Jesus Christ of Latter-day Saints,* 6 vols. (1930; reprint, Orem, Utah: Sonos Publishing, 1991), 1:129. Roberts quotes Harris as saying the stone Smith possessed was a "chocolate-colored, somewhat egg-shaped stone which the Prophet . . . was able to translate the characters engraven on the plates." Other publications verifying Smith's use of this stone include the *Millennial Star* and the *Saint's Herald.*

9. The biblical description of the Urim and Thummim is very vague. What is known is that the name implies "light" and "perfection." While there is no description of what this looked like, Exodus 28:30 and Leviticus 8:8 state that it was stored in the high priest's breastpiece, which was attached to the ephod, a sleeveless vest. It appears this was used to receive revelation from God. However, the Bible never implies that the Urim and Thummim were used for translation purposes.

10. Francis W. Kirkham, *A New Witness for Christ in America,* 2 vols. (Salt Lake City: Utah Printing Co., 1960), 2:417.

11. Smith, *Doctrines of Salvation,* 3:225–26.

12. D. Michael Quinn, *Early Mormonism and the Magic World View* (Salt Lake City: Signature Books, 1987), 194.

13. Smith did in fact have an affair with Fanny Alger. LDS historian Richard Van Wagoner noted that Smith's wife Emma "was searching for her husband and Alger one evening when through the crack in a barn door she saw 'him and Fanny in the barn together alone' on the hay mow." Some believe Alger became Smith's first plural wife.

14. Andrew Jenson, *Latter-day Saint Biographical Encyclopedia,* 4 vols. (Salt Lake City: A Jensen History, 1901–36), see "Cowdery, Oliver," 1:246.

15. *Joseph Smith—History,* 1:19 in *Pearl of Great Price.* Also see 1 Nephi 14:10 and *D&C* 1:30 in LDS scripture.

16. Whitmer, *An Address to All Believers in Christ,* 36, 39.

17. *History of the Church,* 3:228; *D&C* 28:11.

18. David Whitmer, *An Address to All Believers in the Book of Mormon* (Richmond, Mo: David Whitmer, 1887), 56–62.

19. Whitmer, *An Address to All Believers in Christ,* 27.

20. Out of the three witnesses, even Mormon scholars do not dispute that Whitmer was an LDS apostate "who never returned to the Church." See *A Sure Foundation,* 41.

21. *History of the Church,* 2:26.

22. *D&C* 3:12–13; 10:6–7.

23. *D&C* 19:20.

24. *History of the Church,* 2:95.

25. The Shakers were officially known as the United Society of Believers in Christ's Second Appearing. Led by Ann Lee, this faith came to America from England in 1774. The name Shaker was given to the group because of the way the members shook and trembled to rid themselves of evil. James Strang, after the death of Joseph Smith, claimed that the slain prophet had written a letter making him his successor. When his claim was rejected, he left to form a splinter group of Latter-day Saints that settled on Beaver Island, Michigan. Steven L. Shields notes in his book *Divergent Paths of the Restoration* (Los Angeles, Calif.: Restoration Research, 1990), 42, "For several years prior to his death, Strang's following rivaled that of Brigham Young!" Strang was murdered on 16 June 1856.

26. Anthony Metcalf, *Ten Years before the Mast* (Malad City, Idaho, 1888), as quoted in Kirkham, *A New Witness for Christ in America,* 2:348–49. The Brighamite branch refers to the Salt Lake City Church, while the Josephite Church refers to the Reorganized Church based in Independence, Missouri.

27. *History of the Church,* 3:16–20.

28. Wilford Wood, *Joseph Smith Begins His Work* (Salt Lake City: Publisher's Press, 1958), introductory pages.

29. Marvin S. Hill, "Brodie Revisited: A Reappraisal," *Dialogue: A Journal of Mormon Thought* 7, no. 4 (winter 1972): 83–84.

30. On page 345 of *Faith Precedes the Miracle* (Salt Lake City: Deseret Book Co., 1978), Spencer Kimball wrote, "The Lamanite population of the Americas, at the greatest number, must have run into many millions, for in certain periods of Book of Mormon history, wars continued almost unabated and the soil was covered with the bodies of the slain." In Ether 15:2 in the *Book of Mormon,* the Jaredites alone had "two millions of mighty men, and also their wives and their children." With so many people who supposedly lived on the American continent, the artifacts should be numerous.

31. Smith, *Doctrines of Salvation,* 3:232, 239–40, italics his.

32. Ibid., 3:233–34.

33. James E. Talmage, *The Vitality of Mormonism* (Boston: Gorham Press, 1919), 199.

34. The Jaredites were a people group that supposedly came to the Western Hemisphere around the time when God confounded the languages at the Tower of Babel.

35. Benson, *Teachings of Ezra Taft Benson,* 587–88.

36. In a personal letter to Bill McKeever on 11 June 1992, Dr. John Sorenson stated that Joseph Fielding Smith "misread relevant historical documents." While it is certainly

possible that Smith could have done so, we must bear in mind that he held the position of a trusted LDS Church historian for nearly half a century.

37. John Sorenson, "The Book of Mormon in Ancient America," on the FARMS Internet Web site.

38. *Messages of the First Presidency of the Church of Jesus Christ of Latter-day Saints (1833–1951),* 6 vols., ed. James R. Clark (Salt Lake City: Bookcraft, 1965–75), 5:285.

39. *Messages of the First Presidency,* 4:232, emphasis ours.

40. E-mail to Bill McKeever, 16 June 1999.

41. Among Coe's works are *Mexico* and *The Maya,* both published by Thames and Hudson.

42. Michael Coe, "Mormons and Archaeology: An Outside View," *Dialogue* 8 (summer 1973): 41, 42, 46.

43. Ibid., 48.

44. Personal letter addressed to Bill McKeever, 17 August 1993.

45. *Review of Books on the Book of Mormon,* 8 vols. (Provo, Utah: FARMS, 1993), 5:329. Pointing out recent LDS research, including Mormon scholar John Sorenson's 1985 book *An Ancient American Setting for the Book of Mormon,* Norwood notes in a footnote that "it is interesting to note that Coe's essay appeared twelve years before Sorenson's book was published" (330). However, as shown above, Coe (and other non-LDS scholars) *still* rejects scientific backing for the *Book of Mormon.*

46. Stephen Thompson, "'Critical' Book of Mormon Scholarship," *Dialogue* 27, no. 4 (winter 1994): 205.

47. The technology of this age will help scientists understand more in a quicker time. According to the article "From Camels to Computers" in *Biblical Archaeology Review,* "Until very recently, our tools have been modest worker's implements: trowels, picks, levels and buckets. Supplementing these now are a whole array of high-tech machines that are swiftly changing the way we excavate" (vol. 21, no. 4 [July/August 1995]: 45).

48. Benson, *Teachings of Ezra Taft Benson,* 55, 60.

49. Smith, *Teachings of the Prophet Joseph Smith,* 194. *Joseph Smith History,* 1:34, says the *Book of Mormon* is the "fulness of the everlasting gospel."

50. *Conference Report* (April 1902), 38.

51. *Gospel Principles,* 303–4.

52. These points were taken from Art Budvarson's *A Rebuttal to "The Problems of the Book of Mormon"* (La Mesa, Calif.: Utah Christian Tract Society, n.d.), 30–31.

53. *Review of Books on the Book of Mormon,* vol. 5 (1993), 57–58. Peterson admits "several distinctively Latter-day Saint doctrines are not clearly discussed in the Book of Mormon." However, he believes that the book contains "allusions" to LDS doctrines.

54. McConkie, *The Promised Messiah,* 52.

Chapter 9 *The* Doctrine and Covenants *and the* Pearl of Great Price

1. Mormon President Ezra Taft Benson said that the *D&C* was "the only book in the world that has a preface written by the Lord Himself" (*Ensign* [November 1986]: 79).

2. *Ensign* (May 1987): 83.

3. Ludlow, ed., *Encyclopedia of Mormonism,* vol. 1, s.v. "Doctrine and Covenant Editions," 425.

4. See chapter 14 for a full description of the Word of Wisdom.

5. Although the subject of priesthood is not discussed in this book, please see our book *Questions to Ask Your Mormon Friend* ("Is the Mormon Priesthood Really of Ancient Origin'?").

6. Orson Pratt in Watt, ed., *Journal of Discourses,* 13:362.

7. Lorenzo Snow, *Teachings of Lorenzo Snow,* comp. Clyde J. Williams (Salt Lake City: Bookcraft, 1966), 186. Also printed in the *Deseret News,* 15 June 1901, 1.

8. Smith, *Answers to Gospel Questions,* 4:112.

9. Van Wagoner said, "Every age has its delusions. For early Mormons these included eventually discarded communitarian plans as well as hope in the imminent second coming of Jesus Christ. That return, promised by the apocalyptic voice of the young prophet, stranded the Saints in an advent season—the eleventh hour—which has endured for more than a century and a half. These prophetic failures were at the very root of Sidney Rigdon's eventual loss of faith in Joseph Smith." *Sidney Rigdon: A Portrait of Religious Excess* (Salt Lake City: Signature Books, 1994), 90.

10. Talmage, *The Articles of Faith,* 26–27.

11. *Ensign* (March 1994): 4.

12. According to the *Encyclopedia of Mormonism,* vol. 1, s.v. "Civil War Prophecy": "Section 87 was not published by the Church until 1851 and was not canonized until 1876. It was, however, copied and circulated by some Church leaders and missionaries in the 1830s. The Civil War prophecy became one of the most widely published revelations in the *Doctrine and Covenants.* Not surprisingly, it received greatest attention during the Civil War, as many viewed the conflict as a vindication of the prophetic powers of Joseph Smith" (288).

13. McConkie, *Mormon Doctrine,* 564.

14. *History of the Church,* 2:235–36.

15. Ludlow, ed., *Encyclopedia of Mormonism,* vol. 1, s.v. "Book of Abraham," 134.

16. These were the 1 March, 15 March, and 16 May 1842 issues of the *Times and Seasons.*

17. Richard A. Parker, "The Joseph Smith Papyri: A Preliminary Report," *Dialogue* 3, no. 2 (summer 1968): 86.

18. Explanation of figure seven opposite Facsimile No. 2. Key words are an essential part of the LDS temple ceremony.

19. Stephen Thompson, "Egyptology and the *Book of Mormon,*" *Dialogue* 28, no. 1 (spring 1995): 149–50.

20. Ibid., 150.

21. *Ensign* (January 1994): 20.

22. Charles M. Larson, *By His Own Hand upon Papyrus* (Grand Rapids: Institute for Religious Research, 1992), 36. For further study on a fascinating issue, we highly recommend this book.

23. Roberts, comp., *Comprehensive History of the Church,* 2:138.

Chapter 10 *The Atonement*

1. Ludlow, ed., *Encyclopedia of Mormonism,* vol. 2, s.v. "Atonement of Jesus Christ," 84.

2. B. H. Roberts, *Defense of the Faith and the Saints,* 2 vols. (Salt Lake City: Deseret News, 1907–12), 2:513.

3. Benson, *Teachings of Ezra Taft Benson,* 14.

4. McConkie, *The Mortal Messiah,* 127–28, 224.

5. Bruce R. McConkie, *Doctrinal New Testament Commentary,* 774.

6. Ludlow, ed., *Encyclopedia of Mormonism,* vol. 1, s.v. "Atonement of Jesus Christ"; vol. 2, s.v. "Gethsemane; Jesus Christ"; vol. 3, s.v. "Plan of Salvation."

7. Lorenzo Snow in Stuy, ed., *Collected Discourses,* vol. 3, 362.

8. Smith, *Doctrines of Salvation,* 1:130.

9. Romans 3:23 says that "all have sinned" and have therefore broken God's law. "Man's heart is evil from his youth" (Gen. 8:21), "full of evil" (Eccles. 9:3), and "deceitful above all things, and desperately wicked" (Jer. 17:9).

10. Leon Morris, *The Atonement* (Downers Grove, Ill.: InterVarsity, 1983), 50–51. This is an excellent resource on the subject of Christ's atonement.

11. Ibid., 84.

12. A. W. Tozer, *Echoes from Eden: The Voices of God Calling Man* (Harrisburg, Pa.: Christian Publications, 1981), 41.

13. Morris, *The Atonement,* 64–65.

14. *Conference Report* (October 1953): 35.

15. Smith, *Answers to Gospel Questions,* 4:17–18.

16. Bruce R. McConkie, "What the Mormons Think of Christ," 19–20. While McConkie may not like salvation being so simplified, Romans 10:9–10 puts it quite clearly: "That if thou shalt confess with thy mouth the Lord Jesus, and shalt believe in thine heart that God hath raised him from the dead, thou shalt be saved. For with the heart man believeth unto righteousness; and with the mouth confession is made unto salvation."

17. For many years the chorus of this hymn had been sung in the Mormon Miracle Pageant held in Manti, Utah. This annual LDS event is performed before tens of thousands of spectators over a two-week period. The play begins by depicting three different "Christian" congregations that professed conflicting doctrine. All three congregations were singing "At the Cross," off key and in a mocking tone. Numerous Christians complained about the flippant presentation. The pageant director replaced the song in 1993.

Chapter 11 *Grace and Works*

1. McConkie, *Mormon Doctrine,* 669.

2. Ibid., 669, 671.

3. John Taylor in Watt, ed., *Journal of Discourses,* 10:50.

4. Lee, *What Do Mormons Believe?* 38. Such an interpretation makes understanding John 5:28–29 very difficult. This passage states, "Marvel not at this: for the hour is coming, in the which all that are in the graves shall hear his voice, and shall come forth; they that have done good, unto the resurrection of life; and they that have done evil, unto the resurrection of damnation." If this religion is true, we can rightly assume that most of those saved by grace according to Mormonism are actually "saved unto damnation."

5. McConkie, *Mormon Doctrine,* 670–71.

6. This is known as Antinomianism, which is the belief that good works are not important and God's people have the freedom to live life in a hellish manner after conversion. It should be noted that some Mormons privately label evangelical Christians as "gracers."

7. According to McConkie, the first greatest heresy was the doctrine of the Trinity. *BYU 1983–84 Fireside and Devotional Speeches,* "What Think Ye of Salvation by Grace?" 45. Also quoted in *Sunstone Review* (March 1984): 9. According to the *Herald* (Provo, Utah), 12 January 1984, p. 21, "The heresy of being saved by grace is burning like wildfire across the nation. The only 'religious mania' to exceed it was the way the original heresy filled the early Christian church after Christ's death."

8. McConkie, *Mormon Doctrine,* 670–71.

9. LeGrand Richards, *A Marvelous Work and a Wonder* (Salt Lake City: Deseret Book Co., 1976), 25.

10. Talmage, *The Articles of Faith,* 478–80.

11. Richard R. Hopkins, *Biblical Mormonism: Responding to Evangelical Criticism of LDS Theology* (Bountiful, Utah: Horizon Publishers, 1994), 12, 14. While Hopkins says that the Christian view of grace has led many of the "brightest Evangelical leaders" into sin, he fails to point out that many bright LDS leaders have also fallen prey to "serious sin." For instance, George P. Lee admitted to sexually molesting a young girl while he was serving as an LDS Seventy (*Salt Lake Tribune,* 12 October 1994, p. B-1). Another LDS leader, the late Seventy Paul Dunn, admitted to lying in his public talks and in his autobiographical anecdotes (*Salt Lake Tribune,* 27 October 1991, p. B-1). Bear in mind that the above transgressions were perpetrated by those who agree with the view of salvation espoused by Hopkins. No doubt many more examples could be cited on both sides; however, James 1:13–16 clearly shows an individual is responsible for his own actions. An individual's failure does not necessarily prove truthful principles wrong or, for that matter, wrong principles true.

12. Francis Lyman, *Conference Report* (October 1898): 47, emphasis ours.

13. Smith, *Doctrines of Salvation,* 2:15.

14. Young, *Discourses of Brigham Young,* 404.

15. John Taylor, *The Gospel Kingdom,* 3d ed., ed. G. Homer Durham (Salt Lake City: Bookcraft, 1944), 327–28.

16. Orson Whitney, *Conference Report* (October 1910): 53.

17. Brigham Young in Watt, ed., *Journal of Discourses,* 14:133, emphasis ours.

18. Taylor, *The Gospel Kingdom,* 20.

19. B. H. Roberts, *The Gospel and Man's Relationship to Deity* (Salt Lake City: Deseret Book Co., 1965), 136.

20. George Q. Cannon in Watt, ed., *Journal of Discourses,* 16:117.

21. Ludlow, ed., *Encyclopedia of Mormonism,* vol. 2, s.v. "Exaltation," 479.

22. Pride, it should be pointed out, is a sin, clearly showing that an individual has violated celestial law. See Proverbs 16:18; 29:23; Obadiah 1:3; Zephaniah 2:10; Mark 7:22; 1 John 2:16.

23. Alma 5:27–28. Among other *Book of Mormon* passages, 2 Nephi 28:12–15 and Jacob 2:13–22 also warn against the dangers of pride.

24. In his book *Believing Christ* (Salt Lake City: Deseret Book Co., 1992), Stephen E. Robinson mentions numerous examples of Latter-day Saints who have struggled with trying to be good enough for celestial exaltation. A heartrending example of this involves Robinson's wife, Janet. The BYU professor tells how Janet had experienced burnout and one day admitted, "I'm never going to be perfect, and I just can't pretend anymore that I am. I've finally admitted to myself that I can't make it to the celestial kingdom, so why should I break my back trying?" In reading this account, one can't help but feel the pain she must have been going through. Robinson felt that such a reaction was the result of his wife not truly understanding "the core of the gospel" or Christ's role as Savior (17). Why he chose this reason in his wife's case escapes us since he later relates the following: "When I ask my students if it is necessary to keep the commandments to enter into the celestial kingdom, they all answer with absolute certainty that it is. They know that this is true because they have heard Church leaders and teachers tell them so all of their lives" (45). Certainly the LDS leaders are to blame.

25. Smith, *Doctrines of Salvation,* 1:69, italics his.

26. McConkie, *Mormon Doctrine,* 229.

27. Alma 34:32–33. Hebrews 9:27 and 2 Corinthians 6:2 also deny any possibility of any works being performed after death.

28. Kimball, *The Miracle of Forgiveness,* 210, emphasis ours.

29. Ibid., 9–10. This idea is supported by Spencer Kimball, who taught that this is "why we must make our decisions early in life and why it is imperative that such decisions be right" (*The Miracle of Forgiveness,* 244, as quoted in the LDS *Search These Commandments: Melchizedek Priesthood Study Guide,* [1984], 82).

30. Ibid., 354–55.

31. Ibid., 170.

32. *Ensign* (May 1989): 20–21.

33. Kimball, *The Miracle of Forgiveness,* 208–9.

34. *Ensign* (November 1999): 5.

35. Ibid., 34.

36. Robinson, *Believing Christ,* 45.

37. Ibid., 45–46.

38. *Ensign* (November 1995): 88, emphasis ours.

39. Kimball, *The Miracle of Forgiveness,* 165.

40. Ibid., 164.

41. Morris, *The Atonement,* 196.

42. F. F. Bruce, *Paul: Apostle of the Heart Set Free* (Grand Rapids: Eerdmans, 1977), 328. We have heard many Mormons complain about the doctrine of salvation (justification) by faith alone. One question often posed is, "What about those who have never heard?" Our response would be similar to that given by Jesus when the apostle Peter pointed to John in John 21:20–22 and complained "What about him?" when told to feed Jesus' sheep. Jesus answered him, "What is that to thee? Follow thou me." Mormons who have the gospel presented to them are accountable to God. They cannot simply exempt themselves by pointing to others. While it might be interesting to speculate on what happens to those who never hear the gospel, this is in actuality a moot point. Romans 1:18–20 assures us that all men are "without excuse." God has provided for every possibility.

43. Morris, *The Atonement,* 125.

44. Ibid., 11.

45. Ibid., 87.

46. It should be noted that it says to "work out," not "work for," one's salvation. The next verse, verse 13, says that even these works originate from God as He works in the believer for His own pleasure.

47. Morris, *The Atonement,* 204.

48. Bruce, *Paul: Apostle of the Heart Set Free,* 461.

49. Dennis J. Hester, comp., *The Vance Havner Quote Book* (Grand Rapids: Baker, 1986), 105.

Chapter 12 *Heaven and Hell*

1. Smith, *Doctrines of Salvation,* 3:310.

2. Kimball, *Teachings of Spencer W. Kimball,* 50.

3. First Corinthians 15:40 in the JST reads, "Also celestial bodies, and bodies terrestrial, and bodies telestial; but the glory of the celestial, one; and the terrestrial, another; and the telestial, another."

4. Christian scholar Matthew Henry wrote in his commentary, "It was certainly a very extraordinary honour done him: in some sense he was caught up into the third heaven, the heaven of the blessed, above the aerial heaven, in which the fowls fly, above the starry

heaven, which is adorned with those glorious orbs: it was into the third heaven, where God most eminently manifests His glory." *Matthew Henry's Commentary of the Whole Bible* (McLean, Va.: MacDonald Publishing Co., 1706), 6:641.

5. McConkie, *Doctrinal New Testament Commentary,* 3:75. Regarding apostasy, McConkie explained, "Apostates exhibit varying degrees of indifference and of rebellion, and their punishment, in time and in eternity, is based on the type and degree of apostasy which is involved. Those who become indifferent to the Church, who simply drift from the course of righteousness to the way of the world, are not in the same category with traitors who fight the truth, and with those whose open rebellion destines them to eternal damnation as sons of perdition. All apostates are turned over to the buffetings of Satan in one degree or another, with the full wrath of Satan reserved for those who are cast into outer darkness with him in that kingdom devoid of glory."

6. Cannon, *Gospel Truth,* 1:62.

7. McConkie, *Mormon Doctrine,* 757.

8. Ibid., 350.

9. Smith, *Doctrines of Salvation,* 2:220.

10. Smith, *Answers to Gospel Questions,* 2:209. We should point out that covenant breakers are listed here. All Mormons, upon baptism into the LDS Church, make a covenant to keep all of God's commandments. Naturally, this would mean that breaking God's laws should no longer occur in their lives. The fact that all Mormons, like the rest of us, struggle with sin makes it obviously clear that this covenant is broken on numerous occasions. During the sacrament service, all Mormons must again make a covenant to keep all of the commandments. Since no Mormon can persistently keep all of the commandments, it appears that all of them are covenant breakers to some extent.

11. McConkie, *Mormon Doctrine,* 778.

12. Roberts, comp., *Comprehensive History of the Church,* 1:275.

13. Ludlow, ed., *Encyclopedia of Mormonism,* vol. 1, s.v. "Degrees of Glory," 368.

14. Kimball, *Teachings of Spencer W. Kimball,* 48.

15. B. H. Roberts, *New Witnesses for God,* 3 vols. (Salt Lake City: Deseret News, 1911, 1950–51), 1:385. Also see *D&C* 76:79.

16. Smith, *Answers to Gospel Questions,* 1:81.

17. Ludlow, ed., *Encyclopedia of Mormonism,* vol. 2, s.v. "Marriage," 858. This arrangement can only be fulfilled if every single family member is righteous enough to enter the highest level in the celestial kingdom. Any family member who does not meet this requirement will not enjoy the presence of the family unit. For more information on this topic, see our book *Questions to Ask Your Mormon Friend* ("If Mormon Families Will Be Together Forever, Where Will the In-Laws Live?").

18. Bruce R. McConkie, *A New Witness for the Articles of Faith* (Salt Lake City: Deseret Book Co., 1985), 145.

19. Smith, *Doctrines of Salvation,* 2:41, italics his.

20. Brigham Young in Watt, ed., *Journal of Discourses,* 9:102.

21. Smith, *Teachings of the Prophet Joseph Smith,* 312. Smith said some would be "raised to be angels, others are raised to become Gods."

22. Talmage, *The Vitality of Mormonism,* 299.

23. Joseph Fielding Smith, *The Way to Perfection* (Salt Lake City: Deseret Book Co., 1985), 238–39.

24. Pratt, *The Seer,* 37.

25. Ibid.

26. Personal e-mail message sent to Bill McKeever, 19 May 1997.

27. Pratt in Watt, ed., *Journal of Discourses,* 2:345.

28. Smith, *Doctrines of Salvation,* 1:62, italics his.

29. Neal Maxwell, *A Wonderful Flood of Light* (Salt Lake City: Bookcraft, 1990), 25. According to the *Pearl of Great Price* (Abraham 3:2ff), Kolob is the greatest star located "nearest unto the throne of God."

30. According to Mormonism, this planet is said to be a portion of Elohim's inheritance and reward for a life of good works in a previous world. While it is true that Mormonism does not teach that God is physically present, it is taught that He is aware of what takes place on this earth. Given this LDS premise, does it seem reasonable that God is overflowing with joy watching His creation stumble through life? Does He bubble with pride as He witnesses His creation killing each other in war, aborting their babies, overdosing on drugs, and stealing from each other? Only the most sadistic of creatures would define heaven in such a disappointing way.

31. Brigham Young in Watt, ed., *Journal of Discourses,* 14:71–72.

Chapter 13 *Communion and Baptism*

1. Ludlow, ed., *Encyclopedia of Mormonism,* vol. 1, s.v. "Communion," 299.

2. McConkie, *Mormon Doctrine,* 660.

3. Talmage, *Articles of Faith,* 175–76.

4. *D&C* 89:5.

5. Alexander Campbell is credited with popularizing the idea of baptismal regeneration during the early 1800s. Sidney Rigdon, Joseph Smith's right-hand man, was a former Campbellite minister, so it should come as no surprise that this teaching is also found in the LDS Church.

6. Smith, *Teachings of the Prophet Joseph Smith,* 361.

7. Young, *Discourses of Brigham Young,* 15.

8. Woodruff, *The Discourses of Wilford Woodruff,* 19.

9. Snow, *Teachings of Lorenzo Snow,* 96.

10. Heber J. Grant, *Gospel Standards,* comp. G. Homer Durham (Salt Lake City: Improvement Era, 1943), 8.

11. G. R. Beasley-Murray, *Baptism in the New Testament* (Grand Rapids: Eerdmans, 1962), 19. This book is an excellent resource for an overview of the doctrine of baptism found within the New Testament.

12. *Biblical Archaeology Review* (January/February 1987): 58–59.

13. G. W. Bromiley, ed., *The International Standard Bible Encyclopedia,* vol. 1 (Grand Rapids: Eerdmans, 1962), 418.

14. If baptism is really the cause of salvation, it seems strange that Jesus and Paul, obviously the two most visible people in the New Testament, did not regularly baptize others. Instead, they left this job to others. See John 4:1–2 and 1 Corinthians 1:10–17.

15. Beasley-Murray, *Baptism in the New Testament,* 297.

16. Justo L. Gonzalez, *The Early Church to the Dawn of the Reformation,* vol. 1 of *The Story of Christianity* (San Francisco: HarperCollins, 1984), 96.

17. Leon Morris, *The Gospel according to John* (Grand Rapids: Eerdmans, 1995), 215–16.

18. Bob L. Ross, *Acts 2:38 and Baptismal Remission* (Pasadena, Tex.: Pilgrim, 1987), 65.

Chapter 14 *The Word of Wisdom*

1. President Ezra Taft Benson in *Church News,* 20 May 1989, 10.

2. Unless otherwise noted, emphases in this chapter are ours.

3. Brigham Young in Watt, ed., *Journal of Discourses,* 12:221–23. A 5 May 1962 editorial in the church section of the *Deseret News* said those who believe like Cannon did "not state the truth."

4. *Salt Lake Tribune,* 18 August 1991, p. A2.

5. John Stewart, *Joseph Smith, the Mormon Prophet* (Salt Lake City: Hawkes Publishing, 1966), 90.

6. Some issues are areas of freedom. For instance, Paul dealt with the problem of meat offered to idols in 1 Corinthians 8 and 10. In 1 Corinthians 8:8–9 he said it didn't matter whether or not you partook, but you should only do it if you did not offend fellow Christians. For example, if I like to eat meat but know that this causes my vegetarian brother to stumble, I can still partake as long as I am discreet about it in his presence. The same principle can be applied to any number of freedom issues.

7. *History of the Church,* 2:369, 378. In his book *Hearts Made Glad,* LDS author LaMar Petersen documents "the statements and testimonies of scores of witnesses and redactors regarding Smith's interest in 'the fruit of the vine.'"

8. *Life of Oliver B. Huntington,* typed copy at the University of Utah, Special Collections Department (Marriott Library).

9. *History of the Church,* 5:450.

10. *Millennial Star* 21, 283.

11. Brigham Young in Watt, ed., *Journal of Discourses,* 16:238. Young explained that the Church-owned store was selling tobacco for the purpose of killing ticks on sheep. However, some Saints were buying it for personal use, for which he offered a sharp rebuke.

12. Ibid., 8:361.

13. Ludlow, ed., *Encyclopedia of Mormonism,* vol. 4, s.v. "Word of Wisdom," 1584.

14. Brigham Young in Watt, ed., *Journal of Discourses,* 11:140.

15. *A Sure Foundation,* 85.

16. *BYU Studies* (winter 1959): 39–40.

Chapter 15 *The Temple*

1. Jay Todd in *Ensign* (February 1995): 49. The questions asked of potential temple participants have varied over the years. According to BYU law professor Edward Kimball, as quoted in the *Salt Lake Tribune* ("LDS Church Emphasizing Child Support: Revised questions ask all members seeking temple recommends if they are current on payments," 26 June 1999, pp. C1, C3), the 1856 Mormon Catechism included such questions as "Have you cut hay where you had no right to?" "Do you wash your body and have your family do so, as often as health and cleanliness require and circumstances will permit?" and "Do you oppose the hireling in his wages?" Today some of the fourteen interview questions asked by the Mormon's bishop include whether the member is current with his child support and finding out if he abused his spouse. While the payment of tithes "was always important for a temple recommend," "adherence to the faith's prohibition against coffee, tea, alcohol and tobacco varied in strictness. The 1940 and 1944 versions settled for a 'willingness to undertake' to observe" the Word of Wisdom. In 1968, keeping this code meant abstaining from "alcoholic beverages" rather than "liquor" so that light beer and wine would be included. In addition, "while some LDS bishops

and stake presidents have tried to make caffeinated drinks one of the prohibited substances, 'cola drinks have never been included.'" Contrary to what many Mormons may think, "using birth control has never been an explicit bar to receiving a recommend."

2. Smith, *Doctrines of Salvation,* 2:40, italics his.

3. In some temples, two names are used alternately throughout the day.

4. Charles Penrose, *Mormon Doctrine, Plain and Simple* (Salt Lake City: Juvenile Instructor, 1888), 51.

5. Erastus Snow in Watt, ed., *Journal of Discourses,* 5:291.

6. Kimball, *Teachings of Spencer W. Kimball,* 539.

7. Carlos E. Asay in *Ensign* (August 1997): 22.

8. Ibid., 19.

9. Ibid., 20–21.

10. First Presidency Letter, 10 October 1988.

11. McConkie, *Mormon Doctrine,* 226–27.

12. John A. Widtsoe, *Joseph Smith: Seeker after Truth, Prophet of God* (Salt Lake City: Deseret Book Co., 1951), 249.

13. Royden Derrick, *Temples in the Last Days* (Salt Lake City: Bookcraft, 1987), 36. Derrick made this remark only three years before the LDS Church made drastic changes to the ceremony. Mormon Seventy W. Grant Bangerter said eight years before the changes that those members who "wonder if the ordinances can be changed or adjusted" should rest assured that "these ordinances have been provided by revelation" and are therefore "protected from tampering" (*Deseret News,* Church section, 16 January 1982).

14. *History of the Church,* 4:208.

15. For a more complete examination of the changes to the temple ceremony, we highly recommend *Evolution of the Temple Ceremony,* published through Utah Lighthouse Ministry, P.O. Box 1884, Salt Lake City, UT 84110.

16. Smith, *The Way to Perfection,* 153–54.

17. It seems strange that the font resembles Solomon's brazen sea. Joseph Fielding Smith admitted "this font, or brazen sea, was not used for baptisms for the dead, for there were no baptisms for the dead until after the resurrection of the Lord." (*Answers to Gospel Questions,* 5:13). Solomon's brazen sea was destroyed centuries earlier when Babylon captured Judah and did not exist during the time of Christ or after His resurrection.

18. John Taylor in Watt, ed., *Journal of Discourses,* 6:163.

19. Jay Todd in *Ensign* (February 1995): 47–48.

20. Theodore M. Burton in *Improvement Era* (December 1970): 58.

21. *Ensign* (March 1997): 73.

22. LDS general authorities who taught this include: Wilford Woodruff in Watt, ed., *Journal of Discourses,* 13:327; Joseph F. Smith in *Improvement Era* 5 (December 1901): 146–47; Brigham Young in Watt, ed., *Journal of Discourses,* 3:372; McConkie in *Mormon Doctrine,* 73 and *Millennial Messiah,* 673–74.

23. Paul neither condones nor condemns the practice. He merely uses it to illustrate his point. For further information on this verse and topic, see chapter 28 of McKeever, *Answering Mormons' Questions* (Minneapolis: Bethany, 1991).

24. D. A. Carson, "Did Paul Baptize for the Dead?" *Christianity Today,* 10 August 1998, 63.

25. It should be noted that celestial marriage once included plural marriage. See Watt, ed., *Journal of Discourses,* 6:361–62; B. H. Roberts, *Outlines of Ecclesiastical History: A Text Book,* 6th ed. (Salt Lake City: The Church of Jesus Christ of Latter-day Saints, 1950), 424; and Widtsoe, *Evidences and Reconciliations,* 340. This practice is not allowed

today but it is believed that it will one day be restored (McConkie, *Mormon Doctrine,* 578). For more information, see chapter 16 of this book.

26. *Gospel Principles,* 256.

27. Joseph Smith in *History of the Church,* vol. 5, 391.

28. *Times and Seasons* 6 (1 July 1845): 955. Also quoted in Kimball, *The Miracle of Forgiveness,* 245.

29. Kimball in *Ensign* (February 1995): 41–42. He also taught that those who are single or who do not marry in a Mormon temple would not receive the fulness of LDS salvation (Kimball, *The Miracle of Forgiveness,* 245). Despite Kimball's connotation that a temple marriage is "timeless and eternal," divorce is not uncommon in the LDS community. "If the divorce rate is at 60 percent nationally, among LDS couples it is between 40 and 50 percent," said Kenneth A. Macnab, a member of the Association of Mormon Counselors and Therapists (AMCAP). "It is not a whole lot lower with temple marriages" ("LDS Church Emphasizing Child Support: Revised questions ask all members seeking temple recommends if they are current on payments," *Salt Lake Tribune,* 26 June 1999, p. C1).

30. Talmage, *The Vitality of Mormonism,* 229.

31. McConkie, *Mormon Doctrine,* 118.

32. As quoted by President Kimball in *Ensign* (February 1995): 44.

33. Richards, *A Marvelous Work and a Wonder,* 193. Also see Talmage, *The Vitality of Mormonism,* 229.

34. Kimball in *Ensign* (February 1995): 45.

35. Hunter in *Ensign* (February 1995): 2.

36. Smith, *Doctrines of Salvation,* 2:46, italics his.

37. Kimball in *Ensign* (February 1995): 45.

38. Smith, *Doctrines of Salvation,* 2:43–44, 60, italics his.

39. Benson, *Teachings of Ezra Taft Benson,* 559.

40. *Achieving a Celestial Marriage,* 4.

41. Ibid., 4–5. To show that there is no misunderstanding of this key doctrine, a chart is given by them on page 5 to illustrate the order of events preceding "eternal life": birth, faith in Jesus Christ, repentance, baptism, gift of the Holy Ghost, temple marriage, and resurrection.

42. *Conference Report* (April 1957): 20.

43. Widtsoe, *Evidences and Reconciliations,* 340. Widtsoe also explained on pages 342–43 that "after the death of the Prophet, women applied for the privilege of being sealed to him for eternity. . . . Women no longer living, whether in Joseph's day or later, have also been sealed to the Prophet for eternity. The request for such unions has usually come from relatives or friends who would have their loved one share eternity with the Prophet, rather than with anyone else."

44. This story as told in Matthew, Mark, and Luke is the only support LDS Apostle James E. Talmage lists as the basis for the "Law of Eternal Marriage" (*Jesus the Christ,* 278–79).

45. McConkie, *Doctrinal New Testament Commentary,* 1:605–6.

46. David H. Yarn Jr. in *A Sure Foundation,* 115.

47. Talmage, *Jesus the Christ,* 548.

48. Boyd K. Packer in *Ensign* (February 1995): 32.

49. *History of the Church,* 4:550–51.

50. As quoted in Quinn, *Early Mormonism and the Magic World View,* 185. Spelling left as in original.

51. Reed C. Durham Jr., *Is There No Help for the Widow's Son?* (Nauvoo, Ill.: Martin Publishing, 1980), 17.

52. Woodruff in Watt, ed., *Journal of Discourses,* 19:229.

53. Joseph Heinerman, *Temple Manifestations* (Salt Lake City: Magazine Printing and Publishing, 1974), 64–65.

54. Ibid., 66.

55. Ibid., 68, quoting from N. B. Lundwall, *The Vision.*

56. Ibid., 70.

57. Ibid., 96–97, quoting from "Spiritual Manifestations in the Manti Temple," *Millennial Star* 50, no. 26 (13 August 1888): 522.

58. Ibid., 99, as quoted from N. B. Lundwall, *Temples of the Most High* (Salt Lake City: Bookcraft, 1954), 116.

59. For the doubting Mormon, we suggest looking up the book *Temple Manifestations* to see what types of manifestations have occurred to Mormons throughout the years. Perhaps the Mormon's bishop can help confirm these stories.

60. These passages include Leviticus 19:31; 20:6; Deuteronomy 18:10–12; 1 Samuel 28:3–20 (where Saul is reprimanded for dealing with the witch of Endor); 2 Kings 21:6; 23:24 (where familiar spirits are called "abominations" and equated with idols); Isaiah 8:19; 19:3. Even the *Book of Mormon* warns against familiar spirits in 2 Nephi 18:19.

61. Ronald Youngblood, "The Sacrificial System of Mosaiasm" (lecture notes, San Diego, Calif.: Bethel Seminary West, 1986).

62. Since most Mormons are not worthy to attend the temple, those who are not worthy (or who do not regularly attend) should be shown how LDS leaders teach that a celestial glory and the possibility of godhood cannot be attained unless they participate in the temple ceremonies.

63. Second Corinthians 6:2 and Hebrews 9:27. In the *Book of Mormon,* Alma 34:32–35; 2 Nephi 9:38; Mosiah 3:25, 16:5, 11; Mosiah 26:25–27.

64. Temples were built to replace Solomon's temple (in the sixth century B.C.) and Zerubbabel's temple (in the first century B.C.).

Chapter 16 *Lamanites, the Seed of Cain, and Polygamy*

1. Some Mormons claim that the words *white* and *pure* in the *Book of Mormon* are interchangeable. However, Alma 32:42; Mormon 9:6; and Moroni 7:47 show this is not true.

2. *Sunstone* (November 1993): fn. 5, p. 52. While we can understand the possibility of Mormon men taking wives from among the Lamanites, it seems strange that Smith would also include Nephites since they were said to have been completely wiped out. LDS Apostle James Talmage notes that Moroni was the "last Nephite representative" (*Articles of Faith,* 260).

3. Brigham Young in Watt, ed., *Journal of Discourses,* 7:336.

4. *Improvement Era* (December 1960): 922–23.

5. George Edward Clark, *Why I Believe* (Salt Lake City: Publisher's Press, 1989), 129, italics his.

6. Brigham Young in Watt, ed., *Journal of Discourses,* 5:332.

7. McConkie, *Mormon Doctrine,* 114. For more information on the teaching of preexistence, see chapter 4.

8. Smith, *Doctrines of Salvation,* 1:61, italics his. Perhaps this is why the LDS Church has been very slow in integrating its leadership. There had been no nonwhite LDS leader until 1975, when George P. Lee, a Navajo Indian, became a member of the First Quo-

rum of the Seventy. Two years later Adney Y. Komatsu became the first person of Japanese descent to become a Seventy. It was not until 1990 that a person with black skin was made an LDS general authority in the LDS Church. Helvecio Martins, a black Brazilian, became a member of the Second Quorum of the Seventy in 1990. He served his five-year term, which ended in 1995.

9. Smith, *Teachings of the Prophet Joseph Smith,* Section Six (1843–44), 349.

10. Smith, *Doctrines of Salvation,* 1:64–66, italics his.

11. According to Bruce McConkie, a degree of damnation occurs to "those who fail to gain exaltation in the highest heaven within the celestial world, even though they do gain a celestial mansion in one of the lower heavens of that world" (*Mormon Doctrine,* 177).

12. George F. Richards, *Conference Report* (April 1939): 58.

13. *History of the Church,* 5:217–18.

14. Brigham Young in Watt, ed., *Journal of Discourses,* 7:290–91.

15. John Taylor in Watt, ed., *Journal of Discourses,* 22:304.

16. Ibid., 23:336.

17. John Lewis Lund, *The Church and the Negro: A Discussion of Mormons, Negroes and the Priesthood* (Paramount Publishers, 1967), 49.

18. John J. Stewart, *Mormonism and the Negro* (Orem, Utah: Bookmark, 1960), 33, 38. Stewart stresses the point that Carver was a mulatto (meaning, he had one white parent and one black parent), as if this wasn't quite as bad as being fully black. While the black could make up for lost ground in Stewart's theology, he believed that the white person, at birth, was a "lap" ahead of all blacks.

19. McConkie, *Mormon Doctrine,* 1958 ed., 477.

20. This address was given by Petersen at the Convention of Teachers of Religion on the College Level, BYU, Provo, Utah, 27 August 1954. The speech was titled "Race Problems—As They Affect the Church."

21. Ibid.

22. Ibid.

23. Lund, *The Church and the Negro,* 15.

24. Brigham Young in Watt, ed., *Journal of Discourses,* 10:110.

25. Ibid., 2:143. Joseph Fielding Smith also quoted Young's statement on page 106 of his *The Way to Perfection.*

26. Milton R. Hunter, *Pearl of Great Price Commentary* (Salt Lake City: Stephens and Wallis, 1948), 142. Joseph Fielding Smith tempered this by adding how Mormons today believe that "God will reward every man, woman, and child—regardless of his or her color or the land in which he or she lives."

27. Smith, *The Way to Perfection,* 101.

28. Lund, *The Church and the Negro,* 45.

29. Ibid., 47, 104–5.

30. This portion is included in what is known as Declaration 2 found at the end of the *Doctrine and Covenants.*

31. *Improvement Era* (January 1969): 13.

32. According to Lund, *The Church and the Negro,* 91, President David O. McKay wrote a letter on 3 November 1947 in which he said, "I know of no scriptural basis for denying the Priesthood to Negroes other than one verse in the Book of Abraham (1:26)."

33. Widtsoe, *Evidences and Reconciliations,* 391.

34. Richard Van Wagoner, *Mormon Polygamy: A History* (Salt Lake City: Signature Books, 1989), 42.

35. This was especially true among the leaders. Joseph Smith himself claimed in 1844 (*History of the Church,* 6:411) that he had only one wife, but the *Historical Record,* 5:114 published in 1886 shows that he had at least twenty-seven wives at the time he said this! Van Wagoner shows throughout the first half of his book how Smith routinely lied to hide his involvement in polygamy—probably to appease his wife Emma, who was definitely against the practice (Van Wagoner, *Mormon Polygamy,* 50–60). Van Wagoner documents Smith's involvement in polygamy eight years before recording his polygamy "revelation" from God on 12 July 1843.

36. *Comprehensive History of the Church,* 4:57–58. This is also supported by LDS President Joseph F. Smith in Watt, ed., *Journal of Discourses,* 20:29. Section 132 did not become a part of the *Doctrine and Covenants* until 1876.

37. Van Wagoner, *Mormon Polygamy,* 91.

38. Ludlow, ed., *The Encyclopedia of Mormonism,* vol. 2, s.v. "History of the Church," 617.

39. Bear in mind that this denial was a part of the *Doctrine and Covenants* until 1876—twenty-four years after polygamy became an official LDS doctrine.

40. Brigham Young in Watt, ed., *Journal of Discourses,* 11:269.

41. Heber C. Kimball in Watt, ed., *Journal of Discourses,* 5:203.

42. Brigham Young in Watt, ed., *Journal of Discourses,* 11:239. Young also said, "Now if any of you will deny the plurality of wives and continue to do so, I promise that you will be dammed . . ." (*Deseret News,* 14 November 1885).

43. John Taylor in Watt, ed., *Journal of Discourses,* 11:221.

44. Wilford Woodruff in Watt, ed., *Journal of Discourses,* 13:166.

45. Joseph F. Smith in Watt, ed., *Journal of Discourses,* 21:10.

46. Orson Pratt in Watt, ed., *Journal of Discourses,* 21:296.

47. Roberts, *Outlines of Ecclesiastical History,* 437.

48. The Manifesto can be found following section 138 in the *Doctrine and Covenants.*

49. Van Wagoner, *Mormon Polygamy,* 155.

50. Ibid.

51. McConkie, *Mormon Doctrine,* 579.

52. Ibid., 578.

53. Kimball, *Teachings of Spencer W. Kimball,* 447–48.

Chapter 17 *Joseph Smith*

1. D. Michael Quinn, *The Mormon Hierarchy: Origins of Power* (Salt Lake City: Signature Books, 1994), 261–62.

2. Richard Van Wagoner, *Sidney Rigdon, A Portrait of Religious Excess* (Salt Lake City: Signature Books, 1994), chapter 21, "Between Family and Friends," 290–91. *The New World Dictionary* defines *pedantic* as laying "unnecessary stress on minor or trivial points of learning, displaying a scholarship lacking in judgment or sense of proportion. A narrow-minded teacher who insists on exact adherence to a set of arbitrary rules."

3. Van Wagoner, *Sidney Rigdon,* 293.

4. Todd Compton, "A Trajectory of Plurality: An Overview of Joseph Smith's Thirty-Three Plural Wives," *Dialogue* 29, no. 2 (summer 1996): 22. In this article Compton gives the proper definition of polyandry (one woman married to two men simultaneously) but more than once refers to Smith's relationships as "Joseph's polyandry."

5. Ibid., 21.

6. Van Wagoner, *Sidney Rigdon,* 295–96.

7. Ibid., 293–94.

8. *Ensign* (November 1999): 64.

9. Marrying married women was not practiced only by Joseph Smith. LDS historian Jeffery Ogden Johnson wrote:"Twenty-one of Brigham Young's fifty-five wives had never been married, six were separated or divorced from their husbands, sixteen were widows, and six had living husbands from whom divorces had apparently not been obtained. Marital information is unavailable for six" ("Determining and Defining 'Wife': The Brigham Young Households," *Dialogue* 20, no. 3 [fall 1987]: 63).

10. Hugh Nibley, *No Ma'am, That's Not History* (Salt Lake City: Bookcraft, 1946), 46.

11. Richard J. Cummings, "Some Reflections on the Mormon Identity Crisis," in John Sillito, ed., *The Wilderness of Faith* (Salt Lake City: Signature Books, 1991), 61. Cummings refers to Fyodor Dostoyevsky, a nineteenth-century Russian who was exiled to Siberia after being accused of conspiracy. In his book *The Brothers Karamozov* he tells of two brothers, Ivan and Aloyesha. Ivan, the atheist, gives his impressions of what might have happened had Jesus returned during the sixteenth-century Spanish Inquisition. Naturally, Ivan demonstrates that even Christ Himself would be strongly criticized and condemned for His views. The same could be said for Joseph Smith.

12. Quinn, *Early Mormonism and the Magic World View,* 194. Quinn also states that many early leaders in the LDS Church had an affinity for folk magic. On page 195 he says that "the preponderance of folk believers among the founders of Mormonism would seem to justify the conclusion that magic and the occult exercised considerable influence among the first generation of Mormon converts from New York and New England, especially prior to 1831."

13. Ibid., 66. Quinn explained that Wilford Wood purchased the talisman from Charles Bidamon, the stepson of Emma Smith Bidamon, Joseph Smith's widow. In a sworn affidavit, Charles Bidamon stated that he had often heard Emma say that the "piece" was in "the Prophet's pocket when he was martyred at Carthage, Ill."

14. As listed on page 63 of the October 1994 *Ensign,* these were: God the Father (*Joseph Smith—History,* 1:17); Jesus Christ (*D&C* 110:2–10); Moroni (*Joseph Smith—History,* 1:30–49, 59); John the Baptist (*D&C* 13:1; *History of the Church,* 1:39–40); Peter, James, John (*D&C* 27; *History of the Church,* 1:40–42); Moses (*D&C* 110:11); Elias (*D&C* 110:12); Elijah (*D&C* 110:13–16); Adam (Michael); Noah (Gabriel); Raphael; various angels (*D&C* 128:21); Lehi, Nephi (*Journal of Discourses,* 16:266); Mormon (*Journal of Discourses,* 17:374).

15. Brigham Young in Watt, ed., *Journal of Discourses,* 14:203.

16. *History of the Church,* 6:78. The footnote to this passage says that Smith's ending comment was "reverently said," and "not in the blasphemous sense attributed to him by some anti-Mormon writers; namely, that God was subordinate to him—his right hand man."

17. Ibid., 319–20.

18. Ibid., 408–9.

19. Brigham Young in Watt, ed., *Journal of Discourses,* 4:271.

20. Ibid., 7:289. This quotation from Young was reprinted in the LDS Church Melchizedek priesthood manual *Search These Commandments* (1984); as well as in an article "Joseph Smith among the Prophets" printed in the June 1994 issue of the *Ensign* magazine.

21. Cannon, *Gospel Truth,* 199.

22. Smith, *Doctrines of Salvation,* 1:189–90.

23. Andrew Jenson, *Collected Discourses* 2, 16 January 1891.

24. Brigham Young in Watt, ed., *Journal of Discourses,* 8:176–77. Young went on to say in the same sermon that those who refuse to acknowledge that Joseph Smith was sent of God will "never have visions of eternity opened to them." Such people, he said, are "unbelievers."

25. Quinn, *The Mormon Hierarchy,* 91.

26. James B. Allen and Glen M. Leonard, *The Story of the Latter-day Saints* (Salt Lake City: Deseret Book Co., 1976), 82.

27. Ibid., 83.

28. At its peak, Nauvoo rivaled the city of Chicago in population.

29. Smith, *Teachings of the Prophet Joseph Smith,* 302.

30. Let it be said at this point that the authors of this work heartily condemn the persecutions faced by early Latter-day Saints. Physical violence is no way to settle differences, especially those of a religious nature. When scriptural debate fails to sway an individual toward the Christian position, the believer has no retreat but that of prayer. It should be understood that while Christians should "reason from the Scriptures" with unbelievers, it is ultimately God who draws people to Himself. There is no such thing as "strong-arming" a person into God's kingdom.

31. These men were William Law, Wilson Law, Charles Ivins, Francis M. Higbee, Chauncey L. Higbee, Robert D. Foster, and Charles A. Foster.

32. *D&C* 135:4.

33. Roberts, comp., *Comprehensive History of the Church,* 2:231.

34. *History of the Church,* 7:100.

35. Ibid., 7:101.

36. The estimates regarding the size of the mob are subject to debate. The estimates have ranged from as few as fifty to as many as two hundred.

37. *History of the Church,* 6:617.

38. Ibid., 7:100–103. John Taylor wrote this account just four years after the event and he continued to stick to his account of Smith's last moments long after it took place. The actual gun used by Smith (an Ethan Allen Pepper box model) is on display in a museum across the street from Temple Square in Salt Lake City.

39. Reed C. Durham, *Is There No Help for the Widow's Son?* (Nauvoo, Ill.: Martin Publishing, 1980), 28.

Chapter 18 *The Church and Its Leadership*

1. President Gordon B. Hinckley in an interview with the *San Francisco Chronicle,* 13 April 1997.

2. For more information on Mormonism not being the same as Christianity, see our book *Questions to Ask Your Mormon Friend* ("If I Accept You as a Christian, Will You Accept Me as a Mormon?").

3. Kimball in Watt, ed., *Journal of Discourses,* 6:32.

4. Gordon B. Hinckley's address to Ricks College regional conference, Rexburg, Idaho, 29 October 1995, as quoted in the *Ensign* (April 1996): 73.

5. "Mormon President Warns Students of Pornography, Criticizing Church Leaders," *Salt Lake Tribune,* 27 January 1996, p. C1.

6. *Ensign* (May 1996): 4

7. *Ensign* (November 1994): 63, 65.

8. Ezra Taft Benson, "The Gospel Teacher and His Message," 51–52 as quoted in *Teachings of the Living Prophets* (Salt Lake City: The Church of Jesus Christ of Latter-day Saints, 1982), 25.

9. *Ensign* (March 1997): 4. The fourth absolute changes when a new prophet is selected.

10. Apostle David B. Haight in *Ensign* (November 1994): 14–15.

11. Apostle Robert D. Hales in *Ensign* (May 1995): 17.

12. Howard W. Hunter in *Ensign* (November 1994): 87. This statement places an obvious stamp of approval on what L. Aldin Porter said about trusting the First Presidency and Council of the Twelve.

13. *Gospel Principles,* 55.

14. Talmage, *Articles of Faith,* 7.

15. *Church News,* 17 December 1960, 14.

16. *Conference Report* (April 1947): 158.

17. *Living Prophets for a Living Church* (Salt Lake City: The Church of Jesus Christ of Latter-day Saints, 1974), 60, as quoted from a BYU Tri-Stake Fireside Talk ("Beware of Temptation") in January 1963, 7–8.

18. Brigham Young in Watt, ed., *Journal of Discourses,* 16:161.

19. Lee, *Stand Ye in the Holy Places,* 153, 164.

20. Benson, *Teachings of Ezra Taft Benson,* 142.

21. *Ensign* (April 1996): 45.

22. Wilford Woodruff in Watt, ed., *Journal of Discourses,* 5:83.

23. Ezra Taft Benson, "Fourteen Fundamentals in Following the Prophets" (press copy of BYU devotional address, 26 February, 1980), 6.

24. Brigham Young in Watt, ed., *Journal of Discourses,* 1:50.

25. The *Deseret News* of 18 June 1873 (308) records Young as saying, "How much unbelief exists in the minds of the Latter-day Saints in regard to one particular doctrine which I revealed to them, and which God revealed to me—namely that Adam is our father and God." This was only four years before his death. We have found no reference supporting the notion that Young considered this teaching to be just a theory. In his April 1852 general conference sermon he clearly declared it to be doctrine.

26. Wilford Woodruff in Watt, ed., *Journal of Discourses,* 6:120.

27. Brigham Young in Watt, ed., *Journal of Discourses,* 11:286.

28. Smith, *Doctrines of Salvation,* 1:7–8.

29. Bruce McConkie, "Seven Deadly Heresies" (speech given at BYU, 1 June 1980).

30. McConkie, *Mormon Doctrine,* 784.

31. *Ensign* (May 1995): 87.

Bibliography

Achieving a Celestial Marriage. Salt Lake City: The Church of Jesus Christ of Latter-day Saints, 1976.

Allen, James B., and Glen M. Leonard. *The Story of the Latter-day Saints.* Salt Lake City: Deseret Book Co., 1976.

Bavinck, Herman. *The Doctrine of God.* Great Britain: Banner of Truth Trust, 1991.

Beardall, Doug. *About the Three Nephites.* Salt Lake City: LDS Book Publications, 1992.

Beasley-Murray, G. R. *Baptism in the New Testament.* Grand Rapids: Eerdmans, 1962.

Benson, Ezra Taft. *Teachings of Ezra Taft Benson.* Salt Lake City: Bookcraft, 1988.

Bromiley, G. W., ed. *The International Standard Bible Encyclopedia.* 4 vols. Grand Rapids: Eerdmans, 1979.

Brown, Harold O. J. *Heresies: The Image of Christ in the Mirror of Heresy and Orthodoxy from the Apostles to the Present.* Grand Rapids: Baker, 1984.

Bruce, F. F. *Paul: Apostle of the Heart Set Free.* Grand Rapids: Eerdmans, 1977.

Budvarson, Arthur. *A Rebuttal to "The Problems of the Book of Mormon."* La Mesa, Calif.: Utah Christian Tract Society, n.d.

BYU Studies. Provo, Utah: Brigham Young University (published since 1959, there are currently 38 volumes).

Cannon, George Q. *Gospel Truth.* Salt Lake City: Deseret Book Co., 1987.

Church News. Select issues from the weekly LDS newspaper, published by Deseret News, Salt Lake City.

Clark, George Edward. *Why I Believe.* Salt Lake City: Publisher's Press, 1989.

Clark, James R., ed. *Messages of the First Presidency of The Church of Jesus Christ of Latter-day Saints* (1833–1951). 6 vols. Salt Lake City: Bookcraft, 1965–75.

Conference Reports of The Church of Jesus Christ of Latter-day Saints. Salt Lake City: The Church of Jesus Christ of Latter-day Saints, 1889–1970 (139 total conference reports).

Derrick, Royden. *Temples in the Last Days.* Salt Lake City: Bookcraft, 1987.

Deseret News 1999–2000 Church Almanac. Salt Lake City: Deseret News, 1998.

Dialogue: A Journal of Mormon Thought. Select issues from the quarterly journal published by the Dialogue Foundation in Salt Lake City.

Durham, Reed C., Jr. *Is There No Help for the Widow's Son?* Nauvoo, Ill.: Martin Publishing, 1980.

Ehat, Andrew F., and Lyndon W. Cook. *The Words of Joseph Smith.* Orem, Utah: Grandlin Book Co., 1993.

Elwell, Walter A., ed. *Evangelical Dictionary of Theology.* Grand Rapids: Baker, 1984.

Ensign. Select issues from the magazine, published monthly by the LDS Church since 1971. Salt Lake City: The Church of Jesus Christ of Latter-day Saints.

Family Home Evening Manual. Salt Lake City: The Church of Jesus Christ of Latter-day Saints, 1972.

Gonzalez, Justo L. *The Early Church to the Dawn of the Reformation.* Vol. 1 of *The Story of Christianity.* San Francisco: HarperCollins, 1984.

Gospel Principles. Salt Lake City: The Church of Jesus Christ of Latter-day Saints, 1992.

Grant, Heber J. *Gospel Standards.* Comp. G. Homer Durham. Salt Lake City: Improvement Era, 1943.

Heinerman, Joseph. *Temple Manifestations.* Salt Lake City: Magazine Printing and Publishing, 1974.

Henry, Matthew. *Matthew Henry's Commentary of the Whole Bible.* McLean, Va.: MacDonald Publishing Co., 1706.

Hester, Dennis J., comp. *The Vance Havner Quote Book.* Grand Rapids: Baker, 1986.

History of the Church of Jesus Christ of Latter-day Saints. 7 vols. Introduction and notes by B. H. Roberts. Salt Lake City: Deseret Book Co., 1973.

Hopkins, Richard R. *Biblical Mormonism: Responding to Evangelical Criticism of LDS Theology.* Bountiful, Utah: Horizon Publishers, 1994.

Hunter, Milton R. *The Gospel through the Ages.* Salt Lake City: Stevens and Wallis, 1945.

———. *Pearl of Great Price Commentary.* Salt Lake City: Stephens and Wallis, 1948.

The Improvement Era. Salt Lake City: The Church of Jesus Christ of Latter-day Saints (published 1897–1970, when it became the *Ensign*).

Infobases LDS Collector Library for Windows CD-Rom. Salt Lake City: Folio Infobases, 1997.

Jenson, Andrew. *Church Chronology.* Salt Lake City: Deseret News, 1899.

———. *Latter-day Saint Biographical Encyclopedia. A Compilation of Biographical Sketches of Prominent Men and Women in the Church of Jesus Christ of Latter-day Saints.* Excerpts, 4 vols. Salt Lake City: A. Jensen History, 1901–36.

Kelly, J. N. D. *Early Christian Doctrines.* New York: HarperSanFrancisco, 1978.

Kimball, Spencer W. *Faith Precedes the Miracle.* Salt Lake City: Deseret Book Co., 1978.

———. *The Miracle of Forgiveness.* Salt Lake City: Bookcraft, 1969.

———. *Teachings of Spencer W. Kimball.* Comp. Edward L. Kimball. Salt Lake City: Bookcraft, 1982.

Kirkham, Francis W. *A New Witness for Christ in America.* 2 vols. Salt Lake City: Utah Printing Co., 1960.

Larson, Charles M. *By His Own Hand upon Papyrus.* Grand Rapids: Institute for Religious Research, 1992.

Lee, Harold B. *Stand Ye in Holy Places: Selected Sermons and Writings of President Harold B. Lee.* Salt Lake City: Deseret Book Co., 1975.

Lee, Rex E. *What Do Mormons Believe?* Salt Lake City: Deseret Book Co., 1992.

LeSueur, Stephen C. *The 1838 Mormon War in Missouri.* Colombia, Mo.: University of Missouri Press, 1987.

Living Prophets for a Living Church. Salt Lake City: The Church of Jesus Christ of Latter-day Saints, 1974.

Ludlow, Daniel H., ed. *Encyclopedia of Mormonism.* 4 vols. New York: Macmillan, 1992.

Lund, John Lewis. *The Church and the Negro: A Discussion of Mormons, Negroes and the Priesthood.* Paramount Publishers, 1967.

Lundwall, Nels B. *Temples of the Most High.* Salt Lake City: Bookcraft, 1954.

Lundwall, Nels B., comp. *Lectures on Faith.* Salt Lake City: Bookcraft, n.d.

McConkie, Bruce R. *Doctrinal New Testament Commentary: The Gospels.* Vol. 1. Salt Lake City: Bookcraft, 1966.

———. *The Millennial Messiah.* Salt Lake City: Deseret Book Co., 1982.

———. *Mormon Doctrine.* 2d ed. Salt Lake City: Bookcraft, 1966.

———. *The Mortal Messiah.* Salt Lake City: Deseret Book Co., 1982.

———. *A New Witness for the Articles of Faith.* Salt Lake City: Deseret Book Co., 1985.

———. *The Promised Messiah.* The Messiah Series. Vol. 1. Salt Lake City: Deseret Book Co., 1978.

McConkie, Joseph Fielding, and Robert L. Millet. *Doctrinal Commentary on the Book of Mormon.* Vol. 1. Salt Lake City: Bookcraft, 1987.

McKay, David O. *Gospel Ideals.* Comp. G. Homer Durham. Salt Lake City: Improvement Era, 1953.

McKeever, Bill. *Answering Mormons' Questions.* Minneapolis: Bethany, 1991.

McKeever, Bill, and Eric Johnson. *Questions to Ask Your Mormon Friend.* Minneapolis: Bethany, 1994.

Maxwell, Neal A. *A Wonderful Flood of Light.* Salt Lake City: Bookcraft, 1990.

Messages for Exaltation: Eternal Insights from the Book of Mormon. A Gospel Doctrine Class manual. Salt Lake City: Deseret Sunday School Union, 1967.

Mickelsen, A. Berkeley. *Interpreting the Bible.* Grand Rapids: Eerdmans, 1963.

Millennial Star. An official LDS publication that was published in the British Isles from 1840–1970 and later became the *Ensign.*

The Mormon Puzzle video. North American Mission Board (Southern Baptist Convention), 1997.

Morris, Leon. *The Atonement: Its Meaning and Significance.* Downers Grove, Ill.: InterVarsity Press, 1983.

———. *The Gospel according to John: The New International Commentary on the New Testament.* Grand Rapids: Eerdmans, 1995.

Nibley, Hugh. *No Ma'am, That's Not History.* Salt Lake City: Bookcraft, 1946.

Penrose, Charles. *Mormon Doctrine, Plain and Simple.* Salt Lake City: Juvenile Instructor, 1888.

Persuitte, David. *Joseph Smith and the Origins of the Book of Mormon*. Jefferson, N.C.: McFarland and Co., Inc., 1991.

Pratt, Orson. *Divine Authenticity of the Book of Mormon*. From a series of pamphlets. Liverpool, England: n.p., 1851.

————. *The Seer*. Photo reprint of newspapers published between January 1853 through August 1854. Republished in 1990 by Eborn Books (Salt Lake City).

Pratt, Parley P. *Key to the Science of Theology: A Voice of Warning*. Salt Lake City: Deseret Book Co., 1978.

Quinn, D. Michael. *Early Mormonism and the Magic World View*. Salt Lake City: Signature Books, 1987.

————. *The Mormon Hierarchy: Origins of Power*. Salt Lake City: Signature Books, 1994.

Review of Books on the Book of Mormon. 8 vols. Provo, Utah: FARMS, 1989–97.

Richards, LeGrand. *A Marvelous Work and a Wonder*. Salt Lake City: Deseret Book Co., 1976.

Roberts, B. H., comp. *Comprehensive History of the Church of Jesus Christ of Latter-day Saints*. 6 vols. 1930. Reprint, Orem, Utah: Sonos Publishing, 1991.

————. *Defense of the Faith and the Saints*. 2 vols. Salt Lake City: Deseret News, 1907–12.

————. *The Gospel and Man's Relationship to Deity*. Salt Lake City: Deseret Book Co., 1965.

————. *New Witnesses for God*. 3 vols. Salt Lake City: Deseret News, 1911, 1950–51.

————. *Outlines of Ecclesiastical History: A Text Book*. 6th ed. Salt Lake City: The Church of Jesus Christ of Latter-day Saints, 1950.

Robinson, Stephen E. *Believing Christ*. Salt Lake City: Deseret Book Co., 1992.

Ross, Bob L. *Acts 2:38 and Baptismal Remission*. Pasadena, Tex.: Pilgrim Publications, 1987.

Search These Commandments: Melchizedek Priesthood Personal Study Guide. Salt Lake City: The Church of Jesus Christ of Latter-day Saints, 1984.

Shields, Steven L. *Divergent Paths of the Restoration*. Los Angeles: Restoration Research, 1990.

Sillito, John, ed. *The Wilderness of Faith: Essays on Contemporary Mormon Thought*. Salt Lake City: Signature Books, 1991.

Skousen, Cleon. *The First 2,000 Years*. Salt Lake City: Bookcraft, 1979.

Smith, Joseph, Jr. *The Book of Mormon*. Salt Lake City: The Church of Jesus Christ of Latter-day Saints, 1830 and 1981 editions.

————. *The Doctrine and Covenants of the Church of Jesus Christ of Latter-day Saints*. Salt Lake City: The Church of Jesus Christ of Latter-day Saints, 1981.

————. *Joseph Smith's "New Translation" of the Bible*. Independence, Mo: Herald Publishing House, 1970.

————. *The Pearl of Great Price*. Salt Lake City: The Church of Jesus Christ of Latter-day Saints, 1981.

Smith, Joseph F. *Gospel Doctrine*. Comp. John A. Widtsoe. Salt Lake City: Deseret Book Co., 1919.

Smith, Joseph Fielding. *Answers to Gospel Questions.* 4 vols. Salt Lake City: Deseret Book Co., 1957–63.

———. *Doctrines of Salvation: Sermons and Writings of Joseph Fielding Smith.* 3 vols. Ed. Bruce R. McConkie. Salt Lake City: Bookcraft, 1954–56.

———, ed. *Teachings of the Prophet Joseph Smith.* Salt Lake City: Deseret Book Co., 1938.

———. *The Way to Perfection.* Salt Lake City: Deseret Book Co., 1975.

Snow, Lorenzo. *Teachings of Lorenzo Snow.* Comp. Clyde J. Williams. Salt Lake City: Bookcraft, 1966.

Sproul, R. C. *Essential Truths of the Christian Faith.* Wheaton, Ill.: Tyndale House, 1992.

Stewart, John. *Joseph Smith, the Mormon Prophet.* Salt Lake City: Hawkes Publishing, 1966.

———. *Mormonism and the Negro.* Orem, Utah: Bookmark, 1960.

Stuy, Brian H., ed. *Collected Discourses.* 5 vols. Burbank, Calif., and Woodland Hills, Utah: B. H. S. Publishing, 1987–92.

Sunstone. Select issues. Salt Lake City: Sunstone Foundation.

A Sure Foundation: Answers to Difficult Gospel Questions. (Several authors.) Salt Lake City: Deseret Book Co., 1988.

Talmage, James E. *The Articles of Faith.* Salt Lake City: Deseret Book Co., 1987.

———. *Jesus the Christ.* Salt Lake City: Deseret Book Co., 1981.

———. *The Vitality of Mormonism.* Boston: Gorham Press, 1919.

Tanner, Jerald and Sandra. *Mormonism—Shadow or Reality?* Salt Lake City: Utah Lighthouse Ministry, 1982.

Taylor, John. *The Gospel Kingdom.* Ed. G. Homer Durham. 3d ed. Salt Lake City: Bookcraft, 1944.

Teachings of the Living Prophets. Salt Lake City: The Church of Jesus Christ of Latter-day Saints, 1982.

Times and Seasons. A six-volume series that contains copies of the LDS newspaper printed between November 1839 and February 1846.

Tozer, A. W. *Echoes from Eden: The Voices of God Calling Man.* Harrisburg, Pa.: Christian Publications, 1981.

Van Wagoner, Richard S. *Mormon Polygamy: A History.* Salt Lake City: Signature Books, 1989.

———. *Sidney Rigdon: A Portrait of Religious Excess.* Salt Lake City: Signature Books, 1994.

Watch and Be Ready: Preparing for the Second Coming of the Lord. Salt Lake City: Deseret Book Co., 1994.

Watt, George D., ed. *Journal of Discourses.* 26 vols. Liverpool, England: F. D. Richards, 1854–86.

Whitmer, David. *An Address to All Believers in the Book of Mormon.* Richmond, Mo.: David Whitmer, 1887.

———. *An Address to All Believers in Christ.* Richmond, Mo.: David Whitmer, 1887.

Widtsoe, John A. *Evidences and Reconciliations.* Comp. G. Homer Durham. 3 vols. 1943–51. Reprint (3 vols. in 1), Salt Lake City: Bookcraft, 1960.

————. *Joseph Smith: Seeker after Truth, Prophet of God.* Salt Lake City: Deseret Book Co., 1951.

————. *A Rational Theology As Taught by the Church of Jesus Christ of Latter-day Saints.* 7th ed. Salt Lake City: Deseret Book Co., 1965.

Wood, Wilford C. *Joseph Smith Begins His Work.* Vol. 1. Salt Lake City: Publisher's Press, 1958.

Woodruff, Wilford. *The Discourses of Wilford Woodruff.* Comp. G. Homer Durham. Salt Lake City: Bookcraft, 1946.

Young, Brigham. *Discourses of Brigham Young.* Comp. John A. Widtsoe. Salt Lake City: Deseret Book Co., 1978.

Index of Biblical References